A Light to the Nations

To a dear colleague & friend,
Glory Thomas
with all good wishes,
[illegible]

A LIGHT TO THE NATIONS

The Indian Presence in the Ecumenical Movement in the Twentieth Century

Edited by Jesudas M. Athyal

Foreword by Michael Kinnamon

World Council of Churches Publications

A LIGHT TO THE NATIONS
The Indian Presence in the Ecumenical Movement in the Twentieth Century
Edited by Jesudas M. Athyal

WCC Publications is the book publishing programme of the World Council of Churches. Founded in 1948, the WCC promotes Christian unity in faith, witness and service for a just and peaceful world. A global fellowship, the WCC brings together 345 Protestant, Orthodox, Anglican and other churches representing more than 550 million Christians in 110 countries and works cooperatively with the Roman Catholic Church.

Opinions expressed in WCC Publications are those of the authors.

Cover design: Adele Robey, Phoenix Graphics, Inc.
Book design and typesetting: Michelle Cook / 4 Seasons Book Design
ISBN: 978-2-8254-1670-9

World Council of Churches
150 route de Ferney, P.O. Box 2100
1211 Geneva 2, Switzerland
http://publications.oikoumene.org

CONTENTS

ACKNOWLEDGMENTS

This volume is a team effort that cuts across national and confessional barriers. Michael Kinnamon, a scholar who is familiar with the Asian and Indian ecumenical scene, graciously agreed to write the foreword for the book. Throughout the course of compiling this work, he keenly followed its progress and made valuable suggestions. At the early stages itself, Wesley Ariarajah and Deenabandhu Manchala went through the proposal and offered their kind advice. It was a major boost for us when WCC Publications agreed to publish this volume. We are indebted to these friends.

The real strength of this volume lies in the stature of the eminent scholars, from diverse confessional, national, and perspectival backgrounds, who wrote the articles. We are deeply grateful to these dear friends: Roger E. Hedlund, Raj Bharat Patta, Aruna Gnanadason, David Scott, K. C. Abraham, K. M. George, Wesley Ariarajah, Jayakiran Sebastian, George Zachariah, and Daniel Preman Niles.

A number of scholars provided valuable reference materials for the introductory essay (chapter 1) in this volume and later commented on drafts of the essay. Apart from the names mentioned above, they are: Charles C. West, John Webster, Geevarghese Mar Theodosius, Dana Robert, Lois M. Wilson, Raymond Williams, A. George Ninan, Adrian Bird, R. Stephen Warner, Pradip Thomas, Zac Varghese, Jessica Prakash-Richard, George Oommen, Arthur Jeyakumar, and Dinah Oommen. There is little doubt that their valuable input and critical comments helped tremendously to strengthen the clarity and focus of this publication.

I would also like to thank Ninan Koshy for his willingness to be persuaded to be included as the only person still among us that would have a chapter in this volume, and for the advice he was willing to give on the project.

This volume is dedicated to the countless number of women and men, named and unnamed, who toiled, often unsung, for the building up of the ecumenical movement in the church and the world.

CONTRIBUTORS

K. C. Abraham was president of the Ecumenical Association of Third World Theologians (EATWOT) and director of the South Asia Theological Research Institute (SATHRI), Bangalore, India. In the 1980s he was the director of the Ecumenical Christian Centre, Whitefield, Bangalore.

S. Wesley Ariarajah is emeritus professor of ecumenical theology at Drew University, Madison, New Jersey, USA. He was director of the Interfaith Dialogue Department of World Council of Churches (WCC) and deputy general secretary of the WCC.

Jesudas M. Athyal is visiting researcher at Boston University School of Theology, Boston, Massachusetts, USA. He was earlier associate professor of social analysis and Dalit theology at Gurukul Lutheran Theological College, Chennai, India.

K. M. George is director of the Sopana Orthodox Academy, Kottayam, India. He served as moderator of the WCC Programme Committee, executive secretary of the National Council of Churches in India (NCCI), and as principal and professor at the Orthodox Theological Seminary in Kottayam, India. From 1989 to 1994 he was professor at the Bossey Ecumenical Institute, Switzerland.

Aruna Gnanadason was director of the Women's Sub-Unit of the World Council of Churches and coordinated the work on Justice, Peace, and Creation. She earlier served as executive secretary of the All India Council of Christian Women of the National Council of Churches in India (NCCI).

Roger E. Hedlund is director emeritus of Mylapore Institute for Indigenous Studies at Chennai, India. He has taught at Union Biblical Seminary, Yavatmal/Pune, and at Serampore College, Serampore, India. He is the editor-in-chief of *The Oxford Encyclopedia of South Asian Christianity*.

Michael Kinnamon recently retired from his post as Spehar-Halligan Visiting Professor of Ecumenical Collaboration in Interreligious Dialogue at Seattle University's School of Theology and Ministry. He has served as general secretary of the National Council of Churches of Christ in the USA, executive secretary of Commission on Faith and Order (WCC), and visiting professor at the United Theological College, Bangalore.

D. Preman Niles was director for the Ecumenical Process on Justice, Peace, and the Integrity of Creation (JPIC), World Council of Churches, Geneva. He later served as the general secretary of the Council for World Mission, London.

Raj Bharat Patta is a doctoral student at the University of Manchester, England. He has served as general secretary of the Student Christian Movement of India (SCMI) and as executive secretary for the Commission on Dalits, Mission, and Youth of the National Council of Churches in India (NCCI).

David C. Scott is professor emeritus of religion and culture at the United Theological College, Bangalore, and the Leonard Theological College, Jabalpur, India. Scott has lectured in theological colleges in India, South Korea, and the USA.

J. Jayakiran Sebastian is a presbyter of the Church of South India, dean of the Lutheran Theological Seminary at Philadelphia, Pennsylvania, USA, and H. George Anderson Professor of Mission and Cultures and director of the Multicultural Mission Resource Center there. He has served as professor in the department of theology and ethics at the United Theological College, Bangalore.

George Zachariah serves United Theological College, Bangalore, as associate professor in the department of theology and ethics. He earlier taught at Gurukul Lutheran Theological College, Chennai, India.

FOREWORD

Michael Kinnamon

It would be a great mistake to think that this book, which is *about* leaders in the church in India, is only *for* Indian Christians. Anyone who cares about the unity and mission of the church will find much to reflect on in these engaging studies.

For one thing, the very organization of this volume reminds us that the ecumenical movement, so often reduced to a study of texts or a listing of conferences, is actually embodied in persons who carry a vision of the church united and renewed. In many respects, the ten individuals profiled in this book are very different. Some are Protestant, others Orthodox; some have written prolifically, others very little; three are lay, while three are bishops; one was born in 1874, while another remains in active ministry at the time of this writing. And yet, readers will likely be struck by the commonalities that emerge from these very individual lives.

One overwhelming impression is how attentive these leaders were (and are) to local realities. This volume focuses, for the most part, on figures who have been known for their contributions to global ecumenism. But such global leadership is clearly rooted in their response to a context marked by religious plurality, caste oppression, endemic poverty, and the struggle to build a post-colonial nation. Nearly all of these figures saw a strong connection between the reformation of the Indian church and the reformation of the wider Indian society.

As this suggests, a study of these Christian leaders poses a challenge to those who would split the ecumenical agenda. Throughout these pages—including the helpful essay by the editor, Dr Jesudas M. Athyal—readers will see an integration of themes: unity *and* mission, social justice *and* evangelism, spirituality *and* social action, education *and* worship. Holiness, for these leaders, does not mean withdrawal from the social revolutions of their day, but engagement in them on the basis of Christian faith. Unity is not pursued at the expense of justice, but as a sign and instrument of God's reign of justice and peace. Perhaps most significantly, interfaith relations is not, for them, an alternative to passionate commitment to Christ, but an authentic expression of it.

In the same way, this book should help lay to rest certain persistent myths. One of these is that the impulse for unity in the Indian church came primarily from Western missionaries. As we see from these chapters, ecumenism in South Asia was a protest, initiated by Indian Christians, against the imported pattern of denominational fragmentation and missionary paternalism. Another (closely related) myth is that the ecumenical movement, at root, is a European phenomenon whose early intellectual leaders all hailed from the North Atlantic. This volume will do much to help set that record straight. Not only the subjects of these chapters, but also the authors, bear witness to how extensively the movement was and is shaped by Christians from the Indian subcontinent.

I will end on a personal note that reinforces the point I want to make in this foreword. While I have taught, lectured, and traveled in India, I am by no means an expert in Indian Christianity. And I found the book compelling. It gave me fresh insights into persons with whom I was familiar, while also introducing me to persons whose work I barely knew. Most significantly, I found while reading it that I was continually inspired by this witness to what God has done in the lives of leaders from another part of the church, even as I was challenged to think in new ways about my commitment to unity and mission in my own setting.

INTRODUCTION

Jesudas M. Athyal

The address that V. S. Azariah, the first Indian bishop of the Anglican Communion, delivered at the Edinburgh Mission Conference in 1910 to an overwhelmingly Western audience—"You have given your bodies to be burned. We ask for love, give us FRIENDS"—is often cited as a turning point in the history of the ecumenical movement and hailed as "the first shot against missionary imperialism."[1] At the other end of the 20th century, Ninan Koshy, in his capacity as the director of the Commission of the Churches on International Affairs (CCIA) of the World Council of Churches (WCC), led successfully the efforts to bring the church in China back to the fellowship of the WCC. He also initiated and led a process which brought together representatives of churches in South Korea and Christians in North Korea for the first time after the Korean War. The period between Azariah and Koshy saw an impressive line of Indian Christian leaders who left an indelible mark on the modern ecumenical movement. This volume will discuss this remarkable period by focusing specifically on some of these leaders.

It was not merely that some Indians played key roles in ecumenical institutions. There were also historic moments. In 1947 four different church traditions came together to form the Church of South India (CSI), setting in motion a process of organic unity of the churches across the globe. And in recognition of the ecumenical significance of the churches of the nations of the non-Western world, the third assembly of the WCC met in New Delhi in 1961. Further, in the 1970s, when civil liberties and democratic rights were curtailed in the wake of the Indian Emergency, the country's ecumenical leaders were key participants in the movement toward freedom and democracy, and their voices reverberated at the WCC Nairobi assembly in 1975. This volume will also attempt to recapture some of these historic moments.

Again, it was not only that there were certain Indian Christian leaders who contributed to the modern ecumenical movement or that some significant ecumenical developments occurred in India, but also that these developments triggered a process that resulted in a remarkable redefining of the core of ecumenism in our times. In the decades that followed Sarah Chakko's becoming the first woman on the presidium of the WCC in 1951, a sharp focus on women's participation in the church and society emerged and has remained at the vanguard of the ecumenical movement ever since. Further, in response to the increased industrialization of Asia since the 1960s and the widening gulf between the urban and rural contexts, Harry F. J. Daniel and others pioneered the concept of Urban Industrial and Rural Mission at the Asian and global levels, a movement that shaped the Christian response to the challenges of the modern society. Again, Masilamani Azariah's forceful representation at the WCC Vancouver assembly on the plight of the marginalized Dalits of India redefined the Programme to Combat Racism (PCR) to include social discrimination everywhere. These movements set in motion a process that led to a fundamental paradigm shift in the ecumenical agenda from a visibly non-Western perspective. In this publication, we will relive some of those moments as well.

This volume discusses people, movements, and institutions that were trendsetters in the ecumenical movement. While the story outlined here by no means claims to be a comprehensive account of the period, the book does explore aspects of the Indian component that were decisive in the history of the movement. This is a chapter of the ecumenical movement that, we believe, has not yet been fully written, and hence the relevance of this publication.

The editor and contributors of this volume are fully conscious of the many "ifs" and "buts" in this narration. Why the focus on India? Why not the other parts of the world? What was the criteria for selecting these ten persons to discuss in detail? Why not others? We wish to clarify at the outset that by no means do we imply that these particular ten persons were more important than others. We had to make a selection, realizing fully the risk involved. But we believe that during the course of the ecumenical movement, as Christian unity became an important agenda for the church, as justice concerns were recognized as an integral part of unity, and as ecumenism became a truly global movement, these leaders, in their diverse ways, represented important movements and trends in the ecumenical movement in India and Asia. The only person among these ten who is still in our midst at the time of this writing—Ninan Koshy—continues in this great tradition. He can, perhaps, be described as one of the most distinguished ecumenical diplomats in the history of the WCC.

Further, we wish to locate this discussion in the context of the *Asian* presence in the ecumenical movement. Indians were among a galaxy of distinguished Asian ecumenists who led and enriched not only the regional context but provided Asian perspectives to the worldwide movement. In our discussion here, therefore, we stand on the shoulders of D. T. Niles, U. Kyaw Than, T. B. Simatupang, Bishop K. H. Ting, and countless other men and women of God who pioneered the Asian awakening in global Christianity.[2] The Indian contribution was only a part of this larger Asian picture. In the ultimate analysis, therefore, this is not the story of a few individuals; it is the history of the ecumenical movement at the Indian, Asian, and global levels.

The scope of this publication is confined to the mainline Protestant and Orthodox churches and traditions that come broadly within the fellowship of the WCC. This limitation does not disregard other crucial voices in the discussion. Especially following the Second Vatican Council, the Roman Catholic Church—at the Indian, Asian, and global levels—made significant contributions to the ecumenical movement. Of particular relevance is the Catholic Church's work as an active participant in the Faith and Order Commission, in the area of interfaith relations, and the grassroots-level social action and developmental work in the villages and towns, often carried out in an ecumenical spirit. The perspectives of the Evangelical and Pentecostal churches, too, are important. Even though the YWCA and YMCA are integral parts of the ecumenical movement, for logistic reasons, their work could not be included here.[3] While these important angles do not come within the purview of this publication, these remain valuable perspectives that need to be studied in a similar fashion.

In this volume, we deal primarily with ecumenical *thought* and *trends*. Our source of information is, essentially, published literature and ecumenical documents. Biographical notes and incidental details, wherever necessary for such a discussion, along with references needed for further reading, are generally confined to the notes. This pattern has especially been followed in the essay that follows this introduction. The subsequent chapters are focused on certain individual leaders and, hence, they each have a section that serves as a biographical note; but they, too, go on to discuss the thought and trends that person represents. It needs also to be added that, at least in a few cases, the lack of available literature on an ecumenical leader or movement has limited the scope of the discussion in that area. Even with such difficulties, we are convinced that a viable review of the ecumenical movement is possible only within such a framework.

Further, in the last few decades of the past century, a long line of Indian Christians were active participants in the ecumenical movement, at the local, state, national, and larger levels. There were also many who were leaders in their own denominations or confessions, up to the international levels. Attempts to review the contributions of such a large group posed enormous hazards that went beyond the scope of this study. We, therefore, had to proceed in this discussion with some self-imposed restrictions. The decision was to limit the discussion to individuals who played decisive roles in ecumenical institutions, especially at the international level, and to leaders who produced significant literature in this area or on whose contributions scholars had done considerable work.

It needs to be stressed that this volume deals with the ecumenical history during the *20th century*. As such, the scope of this study is essentially *historical* in nature. However, it is heartening to note that today an able team of Indian leaders is carrying forward the rich legacy of the past century. Apart from the names mentioned in this volume, there are several others. In the field of Christian mission, for instance, Geevarghese Mar Coorilose, Sudipta Singh, and several others are making significant contributions. Mar Coorilose, along with Raj Bharat Patta, Shibi Peter, Sweety Helen, and others also provide new impetus to the Student Christian Movement (SCM). In the area of ecumenical theological education, there is a rich team at the national, Asian, and global levels, including such names as Sathianathan Clarke, Jayakiran Sebastian, Wati Longchar, George Zachariah, and Marina Behera. On the foundation laid down by the ecumenical women of the past century, a new leadership consisting of Monica Melanchthon, Priscilla Singh, Evangeline Anderson-Rajkumar, Jessica Richard, and others are charting new courses in women's participation in church and society. In the area of Dalit theology, too, leaders like Peniel

Jesudason Rufus Rajkumar and Philip Peacock are making signal contributions. Dinesh Suna and Sudipta Singh are active in ecumenical social action. And the list goes on. There is no doubt that the work of these leaders, as well as recent ecumenical trends and movements, too, will, in the future, be studied in a similar fashion.

This volume discusses not only the areas of "strength" the Indian presence represents in the ecumenical movement but also the weaknesses. In all humility, we accept that there are areas of crucial importance where the Indian voices have been muted, disinterested, had little to contribute, or were dominated by others. The first chapter in this book mentions two such areas—the Orthodox perspective and women's presence. Despite the long history and rich liturgical and social tradition of the Orthodox Church in India, the Orthodox presence in the ecumenical movement has been more pronounced in other contexts, such as eastern Europe and the Middle East. Similarly, even though an array of distinguished Indian women has been present in the ecumenical movement at various stages, their voices have not yet been fully recognized. As the history of the movement in the 21st century is written, let us hope that these, too, will be among our strong points.

The Chapters

The first chapter in this volume is an overview of the Indian presence in the ecumenical movement during the 20th century and shows how the Indian church helped define and advance central elements of the ecumenical vision. The article draws on both key figures and significant events during this period.

The subsequent chapters focus on ten Indian Christians who contributed significantly to the ecumenical process. They span the spectrum of the 20th century, from the first to the last decade. Let me briefly introduce the chapters:

In his article, Roger Hedlund introduces V. S. Azariah as a leader who was a key participant in church unity discussions that culminated in the formation of the Church of South India (CSI). Azariah's distinctive contribution might well have been his focus on the necessity of an Indian Christian identity, of "church unification as part of a larger program of church indigenization," meaning, a church of India. In that sense, he was a forerunner of the reality of "world Christianity" as it now is seen, its leadership increasingly from India.

Raj Bharat Patta discusses in his article the life and witness of Augustine Ralla Ram, who is considered the architect of the SCM of India, and how, with his farsightedness and pragmatic missiological characteristics, he played an indispensable role in the ecumenical world. Ralla Ram was an ecumenical visionary in a true sense, which he demonstrated throughout his life in all the capacities that he had served. The SCM and churches in India are indebted to him.

While discussing the contributions of Sarah Chakko, who was the first woman on the presidium of WCC, Aruna Gnanadason points out that Chakko's ecumenical formation was culled out of her life story. Chakko's life and commitment stands as testimony to how Orthodox Christian women have stayed in solidarity with women of other denominations, and with the ecumenical movement, over these decades.

According to David Scott, P. D. Devanandan's fundamental concern was to assist the Indian church to understand Jesus, the Christ, as the key to and fulfillment of God's work in and for the world of Indian religion, culture, and society, and to restate and communicate that truth. The theology of religious pluralism is indeed an ecumenical issue of immense importance and consequence to which Devanandan made a significant contribution.

In his article, K. C. Abraham portrays M. M. Thomas as one of the key architects of the modern ecumenical movement. According to Alf Tergel, Thomas, along with Willem Visser't Hooft, has had the greatest influence on the ecumenical movement. Convinced that the gospel offers the dynamics for Christian engagement in politics, he wrote extensively about the political responsibility of Christians with a clarity and commitment that is rarely matched.

K. M. George discusses the life and message of Paulos Mar Gregorios, who was endowed with a rare form of holistic intelligence and broad intellectual curiosity of a polymath, with a sincere quest for a new and just order of the world and deep compassion for the least ones. As a person who was always tormented by intellectual puzzles and internal spiritual conflicts, Mar Gregorios was not obviously a person who would easily fit into ecclesiastical or ecumenical straitjackets.

Stanley Samartha's personal traits and qualities, according to Wesley Ariarajah, contributed a great deal in removing some of the initial hesitations that people of other religions had about Christians wanting suddenly to engage in dialogue with them. Samartha did much to remove the notion among many

Hindus and Buddhists that dialogue is yet another tool in Christian zeal for evangelism. He argued that we "cannot limit the extent or the mode of God's redeeming work, because it is as universal as His love which embraces all humankind at all times." We therefore need to recognize God's saving work in "areas outside the hedges of the Church."

In his article, Jayakiran Sebastian argues that for Russell Chandran, faithfulness to the mission mandate involved both an uncompromised commitment to Christ, as well as the openness to the variety and diversity of the revelation of God in the lives of human beings. As a lifelong proponent of interreligious dialogue, Chandran argued that we cannot absolutize our manner of practicing our commitment as the only possibility for others. Rather, in dialogue one has to be open to a combination of God's self-revelation and human wisdom, leading to the possibility of accepting the diversity of religious faiths as contributing to the beauty and richness of the complex spirituality of the human race, and to the greatness of national as well as global cultures.

George Zachariah, in his article, portrays Poulose Mar Poulose as a prophet who followed Jesus the Christ as his model and, as a leader of SCM, insisted that the ecumenical students should become Christ-centred as they strive to bear witness in our context. Mar Poulose's life was short, "but he still lives in the ecumenical youth and student movements as they continue to remain *out of control*, challenging the ecumenical mafia and the pharisaic church."

Ninan Koshy's main contribution within the Commission of the Churches on International Affairs (CCIA) of the WCC, according to Preman Niles, was in the analyses he had to carry out of critical international situations, in developing theological and conceptual clarity in the area of international affairs, and exploring possibilities for what may be called "ecumenical diplomacy." Almost from the time he joined the staff of CCIA, and certainly from 1979 onward, Koshy drafted the public statements of the WCC on international affairs. This meant that he was actively involved in policy-making on public issues.

Within this overall context, this volume seeks to capture the essence of the Indian presence in the ecumenical movement in the 20th century. The movement, now in the second decade of a new century, is emerging from a Western and institutional framework into a phase that is more catholic, pluralistic, and decentralized. Accounts such as those outlined in this book, of non-Western origin, are especially relevant at this stage. Even with such exciting prospects, we are acutely conscious of the grave limitations in this storytelling. The accounts that fill these pages are mostly that of the privileged;

primarily, upper-caste *men*. Also, despite the increased participation of the Orthodox, Catholic, and Evangelical traditions, the ecumenical movement, we need to admit, is still very much an account of the *Protestants*. Further, the voices of several geographical areas in India—notably, North East India, which has experienced the greatest surge in Christianity in the last century—are not duly represented in the ecumenical history of the past century. Until the last decades of the last century, the Dalits and tribals were almost totally absent from the ecumenical process. We have attempted to include in this volume as many "little traditions"—voices from the margins—as possible, but we sincerely hope that as the history of the ecumenical movement in the 21st century is recorded, we will be able to tell a different story that is more just, participatory, and inclusive.

CHAPTER 1

Jesudas M. Athyal

The Indian Ecumenical Symphony: Significant Movements and Persons

This volume deals with the story of the Indian presence in the ecumenical movement in the 20th century. Its chapters discuss in detail the life and thought of a few key leaders in this process. This introductory essay, however, draws on a wide range of figures and significant institutions and movements and shows how the Indian church helped define and advance central elements of the ecumenical vision. The essay is divided into nine sections covering the following topics: (1) Christian unity; (2) mission, nationalism, and unity; (3) interfaith relations; (4) unity and justice; (5) Dalit and Adivasi context; (6) Orthodox perspective; (7) women in church and society; (8) lay leadership; and (9) ecumenical theological education. This wide canvas sets the story of Indian ecumenism into historical, cultural, and religious perspective.

Christian Unity

The inauguration of the Church of South India (CSI) on 27 September 1947 was undoubtedly a significant ecumenical event during that period. It was "unique in that for the first time in history a church that had maintained the historic succession of the episcopate succeeded in entering into full corporate communion with non-Episcopal churches."[1] V. S. Azariah, the first Indian Anglican bishop, V. Santiago, a Congregationalist theologian, and several other Indians and missionaries were behind the complicated negotiations that led to the new beginning.[2] The union was enthusiastically welcomed, especially in all the newly independent countries, though many Western countries were reluctant to affirm its significance or, even more, to draw the lessons from them. "In its formation, the Church of South India sought to break through Western patterns of denominationalism, seeing itself not as just one more church body, but as a means toward bringing together other churches."[3] The ecumenical momentum from South India, however, galvanized unity efforts in other places—in North India, Ceylon, Nigeria, and elsewhere—with long-lasting theological and ecclesiastical relevance. There is little doubt that it was in recognition of the ecumenical significance of the Asian churches that the assembly of the World Council of Churches (WCC) met in New Delhi in 1961.

While several aspects about the CSI were unique, one element of the unity demonstrates the collegiality, vision, and generosity of the founding fathers and mothers that led to the union. Since different denominations—Anglican, Methodist, Congregational, Presbyterian, and Reformed—had come together in unity at the time of the inauguration of the united church, the new church found itself with both episcopally and nonepiscopally ordained presbyters. As a mark of a new beginning—of not only a new church but also a new era beyond the burden of Western denominational quibbles—the pioneers of the CSI refused to reordain any presbyters (even though it was agreed that in the new church, all the presbyters would be episcopally ordained). Further, the united church "decided not to impose on any congregation an ordained person of another denomination till everyone in the CSI would be episcopally ordinated."[4] The Lambeth Conference, "home" to the Anglican partner that joined the CSI, was concerned about the "cost to Anglicanism" such unity demanded. Although the conference gave "thanks to God for the measure of unity locally achieved by the Church of South India," it could not agree on the "precise status" of its ministers and bishops ordained or consecrated at the time of inauguration or after.[5] For its "defiance," CSI was kept out of full membership in the Lambeth Conference for a while, but of historic importance is not only the spirit of unity that led to the constitution of the united church but also the sense of independence, ecumenical openness, collegiality, justice, and fairness.[6]

The formation of the CSI had a cascading effect on efforts for Christian unity around the world. Participating in the discussions at the Ecumenical Study Conference for East Asia in Lucknow in 1952, David G. Moses[7] expressed impatience with the methodology of the WCC Faith and Order Commission for church unity. He criticized that it was "too leisurely" and had little in common with the urgency of the problem.[8] In India, the Episcopal Synod of the Mar Thoma Church (MTC), under the leadership of Juhanon Mar Thoma,[9] issued in 1952 a statement which was a prophetic call to the churches in India to unite. Parts of the statement are worth quoting:

> We watched with interest and sympathy the Church union negotiations in South India, and we welcome the bold venture of South India. . . . While we greatly value our autonomy and traditional forms of worship, we feel that the time has come for us to make a move towards the realization of a Church of Christ in India. Autonomy, Biblical faith, Eastern forms of worship, and evangelistic vision are our cherished ideals. We feel that our Church must be willing to declare its readiness to become part of the Church of Christ in India . . .[10]

The statement went on to lay down a few conditions for unity. While the organic unity of the CSI and MTC has not yet been achieved, it set in motion discussions at several levels. Especially after the Church of North India (CNI) came into being in 1970, the three churches—CSI, CNI, and MTC—have entered into conciliar unity which, since 2004, is known as the Communion of Churches in India (CCI). The CCI was constituted as the visible organ for common expression of the life and witness by the three founding churches "which recognise themselves as belonging to the one Church of Jesus Christ in India, even while remaining as autonomous churches, each having its own identity of traditions and organizational structures."[11] CCI invites other churches too to enter into full communion with the member churches separately and join the fellowship.[12]

With the formation of the CSI, when denominational differences were sunk in one organic unity, and later, with the coming together of three churches (that continue to be independent churches) in conciliar unity through the

CCI, India demonstrated to the world that there can be diverse and indigenous forms of unity and witness that transcend the established frameworks of "faith and order." In his analysis of the various factors that distinguish churches that have achieved organic or structural unity and churches that are in full communion with each other, Michael Kinnamon argues that while the churches that have achieved organic unity are able to reach common decisions on faith and order matters, mission, and the use of their resources, the churches that are in full communion with each other (also called conciliar unity), retain their separate identities while there is broad agreement among them on faith and order.[13]

Beyond organic and conciliar forms of unity, the churches in North East India have demonstrated their own distinct paths of unity and witness. Diverse denominations and mission bodies from the West—Baptists, Presbyterians, Anglicans, Catholics, and others—introduced the Christian faith to the region during the 19th and 20th centuries. In the socially and politically volatile context of North East India, ecumenical fellowship was not merely unity at the realm of faith and order but it also addressed the acute social and political crisis facing the region. As major social institutions in the region, the churches and, in particular, bodies such as the Council of Naga Baptist Churches, have been key agents in peace negotiations among the various tribes and between the state and the federal government. The unique role of the church and the Christian youth in the region was emphasized by M. M. Thomas who, as the governor of Nagaland, had noted "a new vision of the Kingdom of God taking form in North East India through Christ and a new call to responsible and adventurous participation with Christ in the renewal of society and church."[14] The life and witness of the churches in North East India underscores the reality that Christian unity can also build peace and reconciliation in the wider society.

Mission, Nationalism, and Unity

Historians of Christianity have often been accused of overlooking the role of the "younger churches" in Asia in promoting mission and unity; therefore, it is important to note that in recent years Asian scholars have reiterated the contribution of indigenous movements in building up the ecumenical movement. T. V. Philip sets these discussions in the background of the dialectical tension between the Western churches and the missionary agencies in the past. On the one hand, several missionary societies were voluntary agencies independent of the churches and, consequently, at least some of them "disregarded the denominational and ecclesiastical lines and emphasised the salvation of the individual."[15] On the other hand, many churches failed to develop a missionary spirit and, consequently, drove the missionaries to adopt positions that were unrelated to the established churches. While the missionaries were largely indifferent to any ecclesiastical authority, the churches in the West, in several cases, actively opposed mission.

The disharmony between the Western churches and the missionaries can be overstated; their unity on several vital matters cannot be disregarded. The leadership of the National Christian Council of India (NCCI), dominated in the early decades of the 20th century by these overseas agencies, took an ambivalent attitude to the nationalist movement, as the pungent words of K. Baago demonstrate: ". . . the Council issued two statements on the political situation in 1917 and 1920, using a good number of words, but saying actually nothing. These statements were so vague, wooly and cautious in their choice of words, that they could be interpreted both ways."[16] Baago further stated: "It must be admitted, therefore, that the National Christian Council hardly lived up to the first word in its name at that time, particularly not when we consider what the word 'National' stood for in those days."[17]

Even as the missionary-led NCCI was ambivalent toward the nationalist movement, a steady stream of Indian Christian lay leaders and movements provided the impetus for mission and unity in the country. The All India Conference of Indian Christians (AICIC), founded in 1914, can be considered as the earliest organized response of Indian Christians to the nationalist movement for independence. According to John Webster, in response to Mahatma Gandhi's call to Indians for *swadeshi* (self-sufficiency), the AICIC passed in 1921 a "resolution urging that the *swadeshi* spirit dominate all aspects of Indian Christian life, that Christians wear clothes of Indian manufacturer."[18] S. K. George, an Indian Christian leader of that period, saw in the *satyagraphis'* (participants in the nonviolent resistance or civil disobedience to the colonial rule) "willingness to suffer at the hands of the government for the sake of the poor of India something profoundly Christian."[19] The Madras Rethinking Group, of which P. Chenchiah, Vengal Chakkarai, and others were members, and the influential Christian magazine of that period, *The Guardian*, also provided the framework for a lay and indigenous Christian response to the quest for nationalism and ecumenical unity in the country.

It can further be argued that the participation of the Indian Christian lay leaders in the nationalist movement for independence played an important role in the growth of the ecumenical movement in the country. They saw an integral link between liberation from colonialism on the one hand, and from missionary dominion on the other. As Mathews George Chunakara[20] puts it, the ecumenical movement in India and in wider Asia "came as a movement of liberation, the liberation of the churches from the ecclesiastical, cultural and theological colonialism of the West."[21] It can also be stated that the realization that the nationalist aspirations of the people were integral to mission and unity emerged with the increased participation of people from the South in the global ecumenical movement. In response to the anticolonial and independence movements in Asia, the International Missionary Conference that met in Tambaram, India, in 1938 recognized "the new search by Asian churches for their selfhood freed from the paternalism and domination of missions to be able to relate themselves to the emerging national selfhood of their peoples within the universality of the worldwide church."[22] The conference stated unambiguously that mission and unity were inseparable.

The message from Tambaram that mission and unity were inseparable came in for criticism from diverse sources. On the one hand, the Evangelicals felt that the emphasis on the church would erode the significance of the "kingdom of God" that needed to be preached, especially in a pluralistic society such as India. The fear was that "the substitution of the church for the Kingdom of God might rob the missionary movement of the needed fires of imagination, enthusiasm, and self-criticism."[23] On the other hand, several Indian lay leaders feared that the emphasis on the church might reduce mission to be the business of the ecclesiastical bodies only, in the process leading to the marginalization of the struggles of ordinary people. Chakkarai believed that the church as an organism is constituted "not by mere cultus but by communion with the living Lord for social action." He, therefore, "opposed the CSI scheme of Church Union as a Western imposition on India, and irrelevant to the building up of an authentic Church in India."[24] Chenchiah, on the other hand, went beyond the framework of institutional churches and organized small groups consisting of Christians and Hindus for prayer and spiritual fellowship. As M. M. Thomas summed up the situation, the emphasis at Tambaram on the church came in for criticism later, by the evangelicals who feared that the centrality of the gospel was forgotten, and by ecumenists who stressed the significance of the "agenda of the world" for the mission of the church and the church understood as the sign of the coming unity of humankind.[25] While the conference provided the space for diverse interpretations on the missionary task and unity, the message was clear that mission was integrally related to ecclesiology. From Tambaram on, "it was impossible to speak of mission without directly linking mission to the church."[26]

When the Indians took over the administrative leadership of NCCI in the 1940s, the council "came out unequivocally in support of the Congress" (the Indian National Congress Party) "and its demand for Indian Independence."[27] As the country emerged from colonialism to be an independent nation, the Indian Christian lay leadership could equip the indigenous Christian movement to rise to the challenges of autonomy. Even as the missionaries continued to be in charge of the mission centres in the country, the council spoke up firmly that the church should not be controlled by foreigners. Of particular relevance in this context is the role of Rajah B. Manikam,[28] who assumed the responsibility of NCCI at the difficult postwar period when the missionaries still held leadership positions. Under Manikam's leadership "the Council changed from a kind of missionary institution to a truly indigenous organization."[29]

What is clear in this historical sketch is that in India in the 20th century there was an integral link between ecumenical initiatives and the nationalist movement, and that the driving force for Christian unity, in the country as a whole and especially in the case of the CSI, came from Indians and not so much from Western missionaries. The close alliance between Christian unity and nationalism was not unique to India alone but was a reflection of the rapid changes at the Asian level. In the wider context, the "real impetus for unity came from the Asian Christians who, under the inspiration of the national movement, took the initiative for Christian unity and for the building up of indigenous churches."[30] While Asian Christians recognized that mission and colonialism did not always go hand in hand, to a large extent the growth of the modern ecumenical movement was, on the one hand, the affirmation of the aspirations of the indigenous people for self-rule, and, on the other, a clear rejection of Western domination not only at the political level but also in the church. True, the missionary enterprise played a significant role in the emergence of the modern ecumenical movement, but India—no doubt, as part of the larger Asian context—with its emphasis on self-rule and self-determination, added a critically corrective component to this process.

Interfaith Relations

The work of Indians in the area of interfaith relations is widely acknowledged as having a decisive impact on the programmes and priorities of the ecumenical movement, especially during the last century. Several articles in this volume discuss this matter in detail.[31] The Tambaram Missionary Conference of 1938 was a major milestone in outlining the Christian mission in interfaith contexts such as India. There were, however, voices even before the conference that spoke of a synthesis of the Indian and Western cultural and religious heritages. One of them, K. T. Paul,[32] advocated the "indigenization" of the Indian church: "An indigenous Church rooted in Indian reality and drawing membership from different communities of India and realizing fellowship in Christ and oriented to evangelism and lay witness in secular areas of life, was to Paul the most effective witness of the Church in modern India."[33]

The Tambaram Conference was truly a landmark event as it ushered in a new phase for the ecumenical movement in which interfaith dialogue was an integral part. While making his presentation at the conference on the topic "The Christian Message in a Non-Christian World," the Dutch missionary Hendrik Kraemer asserted that the divine revelation in Christ transcends Western Christianity and that this transcendence makes Asian and African incarnations of Christianity not only legitimate but also imperative.[34] However, it was Kraemer's "concentration on the dangers of syncretism"[35] that won the day and the message that emerged from Tambaram was one which looked suspiciously at Christian involvement in interfaith dialogue. David G. Moses, who participated in the conference, disagreed with the attempts to reduce other religions to mere "human efforts to understand the totality of existence."[36] Moses argued that Christians should be open to the possibility and, indeed, validity, of revelation and the experience of God in other religions as well, and thus make interfaith dialogue a worthwhile experience.

The impact of the "Madras Rethinking Group," which produced the book *Rethinking Christianity in India*[37] just before the Tambaram Conference, also was felt in the discussions during that period. P. Chenchiah, an Indian Christian lay leader and a key participant in these discussions, raised a question that had serious ramifications from an interfaith and missiological perspective: "Why should Hindu converts join the church?" "He criticised the missionaries' dogmatic view and insisted on the necessity of continuity in the life of Indian Christians in a Hindu context."[38] Chenchiah went beyond the framework of institutional churches and organized small groups consisting of Christians and Hindus for prayer and spiritual fellowship. There were others, too, who envisioned Christ-inspired fellowship outside rigid ecclesiastical structures. As a disciple of Christ, Kandasamy Chetty of Madras Christian College kept himself in spiritual fellowship with the fellow disciples yet lived on the margins of the institutional church, as he did not accept baptism and join the church. He maintained that there was "nothing essentially sinful in Hindu society any more than there is anything essentially pure in Christian society—for that is what the Christian church amounts to—so that one should hasten from the one to the other."[39]

T. K. Thomas,[40] too, was persistently critical of a missionary Christianity in India that was wedded to Kraemer's "concentration on the dangers of syncretism." The constant focus of Thomas's writings was on the understanding of authentic mission in the context of plural India: "The God of the tribe may give way to the God of the people. The God of Christianity, for example, if he is the living God, must also be the God of Hinduism and Islam and Communism as well. He must be the God of irreligion as much as the God of religion."[41] Throughout, he grappled with the meaning of being a Christian in both a multireligious and secular context.

Criticisms of the pattern of Christian witness represented by the missionaries resonated well with the Indian ecumenical leadership of the 20th century. Yet, as the nation emerged from colonialism to self-rule and as the leadership of the Indian church moved to indigenous hands, a theological climate that saw the work of both the Westerners and Indians as part of the universal mission of God emerged. As Chandran Devanesan[42] observes, it should be possible for the missionaries to accept our friendship and admiration without expecting us to identify ourselves with them. The missionary should be able to "come as a representative of a different culture and civilization, bringing the best that his background can offer."[43] Underlying this spirit of openness was the grand vision of the universal church of Christ, as Devanesan goes on to say: "Not only is the Christian from the West welcomed because of new insights that he brings to the life of the church, but his very presence is a reminder to the Indians that the Christian Church there transcends national boundaries."[44]

Devanesan's sensitive comments point toward a key element in the transition of the leadership of the churches and the national ecumenical movement from the missionaries to Indian hands. That was the affirmation that both the missionaries and the indigenous Christians were part of a "global fellowship" with the recognition of mutuality and accountability. This position also provided the space for engagement with the missionaries in India long after their domination had ceased.[45]

The emergence of ecumenical study centres was a significant development in free India. Of particular relevance, in this context, is the Christian Institute for the Study of Religion and Society (CISRS) in Bangalore, founded in 1957 under the leadership of P. D. Devanandan and M. M. Thomas.[46] While the study programmes of CISRS had initially focused on Hinduism, in the 1960s and '70s it provided the space for a number of emerging scholars, undertook pioneering research on politics, church, and society in India, and published a number of significant books. The Henry Martyn Institute of Islamic Studies (HMI) in Hyderabad, another such institution, is committed to research, interfaith relations, and reconciliation within an ecumenical framework. In particular, the HMI is dedicated to the objective study and teaching of religions, the promotion of interfaith relations, and reconciliation.[47] Unlike Hinduism and Islam, however, an ecumenical study of Sikhism posed grave challenges. During a visit to Punjab in March 1970, M. M. Thomas observed certain fundamental problems in entering into a dialogical relationship with Sikhism:

> The real problem of Sikh religion today is that there is no Sikh theology of reform which grapples with the movement of secularization and ideologies of liberal or socialist humanism and seeks to interpret Sikhism in terms relevant to contemporary India. Sikhism has no leaders of religious reform to speak of and no tension therefore between dogmatic orthodoxy with emphasis on externalities of religion and religious reform with emphasis on change of non-essentials on the basis of fundamentals.[48]

During the last few decades, however, partly due to the work of institutions such as the Christian Institute of Sikh Studies in Batala, Punjab,[49] interfaith study programmes have also involved Sikhism. Serious theological obstacles in interreligious dialogue remain, and not only with Sikhism. In the context of caste divisions in Hinduism, Dalit theologians have raised questions about the partners in Hindu–Christian dialogue in India.[50] To be authentic, interfaith dialogue in our times need necessarily be open to such critical perspectives on dialogue. And, for that reason, ecumenical theologians may have to go beyond the established religions and enter into dialogue with "popular religions,"[51] especially those represented by the tribals[52] and the Dalits.

Several models for fostering stronger interreligious relations were advocated by Indian ecumenists. For Samuel Amirtham,[53] it was dialogue at the level of practical theology that pleaded for "unreserved openness to people of other faiths." As Amirtham put it, attempts to "clear interreligious misunderstanding and remove interreligious ignorance needs further emphasis with concrete programmes of corporate study of one another's faith."[54] Mathai Zachariah's[55] ecumenical vision, on the other hand, inspired him to found the India Peace Centre in the 1980s as a place for stronger interfaith relations, ecological concern, and the role of religion in building peace and harmony in the society. Through the work of the Peace Centre and in his own writings, Zachariah "emphasized the need for affirming the values of the profound cultural and spiritual heritages of Asian religions, which he said do not see a dichotomy between humanity and nature."[56]

Unity and Justice

It can, perhaps, be argued that the Indian ecumenists pioneered the connection between Christian unity and justice. No doubt, there were inspiring leaders who solidified this link.[57] But, more important, there were people and movements that, throughout the course of the ecumenical movement, raised pertinent questions about whether there can be real unity as long as the church is divided on racial, class, and gender lines. Such questions may be relevant in other societies as well, but they were particularly pronounced in India where traditional hierarchical divisions often overlapped with the notion of equality and justice that was ushered in at the time of national independence. As the country emerged from colonialism to independence, "the development model," based on the values of self-reliance, industrial growth, and economic planning for the establishment of a welfare state, was often projected as the way forward. The Nehruvian path, represented by the first prime minister of India, rooted in these principles and on the values of democracy and secularism, had a great impact not only in the nation but in the thinking of the Indian church as well. "Development departments" under the churches and ecumenical institutions strove to mobilize the students, youth, and others to return to the villages (where, as Mahatma Gandhi put it, resided "the soul of India") and to work among the poor and needy and thus rebuild the nation and the society.

From the beginning, however, there were Indian ecumenists who questioned the development model that did not include a concomitant focus on righting the historic wrong of social injustice and structural violence. At a time when "growth and development" were considered the most essential tasks for emerging democracies, they affirmed that "the notions of social justice and self-reliance have to radically re-define the meaning of development."[58] One of them was Samuel L. Parmar,[59] who questioned the argument that development was possible in the third world without tears. He affirmed: "Rightly understood development is disorder because it changes existing social and economic relationships, breaks up old relationships to create new, brings about radical alternations in the values and structures of society."[60]

The World Conference on Church and Society (Geneva, 1966) was a landmark event where the participants "insisted that the churches should be more active in promoting a worldwide revolutionary opposition to the capitalist political and economic system being imposed on the new nations by the Western industrial countries, which was leading to new types of colonialism and oppression."[61] Occasions such as these provided the opportunities to raise fundamental questions that "further undermined the validity of a secularist model of development which had largely been assumed within ecumenical circles."[62] The 1966 conference and economists such as Parmar truly marked a paradigm shift in the ecumenical movement.[63]

The situation of poverty, inequality, and injustice prompted a Christian response, at several levels, that went beyond the traditional acts of charity or mere "Christian participation in nation building"[64] and became an ecumenical movement that affirmed the building up of a just and sustainable social order and the struggles needed for these. As urbanization and industrialization with their inherent social and economic challenges became characteristics of modern India, the need for urban ecumenical mission was felt in different parts of the country. In Asia, Harry Daniel was one of the earliest to catch the vision of Urban Industrial Mission (UIM) and, as the presbyter of St Mark's Cathedral in Bangalore in the 1960s, he gave concrete shape to this concept.[65] Along with Paul Siromoni and others, he developed the Industrial Team Service that grew out of the urban mission initiatives of St Mark's.[66] As one of the first Indian leaders of the ecumenical movement in Asia, Daniel realized that Asian Christianity has a unique role to play to the rest of the world.[67] In a speech at the annual meeting of the Australian Council of Churches, delivered during a visit to Australia in 1959, he noted: "I am quite convinced that it is as we discern our mission in each of our particular countries and try to fulfil them [that] there will be . . . real co-operation between the countries of Asia, Australia and New Zealand."[68]

Another initiative in urban mission came from Bombay (now, Mumbai) where George Ninan, in partnership with the CNI Bombay Diocese and the other churches of the city, established the Bombay Urban Industrial League for Development (BUILD) as an ecumenical response to urban poverty and inequality.[69] The Urban Industrial Mission in Durgapur, West Bengal, was yet another initiative. Emergency situations, however, called for an immediate response to a mass crisis. During the struggle for independence in Bangladesh in 1971, as refugees flooded into Calcutta and the rest of West Bengal, Canon Subir Biswas, the vicar of St Paul's Cathedral in Calcutta and the Cathedral Relief Services, led a massive operation to provide relief and refuge to the uprooted people.

Situations varied from context to context but the ecumenical response was clear. As Subir Biswas puts it, "Some people in India would be quite happy to see the church just keeping to itself, maintaining the beautiful grounds in the midst of violence and tension. Yet we ourselves who are within this feel we can't do it. We have to expose ourselves, to put our property and our church in jeopardy. It is a way of asking repeatedly, what does the incarnation mean in our lives?"[70] This conviction was reinforced by a significant stream of social thought that Indian ecumenical leaders developed.

The pioneers of urban industrial mission in India integrated their work with the larger vision of the church. According to M. A. Z. Rolston,[71] as India embraced industrialization, the situation presented the church with a great responsibility: to discern and to declare our Lord in the social change wrought by science and technology. "It has to work with Him in response to the needs of the time, and the need in India to-day is for a definition of new social goals and a new direction; to give people, especially those coming under the shadow of industry, a new set of values and to help them to become fellow workers with God."[72]

Apart from the urban and rural mission, the Indian ecumenists also addressed the larger question of global geopolitical and economic developments. The 1960s and '70s were a significant period for Christians who believed that their faith should propel them to address the problems of poverty, inequality, and injustice, and the economic systems under which these breed. The ecumenical document prepared by C. T. Kurien[73] and others affirmed that while growth and development are among the professional categories in the assessment of economic systems, they cannot be assessed as the *norms* for the evaluation of economic systems: "The norm must be the responsiveness of the economic systems to human needs."[74] There were others who raised disturbing questions about the link between poverty and development, at the regional and global levels. The thinking of C. I. Itty[75] influenced and challenged a generation in the ecumenical movement on development, poverty, and justice.[76] Samuel M. Isaac[77] was another leader who enabled "Asian churches to address economic difficulties and poverty in Asia, by facilitating various development programs in Asian communities. He brought his rich experience and commitment to empowering the churches in Asia to respond to the mission of God amidst the sufferings of Asian people."[78] In short, the Indian participation in the ecumenical movement during this period contributed richly to theological reflections on a "spirituality for combat,"[79] with participation, transcendence, and transformation as the three determinants of spirituality.[80]

For Indian ecumenical theologians, the situation of the marginalized people was the foci for theologizing. K. C. Abraham[81] contributed significantly to discussions on mission from the margins. As James H. Cone notes, "For K. C., mission is not just what has been traditionally called evangelism or the proclamation of the Gospel to the unbeliever. Neither is mission simply dialogue with people of other faiths in the hope of bringing them to Jesus. Mission is making solidarity with poor people in their flight for justice. To proclaim Jesus Christ without bearing witness to the justice he brings is to distort the emancipatory power of the gospel."[82] Another scholar who theologized from the perspective of the marginalized people was Christopher Duraisingh.[83] Commitment, for Duraisingh, was to discern ever anew the liberative and "multicolored" wisdom of God in all God's rich diversity through imaginative dialogue with diverse cultural expressions of Christian and other religious traditions.[84]

Concern for the marginalized people also involved ecumenical work for health and wholeness in the total community. In his work in WCC's Christian Medical Commission (CMC), Eric Ram[85] "pioneered early models of integrated primary health care programmes in the state of Maharashtra, where church and government collaborated very closely."[86] Ram also made a deep impact on the wider Indian society as his model of primary health care was adopted by the state of Maharashtra and by the government of India.[87]

While methodical attempts to address the systemic violence and injustice in the society were important, the political emergency declared by Prime

Minister Indira Gandhi on 25 June 1975 provided the Indian church with an immediate situation where the civil liberties and democratic rights of ordinary citizens stood suspended. Many ecumenical leaders found in the situation an occasion to affirm "what it means to be the Church in face of the fundamental ethical challenges of our time or, to put it differently, how church fellowship can be maintained in face of ethical conflicts."[88] According to M. M. Thomas, his opposition to the emergency regime "was just a natural, almost unheroic, response to a political act which cut the ground of the ecumenical Christian concern for human rights and peoples' liberation and of the spiritual vocation of all middle class intellectuals including my own."[89] There were similar initiatives elsewhere. M. A. Thomas[90] transformed the Ecumenical Christian Centre (ECC) as a base for ecumenical reflections and campaigns against the emergency. WCC and its Commission of the Churches on International Affairs (CCIA) and the Christian Conference of Asia (CCA) also protested the regime.[91] The ecumenical response to emergency, however, was not a unified voice.[92] A good part of the official leadership of the established churches of NCCI supported the emergency regime.[93]

The Indian emergency reminded us of how fragile the democratic and secular fabric of the country was, but also provided the occasion for people of faith and others to rethink their priorities and come together to uphold the values of peace, justice, and freedom. Christians who believed that their faith should propel them to address the problems of poverty, inequality, and injustice faced by people in the South felt the need for a common platform for solidarity and fellowship. The 1970s and '80s witnessed the influence of liberation theology and ecumenical social ethics in India, which challenged several seminarians and young people who were inspired by the All India Catholic University Federation (AICUF) and SCM to plunge into the struggles of the unorganized people. Considering social activism inspired by Christ as their vocation, they initiated social-action groups in different parts of the country working with rural poor, Dalits, Adivasis, women, contract laborers, fish workers, victims of mega-development projects, and the like. These expressions of public witness were not only ecumenical, but also instrumental in broadening the understanding of being ecumenical in a multireligious context. M. J. Joseph, Y. David, Rajendra Sail, Antony Murmu, Thomas Kochery, and a host of others were part of this alternative expression of ecumenism. M. M. Thomas recognized the significance of such social-action groups and peoples' movements and called them "secular koinonia."[94] And the Programme for Social

Action (PSA) emerged as a common platform for the various social-action groups that work across the country among the urban and rural poor, displaced people, fisherfolk, and agricultural labourers. These resistance groups repeatedly challenged both the church and the ecumenical movement to maintain a focus on the struggles of the people.

While the response of the leadership of the Indian church to the emergency regime was diverse and ambiguous, clear ecumenical voices emerged out of the situation, in the process providing the impetus for the church to move forward. As the forces of fundamentalism and religious nationalism renewed their presence in India in the 1980s and '90s, threatening the secular fabric of the nation; as large-scale "developmental projects" posed a grave threat to the environment; and as the solidarity of the movements led by the urban and rural poor, women, Dalits, and the other indigenous people gained momentum, the ecumenical movement was constantly challenged to be partners in the process of building a just and sustainable social order.

Dalit and Adivasi Context

The Edinburgh Conference of 1910, the first major ecumenical gathering in the 20th century, was not a widely representative body. The few delegates present "from the colonies" (Australia, New Zealand, and South Africa) and "the new churches" (of Asia—Burma, Ceylon, China, India, Japan, and Korea) provided the lone voices that heralded a southward shift in mission and ecumenism in the following decades.[95] While there were occasional voices "from the South" in the ecumenical movement in the decades that followed Edinburgh, a concerted effort to assert the presence of the marginalized people was visible in the aftermath of the WCC Uppsala assembly (1968). The Central Committee in Canterbury (1969) set up the Programme to Combat Racism (PCR) and approved financial grants to liberation movements in southern Africa.[96] With regard to India, however, a major milestone came with Masilamani Azariah's speech at the WCC Vancouver assembly when he asked for a reference to be made to the "outcastes" in the assembly's report on human rights.[97] In particular, he demanded the insertion of a paragraph on the plight of the Dalits in India. Azariah recalled that there were similarly marginalized groups in other places, such as the Buraku people in Japan. While migrants and refugees were included in the statement on human rights, and their rights were recognized as being under stress, he demanded that the Dalits in India and elsewhere certainly needed special attention.[98] Azariah's intervention at Vancouver was perhaps the first time that the "Dalit issue" was raised on a global ecumenical platform.[99]

Liberative ecclesiology and hermeneutics have been constant themes for the Indian ecumenists who have been involved in theologizing from the perspective of the marginalized people. According to Kunchala Rajaratnam,[100] in this liberation process the Indian church should journey with the oppressed Dalits and Adivasis. The missionary objective of both the churches and the ecumenical movement should be to recognize and affirm this prophetic task in our times. Since the caste system is a self-contained and immutable social order ordained by religious traditions, Dalit theologians have found in the scriptures the resources to analyze and counter the forces of oppression. According to V. Devasahayam, we "need to make it known that in the Indian context, caste system is Satan and the original sin that stands in contradiction to the kingdom Jesus proclaimed and the cross needs to be reinterpreted as the revelation of counter-consciousness to the oppressive caste consciousness."[101] Such biblical insights on the situation of the marginalized people led to the founding of the Dalit Bible Commentary Project that, under the leadership of James Massey, seeks to "enable Dalit sensibility to enter into dialogue with the biblical word/text, making the Scripture more meaningful to their lives."[102]

During the last few decades, programmes that focus on Dalit concerns have been a regular component in ecumenical institutions, but it is debatable if these had any significant impact on the work of the churches. Deenabandhu Manchala[103] reflects thus on both the parallels and the challenges for Dalit theology as it is in dialogue with the theological reflections of the ecumenical movement:

> To some extent, one can say that ecumenical theology too, like Dalit theology, has been a counter-theological discourse, an alternative to the dominant ways of theological reflection that is often grounded in western denominational/confessional ecclesial settings. Likewise, it is also faced with the need to make itself relevant to the changed realities of the 21st century as it is cast in and remains in the methodological mould of the twentieth century western ecclesial reality.[104]

The 21st century has witnessed new perspectives on some of these issues. Emerging ecumenists have argued that treating Dalits, tribals, or women as a collective/essentialist/unitary category and creating solidarity programmes while keeping the paternalist consciousness is untenable. As Y. T. Vinayaraj puts it, in "the changed theoretical-theological-epistemological context, 'solidarity' means a re-imagination of ourselves; not merely a sense of 'standing along with' or 'speaking for' or 'representing somebody'." Rather, it should be a new journey that looks at our own faith, tradition, theology, and ontology.[105]

The Adivasis (indigenous people), who constitute around 8 percent of the Indian population, and who, in large numbers, responded to the Christian faith in the 19th and 20th centuries, stayed in the periphery of the ecumenical movement in the early days but gradually began playing a more prominent role. Nirmal Minz[106] argues that the Christian missions facilitated "a shift in the centre of their (indigenous people's) life from the ageless rhythm of nature to the dynamism of salvation history in Christ." However, he cautions that "the crisis it brought had both possibilities of cultural disintegration and potentialities of cultural growth and reintegration."[107] Minz further affirms that the "Jharkhandi Christian Community needs the experience of the Pentecost so that it will be bold enough to bear witness to Jesus Christ among Adivasis and Dalits and even before the dominant society and fulfil the Mission and Evangelism in this region."[108]

One of the crucial contributions of India to the ecumenical movement was the assertion that Christian unity needs to be a totalizing experience that embraces men and women of all social, ethnic, and racial categories. Inherent in such a recognition is the fact that certain sections of the church and society have historically been marginalized and, therefore, the just and equal participation of all would be a prerequisite for unity. It is the recognition that the ecumenical movement is not only a theological entity but also a sociological one and, therefore, unity in Christ will become a reality only when we are able to negotiate not only our ecclesiologies and orders but also our social identities and distinctions in terms of the identity of Christ.

Orthodox Perspective

It is widely accepted in ecumenical circles that Orthodoxy contributed immensely to the self-understanding of the World Council of Churches.

According to Konrad Raiser, even before the New Delhi assembly where the Orthodox communion became formally part of WCC, there were discussions about the need to revise the basis of WCC. In response to the demand of the Eastern Orthodox churches, the christocentric affirmation in the basis was revised and set in a trinitarian setting. The New Delhi assembly set in motion a long-term study on the theological questions involved in the full integration of the Orthodox communion in the WCC. "Recognizing the central importance given in the Orthodox tradition to the conciliar process in the church of the early centuries, the assembly recommended that a study be undertaken of the councils of the early church and their significance for the ecumenical movement."[109] Over the decades since the New Delhi assembly, the Orthodox contribution to the life and work of the ecumenical movement has developed in fresh and constructive ways.

Several leaders of the Orthodox churches of India have contributed significantly to the life and witness of the ecumenical movement. Foremost among them was Metropolitan Paulos Mar Gregorios (Paul Verghese) who was not only one of the first Orthodox theologians to hold key positions in WCC but, because of his deep theological insights, left an indelible mark on the ecumenical movement.[110] Metropolitan Geevarghese Mar Osthathios, another Orthodox leader, challenged the WCC to have an Orthodox perspective in the work of the Commission on World Mission and Evangelism (CWME). In this context, the Orthodox contribution of establishing within the staff team of the CWME a position for research and relations with Orthodox churches is important.[111] V. C. Samuel, an Indian Orthodox priest, focused his work on the Faith and Order Commission of the WCC. According to Lukas Vischer, the former director of the Faith and Order Commission, Fr. Samuel combined in himself high scholarship, deep humility, and quiet spiritual strength.[112] Sarah Chakko, C. I. Itty, K. M. George,[113] and scores of other Orthodox clergy and lay women and men have, over the years and decades, contributed richly to building up the ecumenical movement, at the national, Asian, and global levels.

Just before the Uppsala assembly, John W. Sadiq[114] had predicted that the Orthodox churches, and newly independent churches from Africa would, for the first time, be able to play an effective part in a WCC assembly. He went on to add: "One could prolong this list considerably. God does not stand still, even though we are tempted to do so. We are convinced that the Holy Spirit has guided this movement towards unity."[115] There is little doubt that this prediction turned out to be true as the presence of the Orthodox churches as an active participant in the ecumenical movement has been essential in shaping the understanding of our common calling for unity and witness. This has not been an easy road, and there have been a number of stumbling blocks on the way. Russell Chandran affirmed that, despite all the questions and hesitation for both the Orthodox churches and the rest of the ecumenical movement, the former "have shown sufficient evidence of willingness to understand and interpret themselves as a Church in via needing the fellowship of other Churches."[116] This dialogue needs to continue, as theology and ethics are inseparable and both belong together in an authentic response to the gospel.

Women in Church and Society

The conviction that the Christian fellowship should be a just and equal community of men and women is one of the cardinal features of the ecumenical movement. Madeleine Barot, who was the first director of the WCC department on the Cooperation of Men and Women in Church and Society, insisted that unity "is not only a matter of Protestants and Catholics being reconciled, but of women and men experiencing the liberating equality and renewing complementarity that is theirs in Christ."[117] Despite such affirmations, however, it was of little surprise that the Indian women were sidelined even as the ecumenical movement surged ahead with *men*, and the institutions and currents they represented. Any history of the church will need to acknowledge this reality and come to terms with it. Nevertheless, despite an intensely dismal environment for women, a few of them did manage to contribute richly during the course of history. Among them, Sarah Chakko undoubtedly played a pioneering role.[118] In the 1930s and '40s she was part of a global ecumenical team that undertook a study covering 58 countries, focusing on the participation of women in the life of the church. Chakko presented the report of the study at the inaugural assembly of the WCC in Amsterdam (1948) and steered the discussion at the plenary there. In response to the discussions at the assembly, the WCC set up an official group titled "Commission on the Life and Work of Women in the Church," with Chakko as the chairperson. In the years between the Amsterdam and Evanston assemblies, under her leadership the commission strove to build a just and sustainable community of women and men in the church and society.[119] It is also important to note that immediately preceding the New Delhi assembly, "a consultation was held in Madras on 'Changing Patterns of Men/Women Relationships,' which prepared the way for the enlargement of the women's department's mandate to include questions specifically relating to family life."[120]

Another Indian leader who attended the Amsterdam assembly and went on to mould generations of women leaders was Annamma George.[121] As Aruna Gnanadason writes about George: "She has left a rich heritage of good works and of women she has nurtured and literally raised. . . . I count myself among those."[122] Some of the other Indian women leaders who played significant roles in the ecumenical movement were Shanti Solomon,[123] Renuka Mukerji Somasekhar,[124] and Daisy Gopalaratnam.[125] Affirming the secular and yet Christian character of the YWCA, Ivy Khan[126] states: "The fact that the YWCA is motivated by the Christian faith forces it to reach out to women of all faiths or none. The fact of its inclusiveness is not an accident. Its inclusiveness, its open-door policy, stems from its Christian faith."[127] Gnanadason[128] locates her reflections in the context of the pathos of the Asian women. According to her, "The majority of Asian women . . . live a life of total powerlessness caught in the grip of poverty and deprivation, denied basic social, political, religious, and economic rights. Twice and thrice oppressed Asian women sell their labor and sexuality to a system that is dependent on exploitation and abuse of large sections of the society, in which women are the worst suffers."[129] Support, understanding, and hope, Gnanadason affirms, sustain women in their search for the answers to these and other questions.

Lay Leadership

In the words of Hans-Ruedi Weber, the history of the ecumenical movement as a whole is the story of the laypeople's commitment to be Christian in the world. The laity's "vocation and experience are marked by the fact that they almost always live in the transient, penultimate realities of this world although as Christians they attempt to live according to what Christian faith teaches about the ultimate reality."[130] Even though the theological discourse on the mission of the laity was less pronounced in India in the past, the country did make significant contributions in this area because of the institutions and movements that evolved in the country in the early part of the 20th century, as well as the visible participation of several Indian lay leaders in the ecumenical movement in the latter part of the century. Virtually every ecumenical institution in India in the early 20th century—the National Christian Council (later the National Council of Churches), the National Missionary Society, the Student Christian Movement, YMCA, YWCA, and also many of the missionary organizations that ignited the Christian Mass Movements in India—were lay initiatives. Throughout the century, as India had an active presence in the ecumenical movement, it was widely appreciated that a strong laity perspective was an integral component of unity and Christian witness, especially in a pluralistic context such as Asia.

Several factors contributed to the key role of the laity in the growth of the ecumenical movement in India. Organizations such as the All India Conference of Indian Christians (AICIC) provided the platform, in the 1910s, for lay Christians to meet, cutting across the denominational divide, and outside the framework of both the churches and the missionaries, to evolve their own patterns of unity, witness, and dialogue. The repeated visits of John R. Mott—about whom the historian K. Baago states, "there is probably no single individual to whom the movement for Christian Unity in India owes more than to him"[131]—to India in the first few decades of the 20th century, and the visit of J. H. Oldham—whose focus, too, was on lay ministry and ecumenism—were important. The task of the laity, as Oldham was fond of pointing out, was restoring the lost unity between worship and work. If the church is to be relevant in our times, "it can only do this through being a living, working faith of the multitudes of lay men and women conducting the ordinary affairs of life. The only way in which it can affect business or politics is by shaping the convictions and determining the actions of those engaged in business and politics."[132] (Incidentally, both Mott and Oldham were laypersons).

While several global ecumenical gatherings, going back to the Oxford World Conference on "Church, Community and State" in 1937, had dealt with the concerns of the laity in their deliberations, an increasing influence of the laity in the work of the ecumenical movement was visible at the WCC New Delhi assembly. The Section on Unity at the assembly asked the pertinent question:

> Ordinary social life already brings men together into various associations—academic, professional, industrial, political, etc. Within these forms of unity there is need for a Christian unity of those who may learn from each other how to bear their witness in those settings. Ecumenical thought in the calling

> of the laity needs to be shared in groups of this kind and it has its own bearing on church unity, for denominational divisions are often found to be quite irrelevant on this frontier. What is the bearing of that discovery upon our inherited divisions?[133]

Even as Christian unity continued to be an important concern for the laity, their primary mission was understood as "being Christian in the world." As Rajah D. Paul[134] puts it: "The effective evangelistic method for the future in this part of the world is the promulgation of the Gospel by consecrated Christian laymen in their secular occupation."[135] In this context, it needs to be emphasized that the Christian student organizations in India were an important factor in equipping the laity to be at the vanguard of the ecumenical movement. The first two visits of Mott "stirred up the entire Christian academic student world and led to the formation of the *Student Christian Movement* and the *Student Volunteer Movement in India*, the early members of which became the ecumenical pioneers in this country."[136] The role of the Student Christian Movement (SCM) in moulding generations of lay leaders in the church and society is of particular relevance. As several articles in this volume reveal, the values represented by SCM—inclusiveness, commitment to the preservation of a secular fabric in the society, and an open and challenging approach to the Christian faith—became strong pillars for the ecumenical movement.[137] In the words of C. I. Itty, who had worked for several years in both SCM and the WCC Laity department, the mission of the ecumenical movement should involve a

> new conversion to the world, a new engagement with social problems and their demand for social change; A conversion to mission; to present the gospel message to those who are not Christians; A new rhythm of life, worship and work, contemplation and action, distance and commitment, social service and social action, suffering and rejoicing, doubt and hope, repentance and pardon; New understanding of the cosmic vision of redemption, the worldwide nature of Christianity, the sacramental character of the church, and the sacramental vision of life and work.[138]

For the Christian laity, "protest" is an inherent part of the "new engagement with social problems." As Michael Kinnamon puts it, "ecumenism, when true to its fundamental vision, is a protest movement."[139] In India, there is a long history of protest initiatives with the active participation of the Christian laity. In the 1930s and 1940s several young people, as members of the Youth Christian Council of Action (YCCA) and SCM, were caught with the vision of understanding the meaning of Christian witness in a country aspiring to be independent of the colonial stranglehold but yet, as a free nation, was faced with the stark prospect of social unrest, oppression, and widespread hunger. These youth belonged to traditional churches that operated largely within isolated community-caste settings and yet were committed to making a difference during their lifetime.[140] This generation of youngsters, it needs to be added, emerged in the following decades to provide meaningful leadership for the ecumenical movement at the national and global levels. As injustice, violence, and caste polarization sharpened in the second half of the 20th century, and as the forces of liberalization and globalization threatened the social and economic fabric of the society, the Christian youth and SCM activists went out and lived with the poor and the oppressed and participated in the struggles of the subaltern, anti-dam, and ecological movements. They focused their attention on understanding the ethics of the subaltern life—their politics, theology, and knowledge mediated through social movements.[141]

The witness of pioneering laypeople succeeded in transcending the divisions in church and society and pointed toward new horizons of witness, unity, and dialogue in India and beyond. In their varied responses to Christ they, and the movements they represented, created the space for Christ-inspired fellowship and unity that built a firm foundation upon which a distinguished panel of lay and ordained Indian Christians emerged to provide creative leadership to the ecumenical movement and evolve relevant structures for witness, unity, and peace.

Ecumenical Theological Education

India has also been pioneering in providing an ecumenical basis for theological education. The United Theological College in Bangalore (UTC)—originally called Theological College of South India and Ceylon—was founded in 1910 "because of the vision of eminent church leaders at the turn of the 20th century to start an interdenominational institution to offer high quality theological education so that leaders with a broader outlook and a deeper commitment to ecumenism could be produced for the churches in India."[142] UTC was established through the cooperation of the London Missionary Society, the Wesleyan Methodist Missionary Society, The United Free Church of Scotland, the Arcot Mission of the Reformed Church in America, and the Trustees of the Jaffna College, and was later supported by several other missionary agencies and mission boards. It was affiliated to the Serampore College, Calcutta, for granting degrees in theology, but became an autonomous college within the Serampore system in 1976. While the regional theological institutions provided theological education in regional languages, UTC served as a national ecumenical seminary in English and drew students from most of the churches in all parts of India and from other Asian countries like Sri Lanka, Myanmar, Malaysia, and Indonesia. There is every reason to believe that the ecumenical theological education and international outlook fostered at the UTC provided an ecumenically conscious ministerial pool in India that made it easier to form organically united churches in the Indian subcontinent.[143]

Among the regional seminaries, the Tamilnadu Theological Seminary (TTS), established in 1969 at Arasaradi, Madurai, is an ecumenical institution that trains ministers, primarily in the Tamil language. TTS signified the merger of two seminaries—(1) the Tamilnadu Theological College, Thirumaraiyur of the Church of South India; and (2) the Gurusala, Tranquebar of the Tamil Evangelical Lutheran Church and the Aroct Lutheran Church. TTS is renowned for its bold experiments in indigenizing and contextualizing theological education in India under its first visionary principal, Samuel Amirtham. Jointly sponsored by the Church of South India, the Arcot Lutheran Church, and the Tamil Evangelical Lutheran Church, the seminary placed enormous emphasis on community-based theological and ministerial formation and theological education that took full account of the social realities of the churches. "Praxis-oriented theology, theological education through involvement, and theology in action have been given practical expression from the early days of TTS."[144] It became a model for theological education in context, based particularly on the experiences of marginalized communities. TTS also played a pioneering role in lifting up the realities of the Dalits in India and providing the space for the emergence of Dalit theology. Amirtham's other important contribution was the creation of the Rural Theological Institute, associated with the TTS, with emphasis on *living theology* done in the midst of the actual realities in which people lived.[145]

Samuel Amirtham left TTS in 1980 to serve the World Council of Churches for ten years, first as programme secretary and later as the director of the WCC Programme on Theological Education and as the director of the Ecumenical Institute, Bossey.[146] His successors at TTS continued the vision of the seminary. Dhyanchand Carr, one of the principals who followed him and an outstanding scholar in New Testament, did pioneering work in interpreting the Bible for the lived realities of the people of India. Before becoming the principal in 2003 he gave ecumenical leadership in the region as the secretary for Mission and Evangelism of the Christian Conference in Asia (1993–1998), enabling churches in Asia to "Read the Bible with New Eyes."[147]

Bringing his experience as student and lecturer at UTC and principal of TTS, Samuel Amirtham, as the director of the WCC Programme on Theological Education, emphasized ecumenical theological education and formation and popularized the concept of "theology by the people,"[148] which insisted that the life experiences of people are one of the sources of revelation for doing theology. Many Indian and Sri Lanka theologians that have made significant contributions to the regional and global ecumenical theological thinking have been deeply influenced by that ecumenical theological education at UTC or TTS.

There are several ecumenical ventures all over India in the field of theological education. The Senate of Serampore College, created through the Serampore College Act, 1918, passed by the Bengal Legislative Assembly, functions as the accrediting body for the Protestant, Orthodox, Evangelical, and Pentecostal seminaries in the country. Federated faculties in various parts of India also provide a common platform for the theological colleges of the different churches to offer courses in theology, especially at the research level.

While the indigenization and localization of theological education was an ecumenical response to the spirit of independence and nationalism in the non-Western world, the criticism has often been raised that Christian ministry in our churches has not effectively addressed the existential challenges and rapidly evolving context of the people. According to Philipose Mar Chrysostom,[149] even though the world around us has undergone significant changes during the last few decades, the content and character of theological education has remained more or less the same, in the process posing serious challenges to the relevance of Christian ministry. "Why are people not interested? Not merely because the liturgy is boring, but because they don't find any relevance for what is said in the church."[150] One of the challenges of ecumenical theological education in the 21st century is to evolve patterns of Christian ministry that are flexible enough to provide a faith response to the rapid changes in the world around us.

• • •

This chapter and the following chapters discuss a number of key players in the modern ecumenical movement. However, many more remain unnamed. As the 20th century spilled over into the 21st, even several names discussed in this volume have gained fresher perspectives and moved on into new challenges. In the ultimate analysis, ecumenism is an ongoing movement, the complete story of which will forever remain incomplete. Yet every milestone counts. And the ten pioneers discussed in the following chapters contributed, with their diverse expertise and strategies, to various strands of the ecumenical movement. Their work often overlapped with that of the others, but all shared a mutual commitment to unity, justice, and peace. Retrospectively, we can say that together they, and the others, wove a tapestry without which the ecumenical movement at the national, Asian, and global levels would have been poorer. We, therefore, have reasons to celebrate. Yet, our primary task today is not to rest on the laurels of the past but to recognize that the task ahead calls for a clearer vision, newer strategies, and deeper commitment.

CHAPTER 2

Roger E. Hedlund

V. S. Azariah: The Forerunner of Indian Ecumenism

Vedanayagam Samuel Azariah, the first Indian bishop of the Anglican Church in India, was born in Vellalanvilai, Tirunelveli district of Tamil Nadu, South India, on 17 August 1874, and died at Dornakal, in Warangal district of Andhra Pradesh, on 1 January 1945. Essentially an evangelist, Azariah guided large numbers of mass-movement converts into the church for nurture and care. As an ardent nationalist and church-union proponent, Azariah was an important figure in early stages of the modern ecumenical movement. He had a leading role in the discussions that culminated in the formation of the Church of South India in 1947, two years after Azariah's death.

Nationalism

Generally speaking, Indian Christians were nationalists who welcomed the end of imperial rule. Indeed, as Judith Brown observes, ecclesiastical "decolonization" had already occurred in 1930 in the formation of the Anglican Church of India, Burma, and Ceylon. Thus, long before political independence, Indian Christians and their missionary colleagues were part of an autonomous church within the Anglican Communion. That was the context in which attempts had been made—not entirely successful—to build up an Indian church leadership.

Indian Christians viewed the prospect of independence and the end of the British Raj as a threat. What might the future hold for indigenous Christians "in an environment where nationalism was shot through with the imagery of Hinduism and the identification of the motherland with the mother goddess, and where many of the local politicians within the dominant Congress party clearly saw India in terms of the Hindu majority"?[1] As the first Indian bishop of the Anglican Church, Azariah, himself of low-caste background, expressed this insecurity in a sermon in Madras Cathedral in 1938: "Nationalism is apt to be identified with loyalty to the ancient religion of the land" and could produce suspicion and hostility toward "any religion which is not supposed to belong to the soil, and which . . . is pledged to propagate itself among all outside it."[2]

Early Ministry

The YMCA: Azariah's ministry began with the Indian YMCA, which he served as secretary for more than ten years (1895–1905). His work entailed considerable travel to many parts of India, providing him exposure to the church and its leaders in a variety of settings throughout the subcontinent. The resulting relationships and contacts would prove invaluable for Azariah's further leadership development.

In 1902 Azariah, along with Sherwood Eddy, visited Jaffna, where he observed the work of the Jaffna Student Mission, which was engaged in missionary outreach to the Tamils in India as well as in Ceylon (Sri Lanka).[3] What he saw apparently made a deep impression. Returning to Palayamkottai in Tirunelveli district, he called for a meeting. There, on 12 February 1903, Azariah challenged the eight clergy and 20 laymen about the need for a structure to enable the church in Tirunelveli to carry the gospel to other parts of India.[4] A draft constitution patterned after that of the Church Missionary Society (CMS)[5] was circulated, a managing committee was formed with Azariah as secretary, and Dornakal, where no other mission was engaged, was selected as the field of the new mission.

Indian Missionary Society: The Indian Missionary Society (IMS) began as a mission of the Anglican Church in India, and in 1947 became the diocesan mission of the Tirunelveli Diocese of the Church of South India.[6] Azariah played a leading role in the formation and development of the IMS and its field. "In 1909, Azariah resigned his YMCA post in order to serve as a missionary priest and evangelist at Dornakal. By 1912, there were 8,000 converts in a great mass movement. Azariah adopted Andhra as his own land and Telugu as his language."[7] On 29 December 1912, Azariah was consecrated bishop with responsibility for Dornakal Diocese, the first *Indian* Anglican bishop. By 1920, membership had increased to 86,000, and ten years later to 158,000. The IMS continues to be active today, with some 500 missionaries serving in 17 states. Its ministries include schools and hostels, clinics and rehabilitation centres. Converts are formed into new congregations.[8]

The IMS might be compared with the Church Missionary Society (CMS) of the Church of England, which Azariah formed in Tirunelveli to inspire and channel the missionary vision and support of evangelical Indian Anglicans, for which the CMS served as model. But there were differences. Azariah is known to have been inspired and challenged by the China Inland Mission (CIM) and sought to replicate its indigenization policy and standards. Founded by J. Hudson Taylor in 1865, the CIM was a "nondenominational 'faith' mission with a conservative evangelical gospel message and a strong emphasis on identifying with the foreign culture through language, dress, and manners."[9] The IMS emulated many but not all of these distinctives. The IMS had a similar evangelical focus, but with strong ties to the Anglican Church in Tinnevelly, which precluded a nondenominational appeal. The CIM's identification with local culture, however, "provided Azariah and the IMS with valuable guidelines for respecting local Telugu customs. All IMS missionaries learned the vernacular and stressed the importance of cultural continuity after conversion."[10]

At Dornakal Azariah advocated both "structural indigenization" by which control of foreign missions should be transferred to Indians, and "cultural indigenization" by which Western-style institutions and religious expressions should be transformed into local equivalents, thus hoping to plant Christianity deep within the Telugu cultural soil.[11] The church, as implanted by Azariah and the IMS, would maintain membership in the multinational Anglican Communion, but also participate in broader expressions of the "universal" church "whose ecumenical character he enhanced as a participant in South Indian Protestant church unity negotations."[12]

National Missionary Society: The National Missionary Society (NMS) came into existence on Christmas Day (25 December), 1905, as an expression of Indian Christian nationalism combined with missionary zeal for spread of the gospel utilizing Indian resources. As with the IMS, it was Azariah who took the initiative and played a foundational role in creating the NMS as a nondenominational society with supporting links to the major Protestant denominations of India, hence becoming an interdenominational agency seeking to spread the gospel to nearby countries as well as in India. Rather than Western relationships, the NMS forged links with Indian churches for finances, personnel, and accountability. NMS missionaries are drawn from Indian churches of various denominations, and NMS-planted congregations "are handed over to the nearby churches in that locality."[13] At one time Sadhu Sundar Singh was an honourary missionary of the NMS. The NMS is supported by Indian giving, and its leaders are chosen from the mainline churches. Its main concern is evangelization of the unreached in India and neighbouring countries.[14]

Unity versus Disunity

Early in his ministry Azariah saw Christian disunity as a serious issue, and battled for unity between the Anglicans and other denominations. "Azariah tried to shock the western church out of its complacency. Denominationalism was taken for granted in the West, but Indian Christians could ill afford divisions, outnumbered as they already were by non-Christians on the subcontinent."[15] He pointed out that Indian converts exploited the shambles of disunity in order to perpetuate caste divisions by joining separate caste-based churches.

> Azariah helped to jump-start the twentieth-century ecumenical movement at a meeting between representatives of the Church of England in India and the South India United Church (a united Congregational-Presbyterian church) at Bishop Whitehead's Madras residence in 1910. This meeting sparked a process that led, after many years of painstaking labor and negotiation, to the first reunification of episcopal (Anglican) and non-episcopal (Congregational, Presbyterian, Methodist) Churches since the Reformation, in 1947. Although the new Church of South India came into being two years after Azariah's death, he participated in virtually all of the major interdenominational meetings leading up to its formation.[16]

As it transpired, the question of church government became the most divisive issue in the unification process. From the beginning of the negotiations, Azariah took a strong position defending the necessity of retaining the historic episcopate. While this supported the Anglo-Catholic tradition, it brought Azariah into conflict with Congregationalists and other non-Anglican participants in the church-union movement.[17] Denominationalism, in Azariah's opinion, was an alien export from Europe and needed to be eliminated in order to achieve a truly indigenous Indian Christian church. Moreover, Indian converts to Christ tended to reify ecclesiastical sectarianism to perpetuate sociological caste divisions. Above all, it was the bishop's observation and experience that disunity was a severe impediment to evangelism as well as a violation of Jesus Christ's prayer for unity among his followers, "that they may all be one . . . , so that the world may believe that you have sent me" (John 17:21).[18]

As Azariah's biographer Susan Billington Harper observes, "The unity movement was one of the primary means by which Azariah became a world-renowned churchman."[19] It remained his conviction that church unification was necessary for church indigenization as well as to remove barriers to evangelization. Azariah and many who joined with him were in fact ardent evangelists. Azariah "regarded evangelism as the single most important instrument of cultural change." He believed that the "social gospel" would never succeed without conversion, and that "the church's primary vocation was to share the gospel."[20]

Caste has been identified by many as a major barrier to the spread of the gospel in India. On biblical and theological grounds, Azariah opposed and rejected caste for its exclusivity. Yet he recognized certain sociological values in caste as an integrative system. His experience in Andhra convinced Azariah that "group conversions along caste lines were much less socially disruptive than individual accessions."[21] It seems appropriate that Bishop Azariah was given the oversight of the Mass Movement Survey that J. Waskom Pickett[22] conducted under the auspices of the National Christian Council of India. The purpose of this survey was to assemble and evaluate information regarding the mass movements taking place throughout India so as to help leaders of church and missionary organizations to think through the issues and to shape policies and programmes accordingly. The outcome was a vindication of the values of such movements together with identification of possible weaknesses and dangers and how best to proceed.[23]

Azariah recognized and appreciated values in the local religious culture and institutions, aspects of which he sought to incorporate into Christian life and worship. He devised "indigenous new forms of liturgy, music, drama, architecture, festivals" and a new Christian marriage ceremony adapting Hindu symbols such as a Christian *tali* "as a substitute for the Western wedding ring."[24] Nowhere was Azariah's indigenization more visible than in the Dornakal Cathedral, "which mixed architectural elements and symbolism from Hindu, Muslim, and Christian traditions into a wholly unique synthesis."[25] Combining the domes of Muslim mosques and the pillars of South Indian Hindu temples together with Christian imagery and the cross required 25 years to complete. "This cathedral, entirely hand-carved and hand-built by local people, was the bishop's most dramatic statement of Christianity's potential as the 'fulfillment'—of good but incomplete Indian faiths and of beautiful but imperfect Indian cultures."[26]

More important was the dynamic of social and cultural change released by the gospel. Azariah waged war against "the four Demons—Dirt, Disease, Debt, and Drink," and introduced a wide range of activities to improve the living conditions of the people, for instance, schools and dispensaries, banks and cooperatives, cleanliness and sanitation initiatives, cottage industries, agricultural and industrial projects, and more.[27] Such projects would benefit not only the Christians but, potentially, also Indian society as a whole.[28] "Christianization, in the Dornakal Diocese with its variety of socio-economic and cultural repercussions is, thus, perhaps best understood as one of many facets of change which occurred in the wider context of *jati* upward mobilization."[29]

Indigenization Resisted

Following his consecration as bishop, Azariah was the sole Indian to serve in that capacity. "No other Indians were made diocesan bishops during Azariah's lifetime."[30] Despite Azariah's popularity and eminent success, indigenization did not necessarily follow. Intercaste and interregional rivalries led many rural Christians to prefer a European rather than an Indian bishop—their presumption being that the former would be less vulnerable to prejudice. Azariah's recommended solution to the problem was the appointment of assistant bishops "as a temporary expedient" to prepare the way for creating additional dioceses as well as for indigenous leaders.[31] Given opportunity to appoint an assistant bishop for Dornakal, Azariah chose an Irish CMS missionary because "he doubted the abilities of Dornakal's Mala, Madiga, and caste converts to handle the responsibilities of episcopal office,"[32] all of whom at that stage lacked the needed education and experience.

Resistance to indigenization continued following Bishop Azariah's death. Rivalry between Malas and Madigas persisted within the church, but both were united in their opposition to further appointments of Tamil bishops for the Telugu church. "The Dornakal church stressed the use of indigenous Telugu musical and dramatic idioms in worship and evangelism, and this may have made Telugu Christians more self-consciously aware of their Telugu heritage."[33] Yet it was Bishop Azariah—a Tamil Nadar missionary from Tirunelveli—who had zealously promoted and adapted local Telugu cultural expressions for Christian use.

Many of the Christians in Dornakal were products of conversion movements in Andhra Pradesh among Malas and Madigas, movements ignited by new converts and spread through networks of relationships, especially of family and caste. Here, as elsewhere in India, the most effective agents for the spread of Christianity were not the missionaries but the Indian Christians who spread the gospel informally among their own people.[34]

Notable people movements in the early part of the twentieth century were recorded by the American Baptist "Lone Star" Mission at Nellore and Ongole, bringing thousands of Madigas to follow Christ. One key figure, Paraiah Yarraguntla, came to know about Christianity through a relative, was baptized, then formed a close relationship with Baptist missionary John Clough at Ongole. Together they toured widely from village to village, preaching the gospel and baptizing thousands of new believers. "The part played by Paraiah in this ministry was very significant. Clough acclaimed Paraiah as his guru (teacher), while Paraiah revered Clough as his spiritual teacher."[35] But it was Paraiah, "already an articulate and trained yogic *guru,* who became the true catalyst . . . for the movement."[36]

A similar movement took place in the Godavari Delta field of the CMS among the Malas, sparked by the conversion of notorious highway robber Pogolu Venkayya, whose changed life and testimony eventually brought thousands into the church.[37] In the nearby territory of the CMS sister Anglican mission, the Society for the Propagation of the Gospel (SPG), near Cuddapah, conversion of another Mala outlaw, Akutu Nancharu, resulted in a movement which by the end of the century brought some 10,000 into the church, increasing to nearly 20,000 by the year 1920.[38]

The rapidly growing Christian movement among the Malas appealed to the Lutheran Mission at Guntur for instruction and assistance. Whole families and villages converted together, thus forming a common front in the face of opposition and persecution, upholding and encouraging one another, with their leaders and structures intact. As with previous movements, each new conversion movement later attracted numbers from the so-called higher castes such as Kammas or Reddis, which saved Lutheran Christianity from becoming exclusively a Mala religion or Telugu Baptists entirely Madiga.[39]

This, then, was the context, dynamic and ever-changing, in which Azariah served. "An ardent nationalist, ready to see the end of British rule, he epitomized the spirit of conversion movements then taking place in many parts of the continent."[40] In 1935 Azariah estimated that there were some "800,000 Christians in the Telugu country, as compared to roughly 200,000 in the Dornakal Diocese," and reported a growing movement among Hindu castes, "about 50,000 Christians of caste origin" in all the Telugu missions at that time.[41]

Dual Identity of Christians

The dual identity of India's Christians is a somewhat confusing reality that is frequently misunderstood. Robert Frykenberg grapples with the supposed contradictions. One persistent misperception assumes "that Christianity is essentially European and that European religion has traditionally been Christian," neither of which is true.[42] An unfortunate corollary is the supposition that India's Christians owe allegiance to some alien power or institution. History, however, reveals that "despite intrusions from the West and from Christians of the West, from cultures that were alien and foreign, most Christians of India have continued to retain their own distinct cultural identities. These identities have remained, in most respects, clearly and predominantly Indian."[43] Frykenberg quotes the words of the bishop of Dornakal, who wrote, "The religion of Christ is one of the most dynamic factors in the world. It always bursts its boundaries, however strong and rigid those boundaries may be. It refuses to be confined to any one race, class, or caste. It seeks to embrace all."[44]

This being so, it is not surprising that Christianity found its way to India long before the advent of European traders and raiders and missionaries. "The emergence of Christian institutions in India occurred long before the arrival of Europeans (*Farangis*) and long before the Raj. Christians and Christian missions in India, in other words, have as much claim to being considered 'Indian', indigenous, and products of cultures that have arisen within the continent as any other socio-religious institution within the subcontinent."[45]

Nevertheless, there has been a considerable anti-Christian propaganda consisting of inflammatory language and unjustified charges. The essence of it is found in recent charges of "forced conversion and proselytization." But as early as 1937 Mohandas K. Gandhi had attacked Bishop Azariah, labeling his attempt to evangelize outcaste Malas and Madigas of Dornakal as "antinational." Ever since then, such rhetoric has been used "to implicate Indian Christians as being alien, anti-national and unpatriotic, or subject to forces from outside of India. The view that Christians in India, one and all, are manifestations of colonialism has remained pervasive, if not dominant, ever since."[46] As a recent researcher, Chad Bauman, observes, "conversion is one of the most politically charged acts in contemporary India."[47] For example, a political cartoon in local Chhattisgarh newspapers lampooned the local Catholic bishop as an "Agent of the Pope—A Servant of Madam [Sonia Gandhi]. . . . Changing religion means changing nationality. . . . Change the government in Chhattisgarh and we can stop conversion."[48]

Conversion movements among the oppressed are very much part of Indian Christian history. Gandhi, however, accused Azariah of "betraying the nation for his leadership of mass conversions in Dornakal."[49] The charge seems ridiculous considering that so-called untouchable groups (today's Dalits) were denied access to wells, temples, roads, education, and possibilities for better jobs and other social amenities. In truth, the bishop of Dornakal was himself the product of so-called mass conversion movements in South India, in Tamil Nadu, his father being a Nadar Christian pastor from Tirunelveli. Azariah's consecration as bishop of Dornakal in 1912 and his leadership of a conversion movement among the Telugu people "symbolized the ongoing consequences of work begun by Tranquebar, Thanjavur, and Tirunelveli disciples of Schwartz, Satyanathan Pillai, and Vedanayakam Sastri a century earlier."[50] This process of evangelization and Indianization was to continue as the advance of the gospel was carried forward increasingly by national Christian leaders.

Counteracting Prejudice

Commenting on the prejudicial view of missionary activity as cultural imperialism, Bengt Karlsson appeals for a more sophisticated approach to correct the misleading portrayal given by various pseudo-scholars. Alongside the dubious tale of missionaries imposing Christianity on the tribals, Karlsson advocates that a parallel story be told, one in which the people themselves are seen as agents who, for various reasons, deliberately choose to become Christians and make Christianity part of their own political and cultural projects and struggles. This other story is largely absent in the literature of tribal India. There are, however, some interesting examples.[51] Karlsson mentions the Nagas, Garos, Khasis, Mizos, and Rhabas, then points out that Christianity helped these and other tribes to maintain a distinct identity and also to develop leaders trained in Christian institutions. Rhabas and other tribes give high priority to education and the advent of modern medicine.[52]

Karlsson's conclusions find support in other recent scholarly research. A cover story in the popular *Christianity Today* magazine engages the demythologizing work of sociologist Robert Woodberry at the University of Texas. Armed with a generous grant from the John Templeton Foundation, some 50 research assistants, and a huge database project, through the wide-angle lens of statistical analysis Woodberry was able to study "the long-term effect of missionaries."[53] The outcome for Woodberry was a shock: "The impact of missions on global democracy was *huge*."[54] The missionaries had not set out to change history, but Woodberry's research shows that they did just that.[55] A number of myths were demolished. Woodberry states, "One stereotype about missions is that they were closely connected to colonialism. But Protestant missionaries not funded by the state were regularly very critical of colonialism."[56] More than that, the data supports the following claim: "Areas where Protestant missionaries had a significant presence in the past are on average more economically developed today, with comparatively better health, lower infant mortality, lower corruption, greater literacy, higher educational attainment (especially for women), and more robust membership in nongovernmental associations."[57]

Woodberry's research is catching the attention of the scholarly world. A summation of his work has won major awards. More than a dozen studies support his findings. "The growing body of research is beginning to change the way scholars, aid workers, and economists think about democracy and development."[58] The social and cultural betterment of the inhabitants of Azariah's

Dornakal Diocese likewise affirms Woodberry's sociological conclusions as does the story of Bengt Karlsson's tribals.

Dornakal and Culture

The political rhetoric of Hindu nationalist attacks against the Christian community seriously misrepresents the reality of Christianity's historic role in India. Christianity was a catalyst for change which has "neither denationalized the Indian Christianity nor diminished communities of other faiths."[59] Interaction between Christianity and India's other religious traditions did not improve one at the expense of the other, but resulted, rather, in a dynamic exchange which has enriched both. This took place despite the fact that "under the leadership of Bishop Vedanayagam Samuel Azariah (1874–1945), Dornakal became the fastest growing Anglican diocese in South Asia . . . i.e. from 56,681 in 1912 to 225,080 in 1941."[60]

Christian schools were beneficial to many upper-caste students enrolled throughout Andhra, "resulting in significant indirect cultural influence of Christianity on elite groups."[61] The impact was undoubtedly greater within the lower strata of society where "the church played an increasingly important role as the bearer not only of the Christian religion but also of social uplift."[62] This was particularly true in Dornakal, which by 1935 had 250 ordained clergy and more than 2,000 village schoolteachers in an extensive network of schools offering elementary education for children as well as literacy and vocational training for adults.[63] A pioneering programme for women's leadership produced nearly 2,000 women elders serving not only in village churches but also in 800 village *panchayats*.[64]

In Dornakal, conversion proved "an effective instrument for improving the status of depressed class groups." The evidence indicates that "conversion movements to Christianity were less a means of rejecting Hinduism and the prevailing caste system than a means by which subordinate groups tried to elevate their rank in the social hierarchy by accommodating and, sometimes, transforming the values of dominant, non-Christian groups."[65]

The process described above is an example of inculturation. "Through the process of inculturation, the Christian faith becomes part and parcel of a culture. It denotes that the grounding of Christian faith in a culture is the model of the Word becoming flesh in Jesus Christ in space and time."[66] Azariah's cultural adaptations caused the Christian faith to take root in the soil of Andhra Pradesh. Azariah himself was an expression of cultural adaptation, "a Nadar Christian from Megnanapuram in Tirunelveli" having offered himself for missionary work in the jungles of Dornakal. "An ardent nationalist, ready to see the end of British rule, he epitomized the spirit of conversion movements then taking place in many parts of the continent."[67] At Dornakal music, dance, rites of passage, and celebration of compatible feasts and festivals were part of the inculturation process. The local culture thereby was enriched and transformed by "the values and worldview of the gospel."[68]

Politics of Conversion

Conversion, in India, is a politically charged event. Mass conversion movements in particular were considered politically sensitive, having the potential to undermine Hindu claims to religious supremacy and hence to subvert the nationalist movement's objective of independence from British rule. As bishop of Dornakal and chairman of the National Council of Churches, Azariah, together with other national Christian leaders, were asked to voice their views on conversion.[69] In their cautious response, conversion was defined as a spiritual event, "a change of heart from sin to God" through Christ alone: "For Christians it is a privilege and a duty to proclaim Jesus and it was right for them to admit converts to the Christian Church."[70] In reply, Gandhi argued that "conversion should be left to God," stated his belief that "there is no such thing as conversion from one faith to another," and concluded that "Christians should confine their work to humanitarian service."[71] Behind this line of reasoning was the Hindu distrust of mass conversions among the oppressed. In response to Gandhi and others' criticism and suspicion of mass conversion movements, Azariah defended the legitimacy of mass conversion by discerning the real motives behind the movement as spiritual, that is, the work of the Holy Spirit.[72] Azariah recognized the need to establish the fact that "Indian Christians are not just a product of outside interference but the outcome of their own search for the new life in Christ."[73] Gandhi, however, continued his attack: "Harijans have no mind, no intelligence," and denounced conversion as the "deadliest poison."[74] Conversion of the untouchables threatened Gandhi's vision of *swaraj* (self-rule), and he viewed the conversion movement as merely a political move. "But he underestimated their resentment of being treated as object rather than subject and their deep desire for human dignity and equality."[75] Indian Christians sought to affirm their Indian heritage while simultaneously maintaining a distinct identity of their own. "Gandhi's suspicions about conversion meant that he tended to regard the Indian Christian community as an appendage of the [foreign] missionaries and not demonstrably a spiritual community."[76]

The Clash with Gandhi

Azariah and Gandhi were contemporaries. In her articulate and carefully documented study of the life and contribution of Azariah, Harper[77] makes the point that in light of his initiatives among India's outcastes, it was inevitable that he would come into conflict with Indian nationalism and its leading exponent, Mohandas K. Gandhi. "Both men were preoccupied with the problems of poverty and untouchability; and both men had devised entirely different strategies for alleviating its hardships."[78] Yet no record of their meeting and clash is found among Gandhi's collected works.

> Gandhi, the apostle of Indian nationalism, was actually educated in London, while Azariah, the supposed adjunct of western imperialism, was educated in India. Gandhi spent the first twenty-one years of his adult career in South Africa during the time that Azariah was traveling the length and breadth of India as a missionary advocate. When Gandhi returned to India from South Africa in 1915, he felt in many ways a foreigner in his own land. By the time the Mahatma began his famous train tour of India designed to reacquaint him with the ways of his own people, the younger Azariah had already spent almost twenty years riding trains, bullock carts, and bicycles throughout the subcontinent meeting with ordinary people and promoting his evangelistic message.[79]

Clearly it was Azariah's "evangelistic message" which formed the basis of their disagreement. What Gandhi called for was a reform of Hinduism, whereas Azariah proposed conversion to Jesus Christ. "Azariah and Gandhi did not clash directly over these issues until the 1930s. But the fundamental religious and philosophical disagreements that lay at the heart of their debates emerged much earlier. Gandhi's position that all religions were equally valid was directly opposite to Azariah's position that Christianity was the only true religion."[80] Azariah, too, was an Indian nationalist who resented the charge that Indian Christians were not patriotic: "If I labour to remove illiteracy, dirt, social enslavement and superstition of the neglected and the unprivileged or underprivileged—am I to be reckoned a foreigner with foreign sympathies with no love for my country?"[81] Gandhi, however, attacked the Christian missions, "implying that their work was secretly political," and this propelled Azariah into heated debate defending the authenticity of conversion movements among the outcastes.[82]

Increasingly, conversion was becoming a political event, and even more so with B. R. Ambedkar's declaration "that he would lead a mass movement of his depressed class followers out of Hinduism into a religion committed to social equality."[83] Azariah's response was cautious; he could not discredit what Ambedkar proposed, but recognized therein a favourable evangelistic possibility. As president of the National Christian Council (NCC), "Azariah became the leading spokesman for the Indian Christian establishment in its development of an appropriate strategy of outreach to depressed classes in search of a new religion."[84] This brought Azariah into direct conflict with Gandhi, "who by now was deeply hostile to Azariah's evangelism," who refused Azariah's invitations to visit Dornakal to see for himself, and became Azariah's vehement critic.[85] A failed reconciliation attempt ended in further misunderstanding and continued tension.

Increasingly, Azariah turned his attention back to the affairs of Dornakal Diocese. "Azariah's chief concern was not the distant world of national politics, but the pressing needs—both material and spiritual—of his depressed class village congregations and of their non-Christian neighbors."[86]

Ecumenical Contributions

Azariah's contributions to ecumenism relate to his passion for the gospel and direct involvement in missionary outreach. Christian nationalist though he was, he has been criticized for lukewarm involvement in nationalist politics. Harper finds the criticism unjust in that it misses the importance of his participation and contribution at a subnational level. "Unlike Gandhi, Azariah was not a politician. . . . He was a missionary and church builder deeply involved in agrarian conversion movements, uplifting depressed classes and promoting inter-church cooperation."[87] As bishop of Dornakal Diocese, his channels of influence were ecclesiastical rather than political—exercising leadership through the NCC, the Bible Society, the Joint Commmittee on Union, church and mission society consultations, major international conferences, and authorship of influential books, articles and pamphlets.[88] "As a Christian in a predominantly Hindu India, as a Tamil missionary in Telugu territory, and as a Nadar amidst Malas, Madigas, and Telugu non-Brahmins, Azariah was a perpetual foreigner in his own country."[89]

Harper reminds us that the roots of the ecumenical movement are in evangelical missions where denominational divisions created obstacles. "Azariah became deeply involved in the beginnings of the ecumenical movement largely because he was a committed evangelical missionary. His work as an evangelist to Telugu outcastes in his vast rural diocese motivated him to become a leader in the negotiations which led to the creation of the Church of South India shortly after his death."[90]

Azariah's involvement in the church-unity movement appears to have been an effort "to recapture the ecumenical spirit that he, like other participants in the unity movement, had encountered for the first time in the YMCA."[91] The South Indian ecumenical movement was inspired by the missionary objective of drawing India to Christ. "The many westerners and Indians who joined Azariah in the quest for Indian ecclesiastical unity were, for the most part, ardent evangelists who recognized that denominationalism was a barrier to the effective propagation of the gospel."[92]

Azariah's distinctive contribution might well have been his focus on the necessity of an Indian Christian identity, of "church unification as part of a larger program of church indigenization," a church of India, a living branch of the holy, catholic, and apostolic church universal.[93] Azariah thereby is a forerunner of the reality of *world Christianity* as it now is seen, its leadership increasingly from India (especially in the World Council of Churches), from Asia, as well as Africa, Latin America, the Pacific Islands and Pacific region.

Edinburgh 1910

Azariah's participation in ecumenical events in India and beyond brought exposure to the world Christian movement. It is not surprising, then, to find that he was a delegate to the World Missionary Conference in 1910 at

Edinburgh, Scotland. There he had been given responsibility to address the assembly. Brian Stanley notes that Azariah had travelled all the way from South India to Edinburgh "in the domineering company of the bishop's wife, Mrs Isabel Whitehead," and that the "stifling experience of being chaperoned by Mrs Whitehead" was almost certainly the background for "what Azariah had to say at Edinburgh."[94] "The Problem of Co-operation between Foreign and Native Workers" was his assigned topic.[95] In his opening statement Azariah acknowledged that "the relationship too often is not what it ought to be." He then hastened to add that "personally my relation with my foreign fellow-workers has been simply delightful, and that in all my travels throughout India I have received nothing but true courtesy and kindness from missionaries all over India"—apparently a bit of tongue-in-cheek hyperbole, followed by reference to "happy exceptions."

Azariah concluded: "Through all the ages to come the Indian Church will rise up in gratitude to attest the heroism and self-denying labours of the missionary body. You have given your goods to feed the poor. You have given your bodies to be burned. We also ask for *love*. Give us FRIENDS!"[96] It was this closing paragraph, and particularly his appeal for "friends," which is remembered as Azariah's charge to the world church, and which established his credentials as a world Christian leader and missionary statesman.

Remembered it is, not least by South Indian Christians who are heirs of Azariah's compelling vision and charge. The appeal for friends is reflected in celebrations of the Edinburgh WMC centennial, including publications such as *Edinburgh 1910 Revisited: 'Give Us Friends!'—An India Perspective on 100 Years of Mission*.[97]

Conclusion

V. S. Azariah died at the age of 70, on New Year's Day, 1945, having served as bishop of Dornakal for 32 years. In London, the Archbishop of York told that Bishop Azariah left "two lasting memorials—a cathedral built in Indian style, and a greater memorial still in the lives of the thousands whom he converted to Christ."[98] At a service of thanksgiving in memory of Azariah held in London, Bishop Stephen Neill remarked that "Vedanayagam Samuel Azariah at the time of his death was far and away the most outstanding of Indian Christians, and one of the most eminent Church leaders in the world . . ."[99]

CHAPTER 3

Raj Bharath Patta

"Lengthen Thy Cords and Strengthen Thy Stakes": Augustine Ralla Ram's Ecumenical Missional Contributions

> "I do not know what the future holds for me, but I know who holds the future and that is Christ my Redeemer who sustains me and with that faith I go forward in life fearless and undaunted."[1]
> – Augustine Ralla Ram

Augustine Ralla Ram has played an indispensable role in the ecumenical world that can be attributed to his farsightedness and pragmatic missiological characteristics. Ralla Ram was an ecumenical visionary in a true sense, which he demonstrated throughout his life in all the capacities that he served. He was a leader who was as good with actions as with words, who brought with him visions of building young people with ecumenical ideals and dedication. Ralla Ram is often referred to as the architect of the Student Christian Movement (SCM) in India, and SCM and churches in India owes greatly to his contributions. From his early days he sought to create greater unity among

Christian churches, to bear one witness to the one gospel and the one Lord in a diverse country like India, and to focus on the spiritual awakening among young people.

This present essay on Ralla Ram's ecumenical missional contributions reflects on his life, witness, and ministry. Most of these reflections are narrative in nature and content, only to highlight the style that Ralla Ram himself used during his speeches, writings. and lectures. Though there are several facets to his work, I have carefully chosen four strands of his missional contributions to demonstrate Ralla Ram's prime engagements: (1) mission as political spirituality, (2) mission as localization of the gospel, (3) mission as organic church union, and (4) mission as deepening ecumenism. These four threads are interwoven to form a rainbow texture of his contributions. This essay has been written from the perspective of one who comes from young, ecumenical, SCMer, and pastoral standpoints. Thus, it is not an exhaustive attempt in itself, but an invitational attempt, inviting ecumenical students and mission enthusiasts to ponder and explore more deeply into the contributions of Augustine Ralla Ram. Ralla Ram has left a rich legacy to our generations and this essay is a tribute to him, celebrating both his contributions and, therefore, ecumenism itself.

Biography

Augustine Ralla Ram was born on 1 September 1888 at Hoshiarpur in the Punjab. As the only son of an orthodox Hindu Brahmin family, Ram was raised going to the temple daily with his father, and spent most of his time as a boy meditating and praying. He was deeply inspired by the preaching of Kali Charan Chatterji, and shortly after his father passed away he converted to Christianity.

In 1911, Ralla Ram graduated from Forman Christian College, and in 1915 he graduated from Saharanpur Theological Seminary. He served as a pastor in Allahabad for three years before traveling to Iraq and Persia to serve as a chaplin to Indian Christian Forces. In 1919 he returned to India where he worked as both a church pastor and professor at Ewing Christian College. From 1923 to 1925 he took a leave of absence to travel with and served as national president of the Christian Endeavor Executive Council.

Ralla Ram was general secretary of the Student Christian Association of India, Burma, and Ceylon (SCAIBC) from 1928 to 1947, and vice president of the World Student Christian Federation (WSCF) from 1932 to 1935, during which time he travelled to Bulgaria, France, Germany, the Philippines, Java, and Malaya. In 1945, Ralla Ram received an honourary Doctor of Divinity from the College of Wooster in recognition of his service to the church of Christ ecumenical. He was elected as moderator in the United Church of Northern India at the 1947 general assembly. Ralla Ram became the secretary of the Uttar Pradesh Christian Council (UPCC) in 1948, a position he held until 1956. He was also editor of *The Christian Messenger* and remained so until his death in 1957.

Augustine Ralla Ram was involved with a number of organizations, boards, schools, and councils throughout his lifetime, and in the later years of his life he served as vice president of the North India Auxiliary of the All India Central Committee of the Bible Society of India, Pakistan, and Ceylon, secretary of the Provincial Committee of the National Missionary Society (NMS), secretary of the Committee on the Study of Hinduism, chairman of the Advisory Committee to the Rajpur Retreat and Study Center, and superintendent of the School and Home for the Blind in Allahabad. He was also part of the executive committee of the National Christian Council and on its committee on public affairs, and served on the subcommittee of the Unification of the Ministry for the Church Union Movement.[2]

C. S. Paul, writing about Ralla Ram, notes his characteristics as follows, which sum up his biography well: "First, his ability to make friends and keep them; second, his ability to spot out young men of promise and build them up to take positions of leadership; third, is the way in which he brought light and cheer into any company he entered; fourth, is his exuberance and conversational ability; fifth, is his whole-hearted enthusiasm for any cause that he espoused; sixth, is his practical concern for those who needed his help."[3]

Ecumenical Missional Contributions

Ralla Ram contributed tremendously in translating faith into praxis all through his life, and tirelessly strived in making the gospel in Jesus Christ more relevant to his context and to his generations. His renewed faith in Jesus Christ was the very basis for his moving forward in life. Most of Ralla Ram's contributions toward church, society, mission, ecumenism, and theology are interwoven and inseparable in all his works and, therefore, we shall summarize his contributions in four prominent missiological categories. Each category should not be viewed independently on its own as a separate layer, but needs to be perceived holistically with the others.

Mission as political spirituality

Ralla Ram in all his capacities—as pastor, lecturer, and organizational executive—always participated in the nation-building process. One has to understand the context in which his ministry and mission engagements continued, predominantly in the pre-independent India and later, during the early stages of nation building, as independent India. As a Christian nationalist, Ralla Ram was always passionate in engaging politically and commentating on issues of national and international significance. He served as a member on the Public Questions of the National Christian Council, and was vocal in challenging the Indian churches to locate themselves actively in the sociopolitical realities of their context.

The following narrative explains well Ralla Ram's political understanding of mission and spirituality, including an instance of his political interpretation of mission and spirituality:

> It was in 1932 the International Missionary Council (IMC) invited a delegation of Indian Church leaders to Britain to speak to a variety of Christian audiences about their experience of the Christian religion. The idea for this "Mission of Fellowship" originated at the World Missionary Conference at Jerusalem in 1928. Among the Indian delegates were Ma Nyein, Headmistress of the American Baptist Mission High School in Burma, A. M. Varki, Principal of Union Christian College in Alwaye, Travencore, Augustine Ralla Ram, General Secretary of the Student Christian Association of India, Burma, and Ceylon and J. S. C. Bannerji, who had just been appointed as the Assistant Bishop of Lahore. The Mission's primary objective was to revitalize the older churches in England by exposing them to the fresh vision of the younger churches, thereby framing the purpose of their visit with a definite spiritual and evangelistic aim. Thereby the organizers thought they could prevent delegates from addressing "political" issues of the Round Table Conference, whose third session was to convene on November 15, 1932.
>
> In the course of time, the word reached the Executive Committee that Ralla Ram was engaged in "political" activities. He had distributed a "political manifesto" during his visits to various churches, was privately meeting with

> Christians throughout England to discuss political issues. He even arranged visits with the Duke of York and the Prime Minister to discuss his political manifesto. The manifesto stressed the need for the immediate acquisition of dominion status for India, and demanded the release of all political prisoners. It also supported the notion that Home Rule ultimately has to be taken by Indians and could not be granted by the British Parliament. It envisioned the drafting of a Constitution only after the acquisition of Dominion status for India. This whole activity was seen as a serious breach of the original understanding regarding the spiritual purpose of the Mission by the organizers. William Paton the chief organizer chided Ralla Ram for his inexperience in practical affairs and criticized Ralla Ram that his Manifesto was both crude and ignorant of the actual processes affecting political change. By such an act Ralla Ram had already made a huge impact on the congregations in England. Ralla Ram had to stress the inseparability of the spiritual from the political in order to justify his activities in England.
>
> The IMC leaders who organized the Mission, as committed as they were to "devolution" within the Church, still believed that Christian identity required no direct engagement with secular national consciousness. It was also later opined that the separation of spiritual from political domains inclined Protestant elites, toward an apolitical interpretation of the Indian Christian community.[4]

This incident explains Ralla Ram's understanding of mission, and exhibits mission as both resilience and as political spirituality. In contradiction to objectives of the "Mission of Fellowship," which wanted a separation of faith of politics, he had to be bold in expressing his faith to explain to the world that spirituality and politics are inseparable. He challenged the dominant paradigm of mission and countered it with his grip on the gospel of Jesus Christ. Ralla Ram was a youth representative to the delegation, and yet, from that marginality, he courageously voiced out and acted according to his commitment to mission. For him, the inseparability of the spiritual and the political in mission was a contextual and theological necessity, and therefore, despite all the interruptions and criticisms, he brought in the relevance of faith by interweaving spiritual and politics.

Ralla Ram, through his writings, always spoke about Christian engagement in the sociopolitical realities of that day. He wrote that, "Members of the Church are urged to practice Christian citizenship by taking part in the political life of the country."[5] He wrote on the Kashmir question, on the United States' aid to Pakistan, the coronation of Queen Elizabeth, the Bandung Conference ("an epic making conference indeed which has given us great satisfaction all round"); on the need for Good Friday as a public holiday ("We beg the Government not on any account to deprive us of leave on Good Friday, a day of fasting, meditation and prayer"); on the disturbances in Hungary, the Nyogi Report,[6] and so on.

As the executive secretary of UPCC, Ralla Ram took up several issues concerning the society to the chief minister of the state, including problems related to the missionary friends from overseas, scholarship money for village children, taxes assessed on schools in rural areas, the standing of the council with the government, and the needs of the School for the Blind in Allahabad.[7] He always had a heart to relate the faith and the concerns of the society and, therefore, held his nerve in expressing his spirituality in relation to the given situation, locality, and context. He had a wide exposure on the issues relating to national and international concerns, and spoke with conviction in addressing them as part of his Christian calling. His political spirituality was one of the greatest traits that Ralla Ram exhibited and he inspired many people, both of his generation and in the generations to come.

Mission as localization of the gospel

Ralla Ram always held his faith in Jesus Christ dear to him, and lived out the values of the Christian gospel all through his life as his father nurtured him from childhood. The name Ralla Ram means "mixed with God" or "thrown into the streams with God"[8] and, therefore, he always had that experience of being in the streams with God, as revealed through the evangelistic fervour that he displayed.

a. Indigenization of ministry

Following his graduation from the Saharanpur Theological Seminary, Ralla Ram came to Allahabad to minister far from his hometown in Punjab. That was the period of nationalism, and the Christian leaders of that generation were speaking about the national Indian church and missions. In that context, the young Ralla Ram, at the age of 26, was fully engrossed and enthused about the National Missionary Society (NMS), which was then a ten-year-old national indigenous movement started by pioneers like Bishop V. S. Azariah and others. As Ralla Ram became the pastor at the Katra Church, he spoke often about the NMS: "He organized young groups, he devised orders of service in which the responses were Indian responses, the music sung to the rhythm of the table drums—services at which the congregation sat on the floor, their leader on a slightly raised platform, worshipping as their forefathers had worshipped for generations. There were many criticisms of his 'Hindu' services but Augustine went on making plans, plans, and plans."[9]

Ralla Ram, as a young seminarian being exposed to contemporary theological articulations, tried to practice what he had learned at the seminary, attempting innovation and the contextualization of liturgy and evangelism through indigenization. Though there were criticisms, he never shied away from his convictions, and carried forward in what he believed.

In other instances, Ralla Ram was dressed in a yellow robe, used bells to ring at appropriate places in worship, and used little clay lamps instead of candles, which brought indignation among some sections of the Indian Christian community. In Dehradun, there were people who came in black flags in protest against Ralla Ram's indigenization of liturgy. For him, indigenization was always a matter of spiritual nourishment and spiritual enjoyment. He translated many English songs to Hindi and later the UCNI asked him to prepare a new Book of Common Worship, *Rasumnama.*[10] For breaking the bread, he, as a pastor, would come down into the pews and break it among the people of God.

Ralla Ram's preaching was also very powerful and made an indelible impact on the listeners, for he spoke through simple illustrations and used some symbols to drive home the point. He was a brilliant preacher, and everyone was inspired by the way he preached the word from the gospel.

b. Localization of church language

Even in his church language, Ralla Ram wanted to use Indian local words. He believed that symbols and spaces explain the ideology, and he therefore wanted such locations also to be indigenized, which he felt was appropriate for his context.

> He even questioned the usage of "Amen" by Indians, asking "what does that mean to us Indians?" He would ask, "Why shouldn't we be saying 'Shanti, Shanti, Shanti (peace)'? And that word 'Padre', which was used for Pastors, we should be called 'Sevak' (servers). The Church music is unspeakable, well, unhearable then—words that cannot move our hearts sung to tunes that

> should all be used for funerals! What we need is some good, red-blooded, soul-stirring Punjabi bhajans of praise sung to the rhythms of our own drums."[11]

Ralla Ram felt it necessary to translate the language used in the churches to be suited and appropriated to the local context, rather than using some strange, foreign words of which one wouldn't know the meaning. Language for him did make a difference, and therefore he consciously saw to it that the members of his congregation were called to locate and own the message of the gospel by localizing the terms that they used in the ministry. The "Word becoming flesh" was best understood by his localization of the gospel, situating it among and within the local communities of his times.

c. Liberation by rehabilitation

Ralla Ram not only preached with simple illustrations, but he made it a point to practice what he preached. There were some Christians who belonged to the "sweeper" castes or, as they were called, *safai karamchari* ("manual scavengers"). Ralla Ram had a special concern for these people and wanted to address their needs and issues. It was recorded that

> He was intensely interested in the rehabilitation of those Christians who belonged to the so-called "sweepers" caste. He wanted them removed from their old situations and new work given to them. He felt very strongly that they should not clean latrines nor eat the food left over from the rich man's table.
>
> One of Augustine's young missionary friends was appointed chairman of a committee to see what could be done for these Christians. After a thorough survey, he came up with plans which could be carried out immediately and in the sweepers' current situation. Augustine violently opposed it. He had no patience with such a plan. He wanted the whole sweeper community lifted bodily from its environment and moved to something better and that done at once, "at one breath."[12]

Ralla Ram's opposition to caste-based and occupation-based discrimination was exhibited by his courageous outrage against the plan and procedure for a committee to rehabilitate the "sweeper" community. All that he wanted was to be done all at once, with immediacy and urgency. He vehemently opposed the attitude of charity toward these people, and upheld that all forms of discrimination are against the very essence of the gospel. He very well knew the tactics of committees and plans for future, and realized that there would be a delay in implementing the decisions or even a push for appendices in acting on such plans; therefore, he called for a quick action on rehabilitating those communities on the margins of his society.

d. Inclusion by solidarity

In another instance, Ralla Ram was keen on affirming equality of all people irrespective of their identities. It was noted that

> The campers at Sat Tal ashram were all gathered together for our final picture. The servants were asked to come into the picture, which they did—all but the "sweepers," who stood off at one side. Padre Ralla Ram called to them to come but they hesitated. He went over and took the broom from one of the "sweepers" and came back and took his place to be photographed holding the broom in his hand. All of the "sweepers" then came into the picture and stood near him.[13]

This incident speaks of Ralla Ram's concern for the equality of all people. His counteraction of holding a broom in his hand when inviting those that were hesitant in joining was a remarkable symbolic act of solidarity to exhibit. It was a Jesus-like quality "in cleansing the feet of the disciples." Ralla Ram wanted to identify with the "sweeper" communities himself by holding the broom; thereby he created a confidence in them that all are equal, and it was an invitation to build a community of inclusivism.

Ralla Ram never showed discrimination toward anyone who came to him for help. His home was always open for all people; he was always eager to extend help, even at busy times and schedules.

> The home of the Pastor of Jamna Church became as busy as a junction of railway station. Yet Padre Ralla Ram had time for everybody. Did a chaprasi (an outcasted person) come with a note into his swirl of activity? Augustine would not keep him waiting first on one foot and then the other while more important business was being transacted; the pastor would dash off a reply at once or, if this were impossible, he would bring the poor messenger in and sit him down in a chair.[14]

Ralla Ram's daughter Sarah Shirin recalls how her father would travel in crowded third-class compartments, even when he was granted first-class travel, so that he could save some money to educate very poor children in the locality.[15] He showed no distinction among people and attended to them on the basis of equality, of course with a preferential option to those on the margins. These are simple narratives, yet they have profound insights of spirituality and convictions for inclusion and in building equality for all people.

Mission as organic church unity

Ralla Ram throughout his life believed, strove, and participated in promoting unity while affirming diversities. He was one of the key proponents in working toward an organic church union movement in North India, and thus paved the way for the formation of the Church of North India. Nurtured in the Presbyterian church tradition, he became a pastor of that tradition and served at the Jumna Church in Allahabad. Later he went as a chaplain to Iraq and came back to work for the ecumenical movement in various capacities. He dreamt of one Indian church, where all the differences would be given up, and thus lead to the formation of a new Indian church free of denominational and doctrinal baggage. Due to his leadership and commitment to such an ideal, the United Church of North India (UCNI) moved from strength to strength in becoming a united and uniting church in North India. Ralla Ram represented the UCNI at its first meeting of Union negotiations and became joint secretary of the Negotiating Committee on Church Union. Later he was on the subcommittee of the "the Church and the sacraments."[16] In 1952, he represented the UCNI at the Conference of the Faith and Order Commission called by the Continuation Committee of the World Council of Churches.[17] Through the positions that he held and by attending various committees and conferences, he strove hard to make church union a reality.

In Ralla Ram's worldview, organic church unity was the need of the hour in the Indian settings and, therefore, he had to be strong in containing all the differences and diversities. He wrote:

> I am afraid that my article as a reply to Dr. Horton's position has to be very militant, for he is an outstanding leader in the Church and the opinion which he holds is entirely contrary to what we are attempting to do in North India by way of organic union. As a matter of fact, Dr. Horton finds it difficult to

> "jump out of his ecclesiastical skin," while we in India, who have been given all the garden of varieties of ecclesiology, can sit down and dispassionately sort out things for ourselves.[18]

Douglas Horton was a Harvard professor, a distinguished scholar on ecumenism, and a Central Committee member of the World Council of Churches, who had spoken extensively on being united as churches, but he had his reservations about organic church unions. In 1937 he edited the book *The Basic Formula for Church Union.*[19] In contrast to Horton's arguments against organic church union, Ralla Ram came out vociferously in support of organic church union in the Indian context. Ralla Ram acknowledged that in India there were varieties of ecclesial traditions, and all could sit down together and sort out things for coming together and for the common good. He quoted Horton's observations: "Fancy this conglomeration of denominations masquerading as the Church of Jesus Christ."[20] Against this background, Ralla Ram proposed the rationale for church union in India as, according to him, it was the Pentecost moment of their time.

a. Moving from federalism to union

Ralla Ram argued that in India, living beside and cooperating with one another, denominations had come a long way in extending friendship with one another. And such a "cooperation," Ralla Ram acknowledged, had yielded great fruits in Indian ecclesial settings. Therefore, he proposed that the Indian church needed to move forward to a new stage toward union, which he called the "promised land of re-united Christendom." India, he believed, had received that "messianic passion" to take it forward. Ralla Ram's friend Stanley Jones was also for federalism—that is, shared life but keeping separate denominational affiliations—among the churches in India, a position he shared with Horton; yet, Ralla Ram continued as a strong advocate for church union rather than federalism.

b. Denominationalism and colonialism as Western imports

Ralla Ram critically observed that denominationalism was an import to the Indian soil from the West, and this was one of the contesting issues against union and unity. He went on to say:

> In the political world we are fighting against the unwanted imposition of the West, namely colonialism, and in the ecclesiastical world we are waging a similar battle against denominational aggrandizement. Not that the denominations have achieved no results: they have given us important emphases, but now having sufficiently emphasized various aspects of the truth, they have begun to go to seed. We are truly appalled at the rapid import of fanciful denominational inventions that emanate from the West all the time.[21]

For him, colonialism and denominationalism were the dominant paradigms which operate on similar mechanisms and, therefore, he had to be again bold and courageous in being critical of these Western imports onto the Indian context. These imported products affected the very ethos of unity in Indian settings. Therefore, for him, church union was a theological imperative and also an adequate Indian ecclesial response to the divisive Western imports.

c. Indian land as spaces for adventures of Christian unity

As much as he critiqued the Western import of denominationalism to India, Ralla Ram encouraged his fellow country people to rise up to the occasion of solving the complex web of ecclesial divisions by attaining church union. He sought the cooperation of his friends in India by affirming the providence of God who had laid in their country a heart for Christian unity. Writing on church union in *United Church Review* in August 1949, he stated:

> It is futile for us who live in India to laugh at our brethren in the West for having brought their divisions to us. I am sure that were we in their places we would have done no better. Most of the divisions that have come to us have human reasoning behind them and that reasoning is fairly representative of humanity at large. . . . If we in the East can make a contribution to the solution of the problem of Church Union, we shall have played our part in the world-wide fellowship. It is to that task that we in India should address ourselves. It is noteworthy that in God's Providence it is in India, the land of castes and inter-communal divisions, that God has set His stage for

> adventures in Christian unity. It is in this land of baffling divisions and strife that the Church of Jesus Christ should stand up for that visible unity for which Christ interceded on the night of His betrayal.[22]

Ralla Ram acknowledged that India, despite all the divisions and splits that happened in the name of caste and religion, still continued to be a space for adventures for Christian unity, and that organic church union was the manifestation of that unity. In a step of moving forward toward church union, he stated that there was a great need for happy amalgamation or blending or combination of good from all the denominations, so that the union would remain intact and relevant for India. Theologically speaking, he asserted that God chooses for Christian unity spaces which are unthinkable and unrecognizable, for efforts for union come from the margins and not from the centres of Christianity.

d. Journeying as pilgrims united and uniting

Ralla Ram identified that the church is called to be a "pilgrim" on a journey toward being united and uniting as a way forward for the future. He was optimistic that organic union was the only available solution in overcoming divisions among denominations, and he believed that this was the ecumenical task for India. He further deliberated theologically on the various issues concerning the episcopal dilemmas, ministerial differences, the missional understandings, and such, which would come in the way of organic union, as each individual church had a different tradition that they followed. Underlying all these differences was the reality that Ralla Ram was fully convinced of and committed to the organic unity of the Congregationalists, the Methodists, the Presbyterians, the Reformed, and the Anglicans for the United Church of North India.

Recognizing the pilgrim nature of the church, he bid adieu to denominationalism, instead marching forward toward union, unity, and a united church in North India. He therefore concluded by telling Horton that

> The time has come for us to begin to say good-bye to denominational Christianity, at which your friends in America are such past-masters, and to fold up our tents and go on our pilgrim way rejoicing at becoming one united people of God. Paul rebuked denominations in the city of Corinth, and in the Celestial City of God, the coming Jerusalem, denominations have no meaning whatsoever; and if that be so, why not begin that heavenly life here

below and thus fulfill the wish of the Master: "as Thy will is being done in heaven, may it also be done upon earth."[23]

Ralla Ram was all out for organic church union, and left no stone unturned in making that a reality, making a great witness to Jesus' prayer, "that they all may be one." The seeds that he had sown did not fall to the wayside, but fell on fertile ground only to see how eventually, years later, the Church of North India was formed and grew from strength to strength, testifying to the discipleship of Jesus Christ. Ms. A. S. Martin acknowledges the prophetic role of Ralla Ram by saying: "in many ways he was ahead of his contemporaries, and most importantly, in his passionate concern for the unity of the Church and the Indianization of the Worship. His election as Moderator of the UCNI was recognition of his services to the Church."[24] It was indeed a befitting tribute to all Ralla Ram's contributions for church union.

Mission as deepening ecumenism

Ralla Ram spent most of his prime time building ecumenism and the ecumenical movement in India. He traveled extensively across the subcontinent and even abroad to several countries, promoting unity and ecumenism to several contexts of students, churches, and communities. He contributed voluminously for the cause of ecumenism from the grassroots to the regional councils to the national movements and, finally, to the global federations. Particularly, his contributions as the general secretary of the Student Christian Association of India, Burma, and Ceylon (SCAIBC) were outstanding in building up the student ecumenical movement that inspired many young people of his generation as well as in the generations to come. Even today, for his tireless contributions for ecumenism, Ralla Ram stands as an icon for the Student Christian Movement of India. He not only worked for the widening of ecumenism in India but equally strove to deepen it, by being rooted deeply in the Indian soil and Indian ecosystem.

a. Ecumenism as building perspective for young students

Ralla Ram's work and mission engagements in and through SCAIBC enormously contributed in shaping new leaders for the church and society. As a general secretary of this student movement, his visions and missional plans were of great relevance and utmost necessity in strengthening ecumenism among young students in the subcontinent. With his five-point programme for the SCAIBC, which were explained as "study, evangelism, Church, university and rural work,"[25] Ralla Ram was focused on his work, and instilled great momentum into the life and witness of the movement. He traveled extensively across the country in building the student movement, and sometimes his travels were elaborate, spanning long periods of time in gathering and building up the university students, and in making faith in Jesus Christ relevant and contemporary. He was gifted in spotting young leaders of promise, giving them sufficient exposure and shaping them to be the leaders of their generation. He laid a sufficient foundation for the movement of students and saw to it that SCM was both a student and a faith movement that made a difference in church and society.

Ralla Ram's final speech at the SCM conference in Tambaram vividly explained the role and nature of the SCM, which would stand as a light to the nations. He went on to outline ten points to the students about the SCM:

> Let us remind ourselves, that the one all comprehensive objective which brings us into the fellowship of this Movement is to accept the discipline of Jesus Christ upon ourselves and to joyously bear his easy yoke, and then to spread the contagion of this discipleship among the fellow-students who are our immediate neighbours.
>
> 1. A Worshipping Community: ". . . I shall never let a morning break without, in the silence of my room, being alone with God."
> 2. A Studying Community: "Let Bible Study become an essential part of our lives. . . . Particularly must we study the Christian faith and realize whether or not it has any uniqueness at all, especially in a country where everyone dins in our ears the heretical slogan, 'All religions are the same.'"
> 3. A Serving Community: ". . . Let us become sensitive to the needs of our fellow-students. Some are poor, some are lonely. . . . Let experiments be made in 'University Settlements' so that groups of students may settle down in needy areas to help their fellow-countrymen."
> 4. A Witness-bearing Community
> 5. A Community loyal to the Church
> 6. A Conference-minded Community

7. A Community for which the World Student Christian Federation has the same place as the Third International to the Communist. "Internationalists first and Nationalists as a result."
8. A Community that heartily believes in fun and laughter: "We must be merry-making disciples of the Lord Jesus . . . but anything cheap should not find a place."
9. A Money-raising Community: ". . . Let there not be a single Union that does not draw up a budget at the beginning of the term."
10. A Community that loves its national heritage.[26]

Ecumenism for Ralla Ram was basically instilling in the young student communities the values of Jesus Christ, so that they would develop a perspective for bringing changes in the society. Throughout his 19 years of work with the SCAIBC, he encouraged young friends to take leadership positions, brought in new horizons of faith and theology, and inspired a great wave of young people to be effective disciples of Jesus Christ in their generations. His ecumenical commitment speaks to our generations also.

b. Ecumenism as forging partnerships

It was Ralla Ram's idea and plan to see to it that the Student Young Women's Christian Association (SYWCA) and the SCAIBC were merged together for greater ecumenical witness. Therefore, he invited the SYWCS to hold their quadrennial conference along with the SCAIBC in 1928 when the world convention of the WSCF meetings were planned to be held at Allahabad. As a result of the joint meeting, they began to publish *The Student Outlook* together. In 1934, both the associations came together and merged into one movement named the "Student Christian Movement."[27] Ralla Ram was the most vocal and convincing voice in the merger, and believed that ecumenism is best communicated by forging newer partnerships and combinations, and in giving up individual choices for the sake of collective and united strength.

c. Ecumenism as empowering women

In a context of patriarchy both in the church and society and at a time when women's leadership was not even in the thought process in India, Ralla Ram overcame those cultural and ecclesial barriers and paved the way in promoting young women's leadership. Sarah Chakko, a young lecturer and later principal of Isabella Thoburn College in Lucknow, as a young girl was inspired by the SCAIBC through Ralla Ram's lectures. She eventually became a strong leader in the ecumenical movement. She was the first woman chairperson of the SCM in its history, and was also invited to be a president of the World Council of Churches. On hearing about the untimely death of Sarah Chakko in January 1954, Ralla Ram wrote: "It was such a pleasure working under her as my 'Boss'." (She had been president of Uttar Pradesh Christian Council). "I could always go to her in the midst of many baffling problems and after I had talked things over with her, I always came out knowing that there were satisfactory solutions in sight."[28] Ralla Ram had high respect for her leadership and both of them also traveled to China to visit and lecture at the universities there. At a time when women's leadership was a far-away reality, the ecumenical movement had women leaders like Sarah Chakko, and ecumenism always affirmed and emphasized that men and women were equals and partners.

d. Ecumenism as enlarging the tents

In 1937, the SCAIBC marked its jubilee celebrations in their quadrennial meeting in Burma, and Ralla Ram invited several senior friends along with students to attend the conference. It was observed there that the SCM work was to be extended, and therefore Ralla Ram recognized the senior friends as "deck passengers" and had an eye on them. He delivered the jubilee sermon on the biblical theme, "lengthen thy cords and strengthen thy stakes" (Isa. 54:2), which had inspired several young people and guided them in their journey of faith.[29] For him, ecumenism was building friendships among all people of God. Friendship among students of different contexts, regions, languages, and even religions was a way forward toward the ecumenical spirit. He also provided opportunities to lessen the intergenerational gap by building friendship between students and senior friends. C .S. Paul, the former general secretary of the SCM, reminiscing about Ralla Ram, wrote: "Before 1932 Augustine Ralla Ram had made the movement sufficiently strong to make the next big bid for expansion. During the preceding years, through incessant travel through the length and breadth of these countries and by building up Christian Unions in every University center and Christian College, he had managed to put SCA on the map."[30]

After serving the first year as the general secretary of SCAIBC in Chennai, in 1929 Ralla Ram and his family moved to Allahabad and rented a house, which they named "Scibac," as the headquarters of the SCM. In the years to come, this house became an abode for several people across the world who received gracious hospitality from him and his wife, Angelina. Ralla Ram could transcend the boundaries of regions, genders, languages, and cultures and display the fact that ecumenism is to enlarge the tents of every boundary drawn. His passion for church union was the best example for his vision of enlarging the tents for the church of Christ in India.

e. Ecumenism as building friendships

Ralla Ram was a member of the Indian delegation at the International Missionary Council (IMC) meetings held in Jerusalem in 1928 and in Tambaram (Madras) in 1938. In *The Student Outlook* magazine of the SCAIBC he explained his experiences of being a delegate at the conference in Tambaram. The major emphasis of the conference was "Christian gospel in a non-Christian world" and the programme brought together around 471 delegates from around the world.

About the participation of the Indian delegates at the Tambaram Conference, Ralla Ram observed that "it is interesting to us that of the one hundred and five delegates present from India, Burma and Ceylon, which number includes missionary members as well, fully fifty-five or sixty have been or are, outstanding leaders of the work of the Student Christian Movement."[31] This observation was only to express that the SCMers had been giving pioneering leadership for mission and evangelism at both the local and national levels, which speaks also to the ecumenical formation that happens at the SCM circles.

On the spirit of ecumenism displayed at the 1938 Conference, Ralla Ram commented that "for seventeen days it throbbed before our very eyes as 'Church unity in action' and what Tambaram says in simple language is that if Church unity could actually be practiced for seventeen days, surely 365 days can also become days of brethren dwelling together in harmony."[32] He could notice a micro-ecumenism being practiced and therefore he had no doubts of ecumenism in reality for eternity if all churches and denominations would come together and dwell in peace and harmony. The IMC in Tambaram was a great experience for Ralla Ram, for the delegates there could speak on various issues of mission and "mission lands." They conversed on various global issues of that period, like Czechoslovakia; discussed theological issues of Christian relation to the non-Christian faiths; had an exposure to the diversified talents of people from all over the world; and were, in general, encouraged by the generosity of the Indian participants in contributing to the IMC. With his vast ecumenical exposure, the conference was for Ralla Ram both a learning experience and also a contributing opportunity. During the conference he could make new friends from different countries and contexts, and make the global mission conference meaningful with local mission experiences.

C. S. Paul further comments on the unique role Ralla Ram played:

> With his remarkable genius for making friends and discovering leaders everywhere, he was able to accomplish in six short years, what very few could hope to do. The next big move was to detach the Student branch of the YWCA from the parent body and amalgamate it with the SCA. Negotiations were started in 1931. It was not by any means an easy matter. But Augustine as usual, proved himself to be equal to the situation. What we take for granted today came after many battles royal with Augustine forcing the pace and winning his cherished object of a united movement of men and women students. Those who were present at those meetings in Madras will remember what an able advocate and negotiator Augustine was. Thus came into existence the SCM which ever since had been an ongoing movement and not merely an association.[33]

This further shows that Ralla Ram's mission of building friendships among all groups of people was an expression of ecumenism, relevant for his times and even for our times today. S. S. Narasaya, a Brahmin who worked as his secretary at Madras testified that, during his six months of work with Ralla Ram, he gained rich experience in his life, which helped him to become a better Hindu.[34] Ralla Ram built ecumenical spirit in his workmanship and teamwork and was a good host for all occasions.

f. Ecumenism as singing a new song in a strange land

Ralla Ram was invited to preach at St John's College, Agra, on 24 February 1957, and he chose the text, "How shall we sing the Lord's song in a strange land?" (Ps. 137:4). He emphatically told the students that they were going into a new land, and that they must sing a new song. He went on to speak of the many circumstances and factors which made India somewhat a "strange land"—the difficulties and problems in the churches, the difficulties in the economic and political situation, and such. He, however, summed it all up with a note of triumph: "You must sing."[35] In a growing context of strange situations creeping up in the country, Ralla Ram challenged the young people to sing newer songs relevant and suitable to the given conditions. All through his lifetime, he sang new songs of liberation, transformation, and solidarity, thus making the gospel practicable and interesting.

Epilogue

Augustine Ralla Ram was one of the most outstanding ecumenical leaders that India has ever produced. All through his life, he was committed to the cause of church, ecumenism, mission, gospel and, unity. Born in the context of pre-independent India, he was surrounded by several complex labyrinths of sociopolitical and ecclesial issues, but he stood with firm conviction in Jesus Christ and in his message, and lived a courageous life with the only aim of living out the gospel appropriate to the context. His passion for mission, for his country, for his church and church union—all speak vibrantly about his contributions.

The four strands of his ecumenical mission contributions communicate the amount and tenacity of his dedication for the gospel of Jesus Christ. His political spirituality inspired several young people to stand up in resilience, to be bold and courageous, and to call on our generation to stand up for justice and justice alone, which is the need of the hour. His creativity in localizing the gospel of Jesus Christ was of pioneering inspiration to several churches of that period. He faced all criticism by risking Christ for the sake of Christ and the Christian church. His enthusiasm and passion for the unity of the church was unparalleled, for not only did he dream of union, but he moved heavens and the earth in making church union a reality. When cynics were pessimistic about such an organic church union, he was optimistic in opening up the tents and in widening it for all people of God, overcoming all denominational divides. His work in deepening Christian and human fellowship through the ministry of SCAIBC and other ecumenical forums were distinctive, for he envisioned new paradigms of ecumenism by attracting both the national and global Christian communities toward his vision.

Ralla Ram continues to speak to the generation today with much vigour and confidence, inviting each of us to join along with him in contemporizing faith in Jesus Christ in a way relevant to our context. He is inviting us to rededicate ourselves in making ecumenism a practice and reality, transcending all dogmatic and doctrinal issues. And he is inviting us to recommit ourselves for the cause of unity of all God's creation, respecting one another and making a new creation. He comes alive today with his simplicity and humility, calling us to locate God among the unrecognized and insignificant categories of life present around us.

I conclude this article with a prayer written by Ralla Ram for India, with my own prayer that this prayer would come true in our generation, and benefit all the generations to come.

A Prayer For India

We intercede before thee for beloved Hindustan
and our prayer is the same
as that of ancient seekers after thee,
"'From darkness lead us to light
And from shadows to reality."
Mercifully grant that millions of this land
forever engaged in arduous pilgrimages
in search of peace and satisfaction
may at last lay down their weary burdens
at the feet of him who gives rest and peace
to all those who labour and are heavy laden.

May they come at last to the haven of peace,
even Jesus Christ,
and find in him thine own response
to their age long quest.

To that end the frankincense of India's meditation,
the myrrh of its renunciation and sacrifice,
and the gold of its devotion
be laid at the feet of Jesus Christ
and may he be crowned Lord of all.
—Augustine Ralla Ram[36]

CHAPTER 4

Aruna Gnanadason

Sarah Chakko: A Woman Who Inspired the Ecumenical Movement

> Women themselves found something in Chakko which drew out of them a fuller and more confident life. The freedom with which Chakko inspired other women always carried with it a larger vision of responsibility and self-giving; and while it encouraged wholeness, it never gave room to cold ambition or self-pity. The growth into humanness was Chakko's achievement.[1]

Her life, from all accounts, indicates that she was like a shooting star— lighting up the ecumenical horizon for just a moment and then disappearing. She died too young, when she was just 49, but from that short life she has emerged as one of the most outstanding ecumenical Indian woman leader of all times. Too little has been written about her and too little is remembered of her in the churches or the ecumenical movement in India or globally, yet the impact she had is phenomenal, to say the least. What makes a reflection on her ecumenical contribution so fascinating is the fact that it has to be culled out of her life story. Most of what is written about her is anecdotal, stories from her brief life. And yet from these accounts what emerges is a story of courage, ecumenical conviction, and exceptional leadership.

The India into Which Sarah Chakko Was Born

Sarah Chakko's story, from her childhood to her emergence as an outstanding teacher and administrator to becoming a world ecumenical leader, is unique, given that she was born in 1905 into an India where women were just beginning to emerge out of domesticity and rigid social and familial strictures. The nation was still in the grip of colonialism and feudalism, though a nascent social-reform movement and freedom struggle was also blossoming. Social reformers in 19th-century India did include the question of women's rights as a central concern. One such reformer was Savitribai Phule (1831–1897), who, along with her reformer husband, struggled against the caste system and for the right to education for Dalits and for women. However, the concerns of women disappeared from the national agenda by the end of the 19th century. Nivedita Menon writes of "the refusal of nationalism to make the women's question an issue of political negotiation with the colonial state."[2] Menon explains why this was so: "the bourgeois leadership of the national movement chose to contest imperialist domination by simultaneously defining the public ('outer') sphere of the citizen as that where 'we' are the same as equal to the imperialist masters, and the private ('inner') domain as that where 'we' are different, thus justifying practices which were discriminatory to women."[3] So, right from that time we discern how the liberation of women was viewed as a "Western agenda" being thrust upon India, a position a few male intellectuals held, even till today. However, there are women who can be counted among the freedom fighters and there were other women (and male) reformers who did put in a considerable amount of effort to ensure the legal and civil rights of women in the newly independent India. Pandita Ramabai, Sarojini Naidu, Annie Beasant, and Aruna Asaf Ali are just a sampling of names of the reformers—they were all born before Sarah Chakko, and were active in the freedom struggle against colonialism, paving the way for women's rights to education, employment, and political participation to be enshrined in the constitution of India.

In the 19th century and in the first half of the 20th century, the Western Christian missionary movement was actively involved in working for the rights of Indian women in close connection with Indian social reformers. Education of women and children was the first open door available to women missionaries themselves, under the new women's mission boards. Teaching in schools, homes, or orphanages was the most frequent role for single missionary women. At that time, not only had the role of teacher functioned as the female parallel to the ordained ministry, but the ideology that prevailed was of "woman's work for women." Education was recognized as key for the liberation of women all over the world. Missionary women founded a full range of educational institutions in response to their faith in education as a means of both evangelism and social uplift.[4]

Chakko's Early Years

Sarah Chakko was born and grew up in a Syrian Orthodox family in Kerala. In a family of ten children, she was the fourth child and the second among five daughters. The family was evidently well off with servants, a big house and compound, and a plantation which they visited, yet she matured into a responsible and disciplined woman with deep compassion for those around her. Her mother, Mary, who was essentially a homemaker, had a deep influence on Sarah, with her simplicity and deep faith. "She did not believe in coddling her children, and gave them as much freedom as possible at an early age."[5] This comment confirms that there was no differential treatment between the sons and daughters in the Chakko home—they were all given freedom. At that period of history this was unusual, as by law and certainly by culture and tradition, males were favoured over females and treated preferentially. References are made to Sarah climbing on to a mango tree and straddling a branch 12 feet from the ground so as to read a book[6] (ironically, girls were not allowed to go to the public library in those times)![7] Her father took her swimming along with her brothers, which also was rare for an Indian girl.[8]

Sarah's father, Avera Chakko, was a graduate of the Madras Christian College and is described as "a man of rare personality, courage and integrity."[9] He was in government service, commissioner of police, and Commandant of His Highness the Raja's Brigade of Guards, the first Indian ever to hold that position. He was often away from home on duty, but saw to it that he spent as much time as possible with the children, developing a deep insight into their personalities and needs. Adored by his children, he became the primary influence in Sarah's life. He was very proud of her and even sought her counsel on occasion. She inherited his fearlessness and strong will, his purposefulness and his optimism. While he was impetuous and excitable, her mother was calm and self-possessed. Sarah got her calmness and poise from her mother and grandmother, after whom she was named. Through the ways in which her father encouraged the children to take decisions democratically, he taught them fairness and justice in all their dealings; this left its mark on Sarah when she took up her own leadership roles.[10]

Of course, there were differences of opinion between daughter and father. As was the custom, the Chakkos found a well-educated engineer who they considered a suitable husband for Sarah, but she had other plans. Her assertion that "marriage did not fit into her immediate plans"[11] was of course not well received by her father. It was indeed rare for a woman to take such a decision in those days, but she insisted that teaching was her life's vocation and that this was what God wanted her to do. A series of unexpected events created the opportunity for Sarah's wish to come true. Her father got involved in a project dear to his heart—to build a girls' residential school to be run by the church—and he was asked if Sarah could teach there. Thinking this would be a passing phase in Sarah's life, he agreed to her spending two years in Madras to teach in the Bentinck Girls' High School, run by the London Missionary Society, while the residential school in Alwaye, Kerala, was built. She did return home to the new school after two years, but soon she felt the need for further education and returned to Madras to complete her master's degree in history and economics. Educating women was her passion and she persuaded her family to let her to pursue her commitment, even if she had to move to the Isabella Thoburn College in Lucknow in the far north of India to do that.

The Educator

Sarah was driven by the commitment to be an "Indian Christian" educator. "She had a concern to create a spirit, a culture and a place which was not only Christian but truly Indian and expressive of an Indian understanding of Christianity. This deep gratitude to her own cultural heritage equipped her well for her pioneering ecumenical and international role."[12]

As an aside, it is important to note that even the government of India acknowledges the role the missionary movement played in encouraging the education of women.[13] The missionaries were "the most important non-official agency"[14] to engage in this work in those days. "They became the initiators mainly because in the early 19th century the officials of the (British) East India Company were reluctant to take up this issue for they feared that it would create unnecessary hostility amongst the people and would amount to interference in their social and religious activity."[15] Unfortunately, the Indian intelligentsia, too, did not want to get involved initially. "The Christian missionaries not only entered the scene but took up the 'dangerous' and sensitive issue."[16] They built institutions and paved the way for women's higher education "with a mixture of evangelical and humanitarian zeal."[17] While conversion was a key part of the early missionary efforts, the fact remains that they saw education as a way to empower women to resist social and cultural practices that denigrated them, such as *sati* (enforced widowhood) and early childhood marriage, as well as a means to lift them out of caste oppression.[18] The missionaries saw the promotion of female education as a way to develop the personality of women, and "essential qualities in women such as tenderness, love, domestic and social virtues and above all to mould the character of their children."[19]

While at the outset the focus was on literacy and school-level education and a commitment to mould women as good wives and mothers, the issue of Christian higher education for women in India was first initiated by American Methodist educationist and missionary Isabella Thoburn, who took a different attitude toward the matter. By the 1890s, the Women's Foreign Missionary Society, with which Thoburn was associated, was pushing its girls' boarding schools to a collegiate level in India, China, and Korea. For Thoburn and the missionary society, the education of women for leadership was a missiological goal in itself; she did not see it only as a way to evangelize Indian women.[20] The college Isabella Thoburn set up in Lucknow in North India was to have a lasting imprint on the life and service of a Syrian Orthodox woman, Sarah Chakko, in Kerala, at the other end of India!

Even as Sarah was completing her studies, a letter was received from Dr Mary Shannon, principal of Isabella Thoburn College, inviting Sarah to teach history there. This time her father recognized that there was no way that he could make Sarah turn back from the path she had chosen, and he agreed to let her go, even though Lucknow was over 3,000 miles away from home, in the Hindi-speaking part of North India. Here Sarah excelled; she was known for carrying to the students the four ideals of the college that she embodied in her own life—loyalty, spirituality, service, and poise. She stood tall and carried herself with such grace that her presence was felt wherever she went. "Students were drawn to her by her beauty that was not entirely physical, but reflected an inner attractiveness."[21] She spoke little, was known for her simplicity in dress, and became a favourite among the students because she challenged their imagination and interest by the way she taught. "Chaks" was the way the students affectionately referred to this teacher who was always available to them even as she maintained strict discipline when it came to studies and reading in the library. She was made chief warden of the hostel because of her rapport with the students and soon became vice principal. A few years later she was named principal of the Isabella Thoburn College; all these roles she played with efficiency and compassion.

It is recorded that one of the heads of department of the Lucknow University had remarked that "no other educationist in India possessed a personality and sense of dignity and self respect like hers. Though a strict disciplinarian, instead of awe she inspired respect, admiration and confidence in the minds of students."[22]

A Life of Faith and Discipleship

Chakko's childhood in the Syrian Orthodox Church and in a family devoted to the church stood her in good stead all her life. She and her siblings were immersed in the spiritual treasures of the church. "The ancient rites were full of movement and colour—lighted candles, swinging censors, fragrant incense, the brightness of the priest's robes. The children listened spellbound to the ancient chants and stood reverently with their elders during the service lasting two hours or more. The richness and beauty of the Orthodox liturgy left a deep imprint on Sarah's mind."[23] It is said that while she was active and engaged in many things all her life, "her public life was fed by springs of private and personal devotion which sustained and controlled her."[24] Sarah remarked that her only theological training came from her mother, who would read the Bible aloud to the family. The Syrian Orthodox Church had no theological college at that time and "much of the credit for its survival from the time of St. Thomas to our own day goes to the women of the church, who transmitted their faith in their families."[25] It was perhaps because she was so deeply grounded in her own tradition that Sarah was so open to ecumenical engagement when she was in Madras and later in Lucknow, and this prepared her well for her role in the global ecumenical movement. As a student in Chennai she worshipped in local churches of other denominations, and as there was no Orthodox congregation in Lucknow in those times, she worshipped at the local Methodist church for the last 24 years of her life.

The Ecumenist

All credit to her ecumenical formation as a young woman goes to the Student Christian Movement (SCM) of India, Burma, and Ceylon, as it was then known. She participated in student conferences in Java, Indonesia (1933) and in San Francisco (1936); she was also on the Indian SCM team which visited students in China in 1946. Additionally, she was a member of the YWCA from the time she was a student in Madras, later to serve on the national committee of the YWCA of India, Burma, and Ceylon; in 1947 she was elected vice president of the World YWCA.

When she received an invitation to attend the first assembly of the World Council of Churches (WCC) in Amsterdam in 1948, she had the courage to insist that the only way she would attend was if she went as a Syrian Orthodox person. She protested the invitation to represent one of the then-named "younger churches" (i.e., the churches newly formed by the missionary movement), as she proudly announced that her church was hardly young, being 1,600 to 1,700 years old! The Orthodox Church agreed that she could attend. As a follow-up to this she took a sabbatical from Isabella Thoburn, spending a year (1950–1951) in Amsterdam and Geneva where she assisted in setting up the Commission on the Life and Work of Women in the Churches. "She arranged meetings and discussion groups and in her wide travelling served as the finest possible public relations person for the Commission. Her personality, her interest, and her ability to interpret between East and West, traditional and new, gave the commission strength, stability and confidence."[26]

At the first assembly of the WCC in Amsterdam in 1948, Sarah Chakko spoke in the plenary about the life of the churches in the newly independent India. She also presented the interim report of the findings on a two-year study that the WCC had conducted to assess the role and status of women in the churches that had been discussed at the preparatory meeting for women held in Baarn in Amsterdam in 1948. She prefaced the presentation with words to the effect that the report was being presented on the basic assumption that this subject is the concern of the church as a whole and not the problem of women alone.[27]

From the outset, the Women's Commission decided to ground all its work on solid theological thought. Karl Barth, who was one of the leading theologians of that time, provoked discussions because of his views on the status of women and on the relationships of the sexes. In 1932, Willem Visser't Hooft's wife, Jetty Boddert, had been in correspondence with Barth protesting his literal interpretations of St Paul's epistles on the subject of women and men.[28] In 1948, at the first assembly of the WCC, Chakko, along with Madeline Barot and other women, asked for a face-to-face encounter with Barth to challenge him. Visser't Hooft recalls, "Barth was one of geniuses of that time. But he was scared. . . . he was *especially* scared of Sarah Chakko, maybe because there was something so dignified about Sarah."[29] Sarah and the other women, while commending Barth for his beautiful exegesis of the creation narrative, said that he "somehow pulled the rug out from underneath" it when he turned to the Pauline teachings on the place of women.[30] So courageous was Sarah Chakko in her commitment to the women's cause that she unhesitatingly took on this renowned theologian.

At the assembly in Amsterdam, in the discussion that followed the presentation of the interim report of the study, she asserted that the issue of the ordination of women was only a minor part of the whole problem. There were many other problems relating to the service of women which it would be good to discuss, and it surely could not be so very dangerous to discuss the ordination of women.[31] It is interesting that this was one of the questions posed to the study, perhaps because she was a woman from the Orthodox Church tradition! The issue of ordination to priesthood "continues to create a number of misunderstandings, gaps and disagreements in ecumenical discussions."[32] Today, however, Orthodox Christian women speak from their own context to the issue, and not "in the framework of the feminist movement nor through the introduction of other confessions."[33] Orthodox theologians such as Elisabeth Behr-Sigel and Kallistos Ware have studied the issue and argue for the ordination of women, not just as deaconesses but to priesthood. In Sarah's time this discussion had not surfaced.

Her impact and contribution was so strong that the Syrian Orthodox Church named her as their delegate for the second assembly of the WCC in Evanston, Illinois, in 1954. This was indeed a great achievement and she proudly announced that this "establishes the principle that women *can* work in an official capacity in the Orthodox Syrian Church. There has never been any rule against it, but it has never been done."[34] Her honesty coming out of a deep love for her church and traditions has been the hallmark of the participation of Orthodox women in the life of the ecumenical movement since then. Susannah Harris-Wilson writes that Sarah did not hesitate in her criticism of the church when necessary, based on her belief that women had a contribution to make to the church and society. She made it clear that "she expected men to behave with more maturity and charity than they often did."[35]

Chakko's Vision of the Role of Women in the Church

It has to be acknowledged, however, that "In Chakko's lifetime feminism had not surfaced in its contemporary form, and to her the 'woman's question' when it arose was not an isolated issue and never a cause."[36] In fact, it is said that to her "love was the incentive in any advocacy for change, her sense that love made certain demands for wholeness, softened the edge of any criticisms she had to make and made it possible for men to accept them."[37] Madeline Barot describes this gift and power with these words: "Sarah never lost her genuinely feminine character, and was able to prove in a particularly brilliant way, by her own personal manner, what women can achieve—this despite the fact that she belonged to one of the most tradition-bound of the Christian churches, in one of the countries where woman is most sheltered."[38]

But she did voice her concerns about the attitude of the Indian churches to women at the first meeting of the Commission on the Life and Work of Women in the Church held in Bossey, in 1950, which she chaired:

> Naturally those of us who were Christian went to our churches asking what the church said about the proper role of women. What did the church say? Nothing. Can you find anything in any of the writings or doctrines of the church about the appropriate place of women other than being a wife and mother? There was no help. And this was upsetting to us. A great many Christian Indian women have been trying ever since to figure out exactly what our role is. We have received an education through the church and could be influential. What are we supposed to do?[39]

Additionally, after her travels on behalf of the WCC Commission on the Life and Work of Women in the Church to several postwar European countries and the USA, she was outspoken in her "implicit rebuke of the institutional church's blatant neglect of women, their needs, and their aspirations."[40] In her words,

> One is very intrigued by the concept of "woman" underlying church and public life in Europe. In countries where women have political rights they are not found in any significant numbers in places of trust and responsibility. In some churches where women were ordained to the ministry during the war and did serve their congregations effectively, a reaction seems to have set in, and women ministers are asked to confine their service to women and children. . . . All this is very intriguing to one who has come from a land where the Christian conception of womanhood has served as a dynamic in social and public life. The church in many so called "mission lands" pioneered women's education and gave them a rightful place in society, and offered them opportunities for service. Many of the European missionary women workers find in these lands greater opportunities for creative service than in their own home countries.[41]

For Sarah, the hope lay in women becoming "more fully ourselves. She saw clearly that this meant giving up a certain kind of power and recognition."[42] In her words, "Don't ever expect the reward for service to be expressed in gratitude or appreciation by those among whom you work. The reward lies in what service does to you yourself—the richness, the sympathy, the humanness it brings you."[43] Susannah Harris-Wilson describes her as one who rejoiced at the "givens" of her life, her own culture, and her own religious tradition.[44]

Her ecumenical formation, her experiences when she visited women in several countries in Europe, the Middle East, and the USA, but also her own life journey, her humility and compassion, and most of all her deep faith from which she drew her Orthodox tradition—all had an impact on what she contributed to the formation of the WCC women's department. It was "characterised by a vision of reconciliation and cooperation between women and men rather than being another women's desk over against all the activities in which men were engaged."[45] It is such a blessing that Sarah Chakko and the women who worked with her—our foremothers—played such an influential role in the directions the WCC's work with women was to take. It has not since then wavered from focusing on the church as a community of women and men as its core theological foundation, while keeping with the times to ensure that the specific concerns of women, in each period of history, are highlighted.

Sarah Chakko, along with Twila McCrea Cavert from the USA, Kathleen Bliss from the UK, and Suzanne de Dietrich and Madeline Barot from France, has to be credited with setting up the Women's Department of the WCC on firm ground. She participated in the first-ever pre-assembly WCC meeting of women in Bossey, in 1950, which underlined the firm conviction of the women in those early times of the WCC's formation that they, along with men, are imbued by God with the gifts to take on both the responsibilities and privileges of participating in the ecumenical movement. The language then was not of "women's rights" but of the desire to accept the will of God for women to serve the church and through the church, the world as equal citizens with men.

Sarah Chakko's life and ecumenical commitment stands as testimony to how Orthodox Christian women have stayed in solidarity with women of other denominations, and with the ecumenical movement, over these decades; from them we have so much to learn. After two major meetings of Orthodox women (in Damascus, 1995, and in Istanbul, 1997) in the context of the Ecumenical Decade of the Churches in Solidarity with Women, I wrote:

> I learnt from my Orthodox sisters what it means for us, as women, to love the Church and respect its great traditions and yet speak with courage and conviction when something disturbs us. All the women I met at these meetings are indeed gifts to the ecumenical movement. The Orthodox women spoke with sensitivity and respect and yet boldness. It taught me that women can speak from within the Tradition, yet also speak to the Tradition and be part of the transformation of the Tradition.[46]

Sarah Chakko in her life and witness embodied this.

Celebrating an Amazing Ecumenical Leader

And so we celebrate Sarah Chakko, our foremother to whom the churches and women in India and the world over owe so much. She has left an indelible mark and will not be forgotten. But, she died too young, when she had so much more to offer! I conclude by echoing the words of M. M. Thomas, another great ecumenical leader from India, who wrote a tribute to her when she died. To his words, I can only say a resounding yes!

> It may be national egoism for me to feel so proud of Sarah Chakko's contribution to the ecumenical movement. The pride remains, and it makes the sense of loss all the more acute. Nevertheless, it is as a world Christian leader that she lived, and it is in this light that her contribution is to be evaluated. The best memorial to her will be our renewed dedication to pray and labour for the ecumenical wholeness of the Church of Christ.[47]

CHAPTER 5

David C. Scott

P. D. Devanandan's Call to Witness: Toward an Ecumenically Credible Theology of Religions

At the end of Western colonialism and the birth of independent India, there was a widespread drawing of distinctions between things Western and those indigenous to India. This was seen in wider sociopolitical as well as religious spheres. Paul David Devanandan, Indian Protestant theologian, historian of religion, ecumenical leader, and noted pioneer in interfaith dialogue, lived through this period and was not only significantly influenced by its values but contributed substantially to this nationalist movement.

Devanandan was born on 8 July 1901 into a Tamil pastor's family in which the religious atmosphere, with its emphasis on the disciplined study of scripture and a sense of worship cultivated through music (in which both parents were proficient), was undoubtedly an early formative elements. He attended school in Madras (present Chennai) and Trichinopoly (present Tiruchirappalli) and subsequently graduated from the Nizam College, Hyderabad. He taught briefly at Jaffna College, Sri Lanka, after which he completed his master's degree from the University of Madras. Here Devanandan became acquainted with K. T. Paul, a prominent Christian social activist and a leader in the Young Men's Christian Association (YMCA), who at the floodtide of the Indian nationalist movement attempted to give it a sense of direction and a Christian content. Paul took part in the first London Round Table Conference, organized by the British government to discuss constitutional reforms in India. Impressed with the young Devanandan, Paul took him as his secretary when he went to the United States in 1924, providing Devanandan the opportunity of extended firsthand contact with the thought, vision, and work of this pioneer. It also gave the young man an opportunity to widen his horizons and deepen his conviction in circumstances very different from those at home. Indeed, it was perhaps Paul's friendship to which we can trace Devanandan's determination to take full part, as a Christian, in nation-building activities.

After his work with Paul concluded, Devanandan stayed on in the USA to pursue theological studies at the Pacific School of Religion, Berkeley, California, where he completed his BD. Subsequently, he was conferred with a doctorate in comparative religion from Yale University in 1931 for his dissertation on the concept of *maya* in the Hindu religious tradition,[1] the subsequent publication appeared under the title *The Concept of Maya.*[2] A number of visiting appointments followed, including William Paton Lecturer at Selly Oak, Birmingham; Henry Luce Professor at Union Theological Seminary, New York City; and Teape Lecturer at Cambridge University.

Upon his return to India in 1931, Devanandan was appointed professor of philosophy and religion at the United Theological College, Bangalore, where today his papers and manuscripts are housed in the college archives. He also had a long and durable association with the Indian YMCA, serving as a secretary at the Delhi YMCA, and later as literature secretary of the National YMCA of India between 1949 and 1956. In the latter position Devanandan augmented the Heritage of India series begun by the orientalist J. N. Farquhar during the latter's earlier tenure in the same post.

In 1954 Devanandan was ordained as a presbyter of the Church of South India, and 1956 saw him appointed as the director of the new Center for the Study of Hinduism, later renamed the Christian Institute for the Study of Religion and Society (CISRS), Bangalore. Through his work at the CISRS and his writings in its journal *Religion and Society*, Devanandan, with his associate M. M. Thomas, sought to guide younger Indian Christian leaders in constructive tasks in newly independent India and to build them into a community of mind and spirit. Here, as well as through his address "Called to Witness"[3] to the third assembly of the World Council of Churches (WCC) at New Delhi in 1961, Devanandan caught the attention of the ecumenical church at large.

Little wonder, in that he took the opportunity to define the nature of Christian witness as "testifying to the reality of the New Creation in the Risen Christ as the one determining factor in world history which gives it significance and meaning, despite the confusion and disorder produced by man's [*sic*] endeavor to divert its destiny towards ends of his own devices." Each Christian congregation is depicted as representing the Community of the New Age, and as therefore having a mission which forbids it to become self-centred or self-contained. "The witness of the Church," he added, "has to do with all the concerns of secular life and must be borne in the context of man's [*sic*] daily life and secular involvement." He gave special attention to Christian witness in a world of other faiths and urged that Christians "take the dominant philosophical and religious concepts of the non-Christian faiths and make them into instruments of interpretation of the Gospel." By way of elaboration, Devanandan went on to observe that traditional Christian approaches, which assume that other religious traditions remain within traditionally accepted boundaries of belief and practice, are inadequate to interpret the modern renaissance of other religions. He asserted that "if religious faith is to be regarded also in terms of response it would be difficult to deny that these deep inner stirrings of the human spirit are in response to the creative activity of the Holy Spirit. . . . The only alternative is to confess either the Christian ignorance of God's ways with people or the Christian blindness in refusing to believe in God's redemptive work with people of other faiths."

Clearly, there can be no escaping the effects of the fact that most of Devanandan's adult life was lived in the days of Western mission hegemony, against which the nationalist in him rebelled. He had, however, learned two important lessons from K. T. Paul. First, it is possible for a Christian to be a responsible nationalist without surrendering Christian convictions and values; and, second, Christians, while affirming their membership in the worldwide body of the Christ, must also take part in nation building with a sense of Christian responsibility and concern. Indeed, he saw more clearly than most in his time that the new day for church and nation was not one of rebellion and revolt, but of reconstruction and reconciliation, whether in theological endeavour, church life, or nation building.

Devanandan was widely known and respected in India and abroad as a Christian thinker and church leader who took a leading part in the life and work of the WCC, particularly, as we have noted, at the third assembly in New Delhi. His published works, apart from *The Concept of Maya*, mainly consist of papers and sermons collected and printed, some posthumously, by the CISRS.[4]

Suddenly, in the midst of an active life, which held great promise of deeper content and greater usefulness, Paul Devanandan was called to his rest. He passed away on the morning of 10 August 1962 at the Dehra Dun railway station on his way to attend a conference at the WCC-related Christian Retreat and Study Centre. For some years he had been troubled with heart disease, on account of which his family and friends had often asked him not to accept responsibilities which required long and arduous journeys. But it was in keeping with his desire and his sense of dedication the he preferred to place the call of duty above his own personal needs that he passed away in the course of service. His life, with its manifold and human limitations, was dedicated to the service of the Christ through the church. At the well-attended service of thanksgiving held in Bangalore, while a deep sense of loss and sorrow was never totally absent, the dominant note was one of joyful thanksgiving for what God had achieved though God's servant.

The Influence of Hendrik Kraemer

The young Devanandan returned from the USA very much a product of the young American society. He emphasized the "ideals of Jesus" as belonging to the core of Christianity and stressed Christian faith in terms of moral and philosophical values. Soon, however, the theologically and politically outspoken Devanandan went through a change in his thinking, as he grew more and more dissatisfied with the theological liberalism which was then in vogue. He finally rebelled against that theological liberalism, which reduced Christianity to a kind of religious philosophy, and found in Hendrik Kraemer, the Dutch Reformed lay missiologist and prominent ecumenical leader, a basis for the renewal of his own theology.[5] He felt drawn to Kraemer as one who represented the cutting edge between what was developing as the distinction between Western and indigenous Christian thought. Not only Kraemer influenced him, however; during this time the neo-orthodoxy of the Swiss Reformed theologian Karl Barth spoke to Devanandan as well.

Both Kraemer and Barth emphasize what they see as the biblical understanding of reality that God is wholly other than humanity, which is both creature and sinner. Indeed, God's self-revelation in Jesus, the Christ cannot, by its very nature, correspond to concept of "natural man" and must remain inaccessible to human beings, thus causing "offense." Kraemer uses the phrase "biblical realism" to indicate that, according to the Bible, reality is theocentric. This means that God is the all-pervading centre in total reality, which is opposed to all anthropocentric endeavours to reduce reality to a body of truths and ideals about the personality of God, the infinite value of the human being, the source of ethical inspiration.

In the last analysis, however, Devanandan rejected Barth and Kraemer's Reformed theology, with its negative attitude to the history of the search for religious truth and the struggle for human values in India's national awakening. He noted that Barth and Kraemer stressed the fact that revelation is from God even though it is to and for the world of humankind. Barth denied the possibility of natural theology based on reason and ordinary experience, distinguished from revealed theology, while Kraemer denied revelation in other religious traditions.

Devanandan's concept of God and revelation does not make the redemptive process in history either totally hidden or totally understandable to faith. It is a reality which faith is able to discern in every human situation, to the extent necessary for human participation in the renewing activity of the Spirit in that situation. Devanandan also asserts that God cannot just be wholly other. After all, "God is the father of our Lord Jesus Christ." Therefore, the mystery of God's ways is not hidden from the insight of those to whom God chooses to reveal them.

The Influence of A. G. Hogg

Significantly, when Kraemer's influence was at its peak at the Tambaram International Missionary Council (IMC) Conference of 1938, this transcendentalism of divine revelation in dialectical theology, unable to become lodged in temporal form to renew it, was criticized from various angles. One particularly trenchant critique is represented by A. G. Hogg, professor of philosophy at Madras Christian College and a contemporary of Devanandan, in his review of Kraemer's *Christian Message in a Non-Christian World*,[6] which appeared in a collection of essays, *Rethinking Christianity in India*,[7] produced by the Rethinking Group in Madras.[8]

O. V. Jathanna, in a doctoral dissertation on *The Decisiveness of the Christ Event and the Universality of Christianity in a World of Religious Plurality*,[9] notes the major elements in Hogg's theology of history:

> (1) History is a development and there is a "purposeful evolution in the process of history. (2) In the process of history the work of the Christ is a cosmic crisis. (3) The purpose of the universe is the evolution of a morally perfect humanity. (4) With Jesus the new age of the Spirit has begun. (5) This new age has been delayed by the lack of human readiness. (6) History is an integrated orderly whole in which the future is bound up with present and past. (7) Teleology, lacking in the Hindu tradition, is vital to the historical understanding of Christianity. History is an adventure in faith, not a rigidly determined process. Finally, Jathanna sums up Hogg's understanding of history as "the experience of and faith in God's absorbed activity in history."

This is the basic framework within which Hogg sees the relation between Christianity and other religious traditions, and he criticizes both J. N. Farquhar's thesis that Christianity is the "crown of Hinduism"[10] and Kraemer's theory of the total discontinuity between the two. For Hogg, Jesus is the self-revelation of God, that is to say, the reality of the Divine Person as "absorbed activity in history," as Jathanna puts it. As the climax of the self-revelation of God, Jesus, the Christ brings a new divine–human reality into being in the historical process. And for Hogg, it is both discontinuous and continuous with the divine self-revelation-cum-human faith response which is the religious history of humankind.

"Christian Attitude to Non-Christian Faith" is the title of the paper Hogg wrote for the Tambaram Conference.[11] The singular here is distinguished from the plural non-Christian faiths. The plural denotes for him those complexes of spiritual, ethical, intellectual, and social elements which we call the non-Christian religions. But the singular faith denotes, in Kraemer's words, "the religious life as present in the non-Christian religions." Is this distinction valid?

This is the first question Hogg discusses. Is there such a thing as a religious faith which in quality or texture is "definitely not Christian," but in which we may recognize "a two-sided communion between God and man [*sic*]"? Is there in such a life of faith not merely a seeking but also a finding by contrast with which a Christian may be helped to make fresh discoveries in his own finding of God in Christ?

Hogg was convinced that the answer to these questions is in the affirmative. Kraemer's general attitude to non-Christian faiths tends to exclude the possibility of anything really deserving the name of non-Christian faith by suggesting that these religions are a purely "human phenomenon," and in no sense "an experience of Divine self-disclosure." Hogg repudiates the adequacy of a purely humanistic conception of non-Christian faiths. He believes that the universal religious consciousness is the universal manifestation of a human response (however deplorably crude, wayward, and reluctant) to God's continuing endeavour to reveal Godself to humankind, and in that sense every religious tradition is founded on what is, in some sense, revelation, a divine effort of disclosure.

Aligning himself with the views of Hogg, Devanandan felt compelled to a post-Kraemer approach to the relation between the Christian religious tradition and those of other religions; an approach that would restore the balance by making a detailed and sympathetic study of humanity and society in modern India. Whereas the neo-orthodox impulse rejected "culture religion" and any programme of merely earthly betterment, insisting on the "radical otherness of the Gospel," Devanandan argued for a Christian concern in society and called for a theology which regards a positive approach to other religions and cultural contexts. He called on his fellow Indian Christians, saying:

> We as Christians ought to act as pioneers in radically removing the more important social evils in India by personal example. One of the primary tasks of Christian evangelism in India as elsewhere in our modern world is to make clear to the mind of thinking people that religion is relevant to life; that Christianity concerns this life as much as the life everlasting; that ours is a revolutionary faith which asks to realize here on earth abiding standards of righteousness and justice because these are the very nature of the Church.[12]

Devanandan believed that Christian concern in society was not merely political or economic but primarily theological, rooted in and governed by the insight that our faith stands for "the redemption of the whole man [*sic*]" here and now. Thus he began his search for an approach to the relation of Christianity to religious and secular history which went beyond Kraemer and Barth and would incorporate the insights of K. T. Paul about the Christian significance of participation in the national movement. Arend van Leeuwen pointed the direction: "Christianization and secularization are involved in a dialectical relation."[13] We shall have more to say about this dialectical relation.

Theologically, Devanandan's perennial theme was Jesus the Christ in the contemporary world of religion and society. This, and his many contacts with people of faith in other religious traditions in and through whom he experienced "the surging new life" manifest in other religious traditions as the creative activity of the Holy Spirit, gave him a clear conviction of the significance and necessity of dialogue with the living religious traditions and secular faiths in order to understand the ultimate questions they ask and the meaning of the Christ in relation to them. At a time when conversations between Christians and persons of faith in other religious traditions were primarily contentious or, at best, parallel monologues, Devanandan initiated a series of dialogues with Hindu scholars and thinkers. His intention was to facilitate a deeper understanding of religion based on the actual experience of dialogue. His persistent emphasis on the fact of Jesus the Christ reinforced and clarified the common humanity of all women and men. On this basis, he was convinced; all dialogues about humankind, faith, culture, or society become real conversations in Christ and about Christ.

For Devanandan, the divine activity in Jesus the Christ for the world is from beginning to end a divine–human activity, and therefore an integral part of history, both religious and secular. Here is a new dimension in history which rules and overrules it and leads it to its future. No doubt the faith response on the part of human beings to the divine activity is also God's work. Only God can create the response of faith in human hearts through the Holy Spirit. However, that faith response is part of the cosmic historical process which is renewed by it. As such, it has fundamental this-worldly implications. Thus, Christian evangelistic witness is at the same time and for all times a cosmic process, a divine activity, a historical reality, and a people's movement that is missionary in origin and intention, and congregational in purpose and design.

Devanandan's Originality

In the pre-independence era of Indian nationalism, the originality of Devanandan's thought, then, is not to be found in any indigenous reinterpretation of the basic doctrines of the Christian religious tradition such as we find, for instance, in Brahmabandhab Upadyay's treatment of the Trinity, A.

S. Appasamy's exposition of the Christian tradition as *bhakti marga*, or Vengal Chakkarai's formulation of Christology. Rather, it is in relation to this universal, cosmic, historical, and people's movement for the renewal of all things that the church, as the household of faith, works together with God, insofar as this is possible for human beings, in the task of extending the kingdom. Here the church becomes the mission, "the outreach of God towards the world," the earnest of the new creation in the Christ. Devanandan emphasizes the historical corporate concreteness of the local congregation as representing "the community of the New Age" in the context of the world-life in which it is placed. Only through the worship, the fellowship, and the service of the local churches can the saving power of God become manifest. The fellowship of the local congregation serves as the instrument of divine renewal. Where the local church becomes a genuine and dynamic community in the Christ, it will spiritually penetrate its secular environment and draw those outside into its *koinonia*.

For Devanandan, social action and dialogue are significantly central to the reaching out of God to the world. His this-worldly orientation was also influenced by neo-Hinduism, especially that of S. Radhakrishnan and Sri Aurobindo Ghose, both of whom emphasized *lokasamgraha*, a Sanskrit term meaning "the maintenance of the coherence of the world."[14] The concept of *lokasamgraha* is central to Krishna's message of *nishkama karma* ("selfless action") in the *Bhagavadgita.*[15] Radhakrishnan observed that *lokasamgraha*, or working for the welfare of others, demands a change in the whole pattern of human existence, wherein one is continuously active.

Sri Aurobindo understood human personhood through one's relations with one's environment and through world harmony. Devanandan linked up with this trend in neo-Hinduism. Since secularization brought on dissolution of traditional Indian society, there developed a contextual concern in post-independence India for finding "new foundations for her political and social structures" and "an adequate social philosophy."[16] This search is a common search of all Indians, and Devanandan insisted that Christian participation in this search should be the way forward for relevant Christian mission in India. Such participation in a common concern, however, sets prerequisites. On a theoretical level it demands a concern for the individual and a dynamic understanding of history—a new anthropology and a historical consciousness, and on the practical level an active interreligious interaction (dialogue) and cooperation in social action.[17]

In a remarkable partnership with M. M. Thomas, his associate and successor at the CISRS, Devanandan concentrated on the content of interreligious interaction and Thomas focused on the implications of Christian cooperation for social action. Thus, together they spearheaded the development of an ecumenical theology of mission in India, centered on a CISRS group of thinkers and influencing the church in India through the National Council of Churches and the Serampore Senate structures. To Devanandan, mission as *lokasamgraha* means the production of a community of human being with human being, of human being with God, "a triangular community," the "true community" in which alone a person finds oneself as a person among persons in relation to *the* person.[18] His theocentric perspective accommodates all religious traditions within the common search for community in the one God spoke of "God's redemptive activity outside the church," with a theocentricity transcending all confessionalism.

Within the framework, then, of a theology of "new creation" that relates the revelation of God in Jesus the Christ to the universality of the historical movement of divine grace renewing persons, cultures, and cosmos, Devanandan develops his theology of religion and religious pluralism. Here Devanandan's starting point is dialectical theology, that is, the revelation in Jesus the Christ, which justifies humanity by grace through faith, exposes religion as sinful humanity's search for self-justification through idolatry, and abolishes it. As we have suggested earlier, this was the starting point for Barth and Kraemer to move in the direction of revelation justifying and sanctifying Christianity as the true religion, as the means of grace. Subsequently, however, there were Dietrich Bonhoeffer and Arend van Leeuwen justifying by faith a religionless[19] or a secular Christianity.[20] Devanandan takes a third path which explores the possibility of revelation judging, justifying, and renewing other religious traditions also, so as to make them true religious partners, with justified Christianity and justified secularism in witnessing to and participating in the recreation of the world in the Christ.

Meaning of the Cross

The central emphasis in Devanandan's theology of religion is on the meaning of the cross as exposing all human search for justification by the works of the law, including religion, as hostility to God. Simultaneously, the cross also reveals free divine forgiveness which breaks the hold of law, breaks all middle walls of partition between people set up by law (religion), and unites them in a new plane of being in Christ's new humanity.[21] The cross of Jesus the Christ is thus the vision of a common humanity, a *lokasamgraha-koinonia* transcending religions and secular quasi-religions, and of a power to break down their rigid boundary walls and to participate with each other in witness to the new humanity in the Christ.

Of course, the order of new being in the Christ will coexist with the old order of religion until its consummation in God's reign. But even in this stage of coexistence of the two orders, the cross provides a permanent critique of religion and the powers, to renew it constantly toward converting it into the true religion mediating grace. This is real not only for Christianity. So long as it is the divine grace in the Christ that justifies and transforms idolatrous Christianity into true religion, such renewal can happen to any religion or secularism, provided it opens itself to the ferment of the cross within it. It also means that where people are drawn to the divine humanity of Jesus revealed on the cross, we should expect the religious walls separating them to be demolished, making possible a new *koinonia* community of dialogue. Devanandan demonstrates not only that such renewal can take place, but that this is the trajectory along which things do happen in the present renaissance of other religious traditions and secular quasi-religious traditions.

> The word of the cross needs to be preached today in the conviction that because Christ rose again, what man [*sic*] calls religion—the reign of law—is of the earth . . . of the old things to pass away. This is a daring thought; and it may well be fraught with dangerous heresy. But Christians of this generation may give heed to it. As we enter a new era in world history, we need to question ourselves whether we witness to a gospel that perpetuates this very enmity which God in Christ has destroyed, or do we proclaim the word of reconciliation?[22]

For Kraemer, this necessitates absolutizing the distinction between the Christian religious tradition and other religious traditions. Devanandan, however, contends that it need not and sets out to demonstrate that the various streams of religious life and tradition are too internally diverse, too richly various, and too subject to historical change to be characterized usefully in terms of some enduring and distinct essence. It is not adequate to the almost infinitely complex character of the immensely diverse, fluid, and subtle data of the religious life of humankind in history to assert that there are in the world absolutely distinct unitary entities called Christianity, Hinduism, Buddhist, Islam, and so forth. He recommends that we try to abandon this way of thinking and speaking. The concentric circles of creed, cultus, and culture altogether comprise the total area of outreach and influence of any religious tradition. Faith is nurtured by and expressed in and through these circles and hence they are tied to faith. But they are not identical with faith and should not be absolutized.[23] As Devanandan puts it:

> All religions are historical phenomena and Christianity is no exception. As any religion, it has also been subject to the process of change in human history. Its organizational structure, its interpretation of the fundamentals of the Christian faith, have all been subject to limitations of the human mind and of human effort. But it is not Christianity that is preached as against other religions. The message of the Christian witness is the gospel around which Christianity as a historical phenomenon has developed.[24]

The message is the person of Jesus crucified, understood as the divine re-creation of humanity. Insofar as other religious traditions have been grappling with Jesus and his cross and his humanity, any easy distinction set up by Christians between the "believer" and the "nonbeliever" based on Christian doctrine breaks down. The insidious danger lies in forgetting that doctrines are also symbolic. They stand for a reality which they do not always fully represent nor totally exhaust. Therefore, to reduce the distinction between a believer and a nonbeliever by the rigid pattern of a creed or the externals of a ritual act is to fall into the same error which persisted in distinguishing Jew from Gentile in the early church.[25]

Faith is seen at the level of self-commitment. As a particular example, Devanandan contends that God gave Gandhi enabling grace to live the Sermon on the Mount to the extent that he did as a *satyagrahi*.[26] Here Devanandan discerns a partial acknowledgment of the Christ in Gandhi, not in his doctrine or ethical interpretations of Jesus, but his grappling with and his positive life response to the person of Jesus and his new humanity, though this is done within his own Hindu religious tradition. If Christian faith is the acknowledgment of the Christ's lordship in human self-commitment, one meets it among the adherents of other than Christian religious traditions, often in periods of renaissance. What, then, is Devanandan's theological interpretation of the resurgence and restatement of all religions? This is an ongoing process resulting, in part, from the meeting of living faiths on the plane of religious tradition and culture and partly because of the struggle in all religious traditions and cultures for full human life through a greater mastery of nature, a recognition of the fundamental dignity of human persons and deeper interpersonal relations in social institutions, and through the development of human community. But what do the rapid changes taking place imply for the self-understanding, self-transcendence, and self-commitment at the core of personal faith and religious traditions? Does the contemporary resurgence of Asian religions and their restatement under the impact of the Christian religious tradition and secular humanism informed by the gospel of the Christ indicate an activity of the Christ to destroy the "middle wall of partition" between religious traditions in order to prepare them for an all-transcending new humanity in the Christ?

Seeming to answer, Devanandan describes a renascent Hindu religious tradition engaged in the task of integrating the values of Western science and humanism in its own theological foundations, and concludes: "One cannot resist the impulse of faith that believes in a God who is also the Lord of history, and in a creative Spirit who is ever at work in the world of men [*sic*], redeeming it even in its present involvements and directing its course to the ultimate fulfillment of his [*sic*] purpose, that in all religious revival God is somehow at work."[27]

The Influence of William E. Hocking

Devanandan sees the discernment of the work of God and the relating of the church to it as a significant challenge to the church. Here Devanandan follows William E. Hocking, the American historian and philosopher of religion and chair of the Layman's Foreign Mission Enquiry,[28] in advocating a process of "reconception" of the Christian religious tradition intended to make it a vehicle for the creation of world community.[29]

Incidentally, in 1938, the same year that Kraemer published his *The Christian Message to the Non-Christian World*, Hocking delivered the Hibbert Lectures, dealing with "Living Religions and a World Faith."[30] These lectures present his mature conclusions after his experience as chairman of the Laymen's Foreign Mission Inquiry and the rather stormy reception of its report.

In them he examines and rejects both the principle of the radical displacement of other religious traditions by any one tradition considering itself to be the only true and absolute one, as Christian extremists consider it to be; and that of a synthesis of all living world religious traditions in one. In contrast with these, he presents the principle of the radical self-reconception of each of the great living religious traditions, not alone, but in vital reciprocity with the others. In this reciprocity they should all shun competition and rivalry with one another; purify themselves of all transient elements; cultivate the permanent; and assimilate such true insights of other great religious traditions as could be incorporated into the organic wholeness of their own living religious culture.

The particular strength of Hocking's position is that he had devoted his life to the study of the philosophy of state as well as to the study of religion, and was constantly concerned with the impact of religious faith and principle upon the whole fabric of culture, society, and civilization as it was developing in history. In this process of self-reconception in the great religions, Hocking believes that Christianity would out-match all others. This is the major premise of his *The Coming World Civilization*.[31]

There can be no gainsaying that the Christian missionary movement has historically been insensitive to non-Western cultures and Christian theology has been exclusivist in relation to other religious traditions. Devanandan was persuaded that the integrity of the Christian message could be maintained without violence to other religious traditions through Hocking's "reconception" relational model that is neither the indiscriminate amalgamation of synthesis, nor the exclusivism of radical displacement of other religious traditions by the Christian tradition, which was the usual Christian mission effort. Indeed, Devanandan was convinced that such exclusivism is a disservice to the living religious traditions of indigenous peoples, as well as to the Christian tradition because it does not demand that Christian thinking continue to develop and mature. Encounter causes each religious tradition to rethink its basic positions, leading to a future in which the natural religion of humankind and the substance of Christianity will be conjoined, providing the binding ingredient for cultural and religious pluralism in the coming world civilization.

In and through it all, three fundamental concerns in Devanandan's understanding of "reconception" stand out clearly. First, there is a movement toward a composite culture inspired by a common humanity with openness toward different religious traditions and their contribution to the common pool. Second, he proposes a more radical interpretation at the level of religious creed and cultus of each religious tradition absorbing elements from other traditions and integrating them in its core and within the context of the struggle for a common culture. Third, there is the ideal of a meeting of different religious traditions at their fundamental core, leading to greater mutual understanding and openness, even to conversion.

Conclusion

Finally, a couple of noteworthy questions have been raised related to Devanandan's emphasis on the historical particularity of Jesus and on the historical and personal categories of humanness in his theology of dialogue. First, does Devanandan's dominant missionary motivation, in fact, make justification of Christianity its final aim? Does this not preclude the very openness and willingness necessary for understanding the other as an equal partner in dialogue? Second, and even more telling, does Devanandan's preoccupation with personal and historical categories make his theology inadequate to meet the metaphysically oriented Hindu partner in dialogue on a conceptual level?[32]

When all is said and done, however, Devanandan succeeded in preparing the way for a credible theology of religions whose major themes may be summarized in three basic affirmations. First, the redeeming work of Jesus the Christ, in a world where persons are involved in nature, society, and history, is all-inclusive in that all things are summed up in the Christ. Second, while believing that God's work is continuing in the world, Christians must never forget that it is not ultimately of this world. The gospel must never be identified with any particular cultural system of thought or moral ideal. Third, the ongoing work of the living Christ, bringing healing and wholeness to broken humanity, is work in which Christians are called to be humble participants. In and through it all, Devanandan's fundamental concern was to assist the Indian church in understanding Jesus the Christ as the key to and fulfillment of God's work in and for the world of Indian religion, culture, and society, and to restate and communicate that truth. The theology of religious pluralism is indeed an ecumenical issue of immense importance and consequence to which Devanandan has made a significant contribution.

CHAPTER 6

K. C. Abraham

Explorations into Spirituality and Humanization: The Revolutionary Thought of M. M. Thomas

M. M. Thomas was one of the chief architects of the modern ecumenical movement. Professor Alf Tergel, the Swedish church historian, has written: "Along with Visser't Hooft, M. M. Thomas has had the greatest influence on the modern ecumenical movement." An outstanding theologian, his original and rather unconventional explorations into ecumenical social ethics remain highly relevant even today. Long before liberation theology burst on the scene, M. M. Thomas raised his prophetic voice for the liberation of humanity from the dehumanizing structures.

Born in 1916 into a devout Mar Thoma Church family in Kozhencherry, in Kerala, India, Thomas maintained throughout his life the spirit of reformation that guided the establishment of the Mar Thoma Church. From the life and work of the great reformer Abraham Malpan, who was a precursor of the Kerala renaissance, he knew how reformation in the church could influence reformation in the larger society.

Thomas was secretary of the Youth Christian Council for Action, a progressive movement of Christian youth under the strong influence of Marx and Gandhi. He became secretary of the Student Christian Movement (SCM) in Madras (now Chennai). He also served as the secretary of the Mar Thoma Church's youth movement.

From 1947 to 1952 he served on the staff of the World Student Christian Federation with special responsibility for its political commission. He was one of the very few from what he called "the two-thirds world" involved in the preparations for the inaugural assembly of the World Council of Churches (WCC) held in Amsterdam in 1948. Within the council he became closely associated with the Department of Church and Society and served as its chairman in the 1960s. His leadership at the World Conference on Church and Society in 1966—a landmark in the path of ecumenical social thought—was remarkable.

He was elected moderator of the Central Committee of the WCC at the Uppsala assembly in 1968. It was with much reluctance that he accepted the position, and it is known that it was the persuasion or, rather, friendly direction of Willem Visser't Hooft and the encouragement of Rt. Rev. Philipose Mar Chrysostom, bishop of the Mar Thoma Church, that made him do so. Among the considerations that Visser't Hooft probably had was the fact the general secretary, Eugene Carson Blake, was new to the WCC, while Thomas had been closely associated with it from its inception. Blake had been an outstanding leader of U.S. churches who very soon began to give dynamic leadership to the ecumenical movement. His bold criticisms and actions against apartheid in South Africa and the U.S.-led Vietnam War earned for the WCC international approbation. Blake had Thomas's full support for his stance.

M. M. Thomas was the first layperson to be elected to the position of moderator of the Central Committee and the first from outside the Anglo-Saxon world. Thomas influenced the policy and direction of the WCC for many years. His addresses to the Central Committee and assembly broke new ground, as they were "State of the Ecumenical Movement" addresses rather than reports about the activities of the council. In short, Thomas was one of the pioneers that gave shape to the conception of framework of the ecumenical movement. This article will discuss a few key points in that context.

Building the Asian Ecumenical Movement

Thomas's contribution to the building of the Asian ecumenical movement is as important as his contribution to worldwide ecumenism. D. T. Niles, one of the most distinguished ecumenical leaders of the twentieth century and the first general secretary of the East Asia Christian Conference (later Christian Conference of Asia), was his collaborator. The distinctive feature of the Asian ecumenical movement was that it was essentially an expression of Asian nationalism. It was shaped during the period of the Asian revolution. One of Thomas's signal contributions was his interpretation of Asian nationalism and Asian revolution.

At the inaugural assembly of the East Asia Christian Conference in Kuala Lumpur in 1959, Thomas made some profound observations in a speech modestly entitled "Some Notes on Christian Interpretation of Nationalism." Nationalism was an important issue before the churches in Asia. Thomas defined nationalism as the struggle for nation building, rather than primarily a struggle against outside forces. Thomas said, "In every national movement and pattern of social change and in the cultural transformation of every country, people are led to a decision for or against Jesus Christ, because the situation raises fundamental questions of God, man and the world in more or less Christian terms."[1] He warned against the possibility of nationalism being misused to suit the interests of the politically powerful.

After describing the Asian revolution as the bearer of humanism, as the instrument of technological development and as the means of enhancing the unique selfhood of peoples, Thomas attempts to answer the question: What is God doing in all this?

> First through the revolution, God in his providence is creating in Asia the basic conditions for greater human dignity, enhanced human creativity and mature human living. Personal freedom and social justice and higher standards of living and sense of national identity do not guarantee personal fulfilment in a responsible society, but they are certainly necessary conditions for the same.
>
> Secondly, through the Asian revolution God is preparing the Asian people to face up to the challenge of deciding for or against Jesus Christ. A new stage of creativity and the problems of the spirit, it gives a new relevance to the gospel of Christ.

> Thirdly, through the Asian revolution, God is judging and recalling the Church in Asia to repentance and renewal in a new way. It was Asian nationalism that broke the too close identification of the gospel with Western culture and imperialism and brought the awareness of the transcendence of the gospel over all cultures and historical movements and the possibility, as General Simatupang of Indonesia puts it, of relating itself positively, creatively and realistically to indigenous cultures and national goals.[2]

Thomas warned against the possibility of the betrayal of the revolution from within.

Charles C. West points out how Asian church leaders, the young M. M. Thomas among them, repeatedly brought home to Westerners the exhilaration and challenge of societies emerging from colonialism and going through in two generations the multiple revolutions that had taken Europe four centuries. The question was how these revolutions are to be understood in the purpose of God. West writes,

> It is M. M. Thomas, however, in his many writings out of the Indian scene, who seeks to work on all frontiers at once, redefining ecumenical social ethics for an Asian context but in the light of global forces and ideologies, guiding the ancient churches of Christendom towards ecumenical renewal, and exploring ever fresh the form of the gospel for non-Christian cultures which are themselves being transformed in encounter with the post-modern world.[3]

India: Thomas's Base

M. M. Thomas always believed that the base of his work was in India. That is where the centerpiece of his work was. From the time of the independence struggle, he was not only a keen observer of political developments, but participated in many of them on the side of the people. He was a guide to a whole generation who explored the meaning of faith and politics. His main center of activity was the Christian Institute for the Study of Religion and Society (CISRS) in Bangalore, which was founded in 1957 by P. D. Devanandan and himself. He served on its staff first as associate director and then as director until his retirement in 1976. His bold stand criticizing the emergency in India in 1975, which was an onslaught on democracy and fundamental rights, brought him into national prominence. His insightful commentaries on the emergency, most of which had to be circulated privately, continue to be relevant for all situations where human dignity is under threat.[4] He was appointed governor of the state of Nagaland where he served with distinction. Perhaps equally significant was the in-depth study he made on Naga culture.

Political and secular ideologies played a major role in Thomas's theological framework. The ideology of Marxism began to influence him from his contact with Father Leonard Schiff. Thomas believed that faith without ideology leaves little scope for action, and ideology without theology leaves little room for hope. Thomas understood "Theology as faith seeking rational understanding of the truth and meaning of its commitment."[5]

At one point in his youth, he applied for ordination in the Mar Thoma Church and for membership in the Communist Party of India. The church rejected him because of the Marxist leanings of his social ethics and the party rejected him because of his Christian faith. One cannot claim that even today the church knows how to deal with members with Marxist orientation or the party knows how to deal with Christian believers.

Thomas's writings on state and politics span a period of more than fifty years. His thought on politics and state is an integral part of his theological-ideological quest of his faith, which in his own words was a neverending one. In *Ideological Quest within Christian Community*, Thomas describes his ideological evolution. Starting as a Gandhian, a combination of liberal theology and Gandhian idealism informed his social work and thought. His studies and discussions in the Kerala Youth Christian Council for Action led him to Marxism. He describes his approach in the 1950s as an attempt to redefine the dialectics of Karl Barth within the neo-orthodox theology of Karl Barth, Reinhold Niebuhr, and Nicholas Berdyaev. From 1947 he was led to further theological ideological exploration in a world setting through the Political Commission of the World Student Christian Federation (WSCF) and the Study Commission of the WCC.[6]

World Conference on Church and Society

It was the 1966 World Conference on Church and Society that led to the recognition of the genius and greatness of M. M. Thomas. Paul Abrecht, who was the organizer of the conference and Thomas's close collaborator over the years in Church and Society, has written: "Remembering M. M. Thomas is an ecumenical celebration. Few other persons have made such a notable contribution to the social thought of the World Council of Churches for so many years."[7] Thomas chaired and led the conference, Albrecht has said, "and the result was a conference which went far beyond any previous ecumenical effort in seeking to discern the Christian social responsibility in a world context."

Speaking of the conference at the Uppsala assembly of the WCC in 1968, Thomas said,

> And it seems to me that the significance of the Conference for the Churches lies precisely in that it has the potentiality of bringing them to an awareness of the radical changes taking place in men's relations to nature and to their fellowmen, through the technical and social revolutions of our time, and of the spiritual depth of the revolution in spiritual self-understanding which has taken place in man himself. And the impact of it all on the theological leadership of the churches and ecumenical movement shows that the conference focus on the human and the human situation has become the turning point for ecumenical rethinking, not only of social ethics but also of mission and service.[8]

His interpretation of the Uppsala assembly, at which he was elected moderator, gave new insights about the ecumenical movement:

> Uppsala 1968 has highlighted the theological and ethical basis of the struggle for human community at the local level as well as the world level. It affirms the Catholicity of the Church given in Christ as the source and criterion of the unity of mankind.
>
> Thus the WCC sees that it is committed in its central confession of Christ and his church and as one of its essential commitment to a new ethics of Catholicity by which we must judge and repudiate the tragic distortions of humanity. It is this faith-ethics commitment that Uppsala considered the very centre of the Council's fellowship, because the unity of mankind is part and parcel of God's own revelation.[9]

The Church and Revolution

I have referred to the interpretation Thomas gave to the Asian revolution. The church and revolution is a topic that he dealt with in depth, and his rich theological insights on this have continuing relevance.

Thomas spoke about the continuing revolution in science and technology, the new revolutionary awakening of people who have hitherto remained submerged or suppressed, and the worldwide process of secularization. He said that these three revolutionary realities are closely related. His emphasis was on the revolutionary upsurge of our times "because it demands radical changes in the traditional power structures and their supporting theological and religious sanctions within every national society where power is exercised."[10]

At the theological consultation held in Zagorsk, near Moscow, following up the Church and Society conference, the double interaction between technological development and the self-awakening of the people found expression. The statement emerging from this consultation says, "It is in this context of the demand of peoples for radical changes in the status quo and for the establishment of greater justice that the word 'revolution' has acquired in the twentieth century a worldwide emotional importance as universal and comprehensive as the word 'democracy' in the nineteenth century."[11]

Thomas criticized the false approaches to revolution which go by the name "Christian." The first of these is the approach of pietism which sees Christ and his gospel of salvation in terms of pure spirituality and a certain kind of "revivalism," keeping away from what is happening in the world. True piety and holiness should not mean withdrawal from the realities of the revolutions of our time, but engagement with them in the name of the salvation offered in Christ. The second approach considers the revolution and the secularization associated with it as a revolt against God and God's orders and asks for a return to religion and the organization of political and social life on the basis of religious principles enunciated by religious authorities. The third is to give Christian benediction to the revolution, considering it as in itself a scheme of redemption. This is to affirm that history has within it the capacity finally to overcome its own inner contradictions and bring about its fulfillment, which is tantamount to denying the fact of sin and humanity's need for Christ's salvation.

Giving the true Christian interpretation, Thomas affirms that "Under the creative providence of God, the revolution of our time has within it the promise of Christ for a fuller and richer human life for men's societies."[12] He says the postwar revolution is the expression of the creativity of human freedom. He adds that the revolution has enhanced humanity's sense of history and destiny. "We should see the revolutionary hand of God in Christ, carrying history forward through judgement and redemption to the consummation of the Kingdom and calling the Church to participate with him in it."[13] Thomas then goes on to say that the revolution has inherent in it evil powers of both individual and collective egoism, selfishness, and idolatry. The revolution can be betrayed from within. Jesus Christ, who is present in the revolution, is victorious over these evil powers through his cross and resurrection and his kingdom. Thomas explains the mission and witness of the church in relation to the revolution:

> Thus for the very sake of the fuller realization of the humanity of man, the witness of the Church to Christ's presence creating, judging and redeeming the revolution is urgent within the revolution. This witness involves, first, participation in the revolution, second, prophetic criticism of its idolatry and third, the exercise of the ministry of reconciliation. It is thus that the Church can help the creation of those secular conditions of true responsible human living which is the promise of God for men in and through the revolution.[14]

The church is called to participate in the revolutionary struggle for a just society. The church should be ready to accept that such a struggle may necessitate revolutionary changes in the structures of society. These changes have to become the instruments of justice for all rather than of privilege for the few.

One of Thomas's major propositions is that the revolution is God's preparation of people and societies for facing the challenge of the gospel. Through this revolution, Christ raises fundamental questions about freedom and responsibility, the human person and his or her destiny, the relation between law and love in community, the meaning of history in tragedy and fulfillment—questions from the depth of existence in the context of which the gospel of Jesus Christ, the crucified and risen one, acquires a new relevance.

For Thomas, the confession of Christ and the defense of the dignity of and justice for the human being are integral to each other: "It is a confession which involves active participation in the creation and preservation of structures of thought, special institutions and cultural ethos necessary for human living, constantly resisting the idolatries and forces of self-righteousness which appear within them which are imperceptible except to the participants. This is the confession to which the church is called in the revolutions of our time."[15]

The meaning of confessing faith in Asia was distinct from the historical confession of faith in the West in traditional faith and order circles. The East Asia Christian Conference redefined as the church's response to the Asian revolution by involvement and participation as well as courageous action "to resist every form of belief and ideology which denies people their essential dignity, every form of social structure in which a person lives at the expenses of fellow people."[16] It is this concept of confession that Thomas articulates here about the response of the church to all revolutions.

Strategy of the Revolution

Thomas's elucidation of the distinction between the basic revolution for participation and justice and the more ambiguous strategy of the revolution is significant. On this matter, which often causes confusion, his explanation is clear: "While there could be general Christian agreement about affirming the revolutionary ferment and goal as valid expression of human dignity, the strategy is the focus of danger and ambiguity." He is emphatic that we should not make the strategy of violence the essence of revolution. Counterrevolutionary forces are most often not amenable to moral, legal, and nonviolent forces. In the struggle against the coercion and violence of the established power structures, revolution has often involved violence.

It is the established order that illustrates the strategy of those in the struggle. Thomas quotes from the famous statement of Nelson Mandela at the Rivonia trial to prove his point. There Mandela said that at a point when violence by the African people had become inevitable, it was necessary to channel and control it rather than allowing it to deteriorate as terrorism. After having attempted all legitimate and even illegitimate nonviolent means and failing, leaders like Mandela came to the conclusion that without violence there would be no way open to the African people to succeed in their struggle against the principle of white supremacy. Therefore, Thomas wrote, "We must realize that the call to Christians for identification with the social ferment and for participation in the revolutionary strategies will lead some Christians to decide to participate fully in strategies of revolution involving violence. In such situation they will need all the understanding, sympathy and prayer of their Christian brothers. Indeed the Church has a pastoral ministry to Christians who are involved in all strategies of revolution."[17]

The Uppsala assembly marked a turning point in the life of the WCC, as it entered a phase of what might be called "ecumenical activism" which supported revolutionary movements, especially in southern Africa. The Programme to Combat Racism (PCR) was the challenging expression of this. Thomas's speech at the Uppsala assembly on the topic "Issues Concerning the Life and Work of the Church in a Revolutionary World" gave the conceptual and theological basis for the involvement in and support to the struggles for justice and liberation, especially in southern Africa. He spoke of the possibility of "just revolution" and dealt with the problem of violence and nonviolence in the struggle for justice. He quoted from the Zagorsk consultation: "Even where the effort to make violence unnecessary for the political and social revolution fails and Christians concerned with justice find themselves called to participate in strategies of violence, the universality of the Christian fellowship and common membership in an inclusive church should remind them and others of the 'full humanity of the political adversary or the enemy.'"[18]

He presided over the Canterbury Central Committee, which approved financial grants to liberation movements in southern Africa, a decision which became controversial within the churches and outside. It was the WCC, undergirded by Christian conviction, that affirmed the legitimacy of the liberation movements at a time when "in the West" generally they were dubbed terrorists. In making this affirmation, Thomas's theological insights played an important role:

> As long as the Council has not been able to develop a common mind on the issue of violence and war and so long as such a situation exists in Southern Africa, the Council cannot deny its moral support to liberation movements which have resorted to illegal means, or its help in the humanitarian, educational and social aspects of their programme for combating racism. In fact such support is nothing more or less than the protest of the WCC against the *status quo* ideology of violence and an attempt to break the moral and religious sanctions behind it.[19]

The Uppsala assembly highlighted the integration of unity and justice. Thomas's significant contribution in this regard has been widely recognized. The real revolution of ecumenism in the 1960s, he told the Central Committee in 1973, was the integration of unity, witness, and service. "They have interpenetrated each other so much that Church unity, world mission and the struggle for social justice and world community are now seen as impossible to deal with in isolation from each other."[20]

Thomas's theological explorations have been path-breaking and innovative. The profound insights he provides through his reflections on spirituality, new humanism, and salvation and humanization illustrate this. Humanistic in its thrust, his work is decisively informed by the Christ-event.

Human Spirituality

Thomas said there must be a fundamental change in the understanding of human spirituality. The primary concern for Christian mission, he argued, is the salvation of the human spirituality with people's right choices in the realm of self-transcendence, not in isolation but "in relation to the material, social and cultural revolutions of our time." It was not just at the theological level that he raised the question of spirituality. This was prominent in his interaction with action groups, several of which he inspired. Thomas felt that there was need for a theology of political engagement that would help Christians and churches in such participation, a theology that would clarify the dialectical relation between faith and ideology in the light of the cross and the resurrection. He said at the Nairobi assembly in 1975:

> All these issues bring us to the need for a "spirituality for combat"—an expression that comes from David Jenkins. In his address on the theological enquiry on human rights Jenkins says; "perhaps what Christians are particularly called to work out . . . is what might be called a spirituality for combat. . . . Can our very struggles become part of our celebration of man as we understand him, in the image of God and died for by the Son of God? How might we help one another to so conduct our struggles that they become part of our worship?"[21]

Thomas quoted, in this connection, Hans-Reudi Weber, who described the spiritual vocation of the laity in the secular world as "holy worldliness."

Thomas emphasized the necessity to enter the Asian struggle at the level of spirituality, which is the structure of ultimate meaning and sacredness within which the human being lives and enters into relationship with nature and with fellow human beings in politics, economics, and culture. He argued that the church's central mission is the mission of presenting Christ as the saviour of the human spirit. He said: "The central task of those who would discover a spirituality in the midst of Asia's struggles, is therefore the linking of radical social involvement with a continuing exposure to biblical truth and sacramental action," adding, "In other words an important aspect of Christian spirituality is the sacramental dimension of the struggle for social justice."[22] For Thomas, the word *spiritual* denotes a fundamental framework of meaning which is assumed by a society and the beliefs about ultimate reality which reinforce the assumption.

New Humanism

In other words, Thomas argues that the spiritual awakening of the people of Asia should be understood in humanistic terms—as a search for a new humanism: "It is evident that at the spiritual centre of the Asian ferment today, there is a new human self-understanding or vision of a new dimension of human existence, or if you will, a new humanism. One may speak of this new dimension in many ways—one way is to define it as vision of man as personal being, that is man as freedom-in-responsibility, called to be dynamism of a purposive historical destiny."[23]

Thomas links this to a new vision of humanism. He attempts to delineate three aspects of this vision of new humanism. First, there is human awareness of his selfhood as distinct from nature: "Only a being which has self-awareness can be called spiritual. . . . It is the distinctive character of being human. Man is certainly part of nature and involved in the necessities of mechanical and organic processes of nature; but he is aware that while he is thus involved, he also transcends them, and is capable of relating himself to them, in terms of a structure of meaning and sacredness which he perceives as impinging on him, calling for his response."[24]

The second aspect of new humanism Thomas describes as "the search for purpose in history which gives meaning and specific vocation to individuals, groups, and nations. History is defined as humans creating themselves by creating their world. Involvement in history is described as a movement for human liberation related to human creativity, which consists of a person consciously participating in decisions that affect his future."

Third, the new humanism is itself expressed "in the search for new forms of community which recognised individual freedom, equality between man and woman. A community of interpersonal responsibility in love is the final goal of personal self-awareness, self-determination and self-direction. Radical personal individuality and community of persons are thus two sides of the same coin."[25]

Thus we see self-identity, historical consciousness, and community as characteristics of new humanism. Sometimes they are asserted negatively, as protest against and rejection of authoritarian structure of the traditional society, but often as a search for a fuller and richer human life.

The new sense of history, an awareness of the personal dimension of human existence, and a consciousness of the rights of the individual are all the result of Western ideologies which are inspired by the gospel or Christian missions. For this reason, says Thomas, "We are talking about human strivings which are in one sense or the other the creation of the Gospel, or at least the ferment of the Gospel integral to them, though I admit, not always the gospel in its purity and certainty."[26] Christian witness, holds Thomas, is primarily an effort to interpret the new self-understanding of human in the light of the gospel.

According to Thomas, as we have seen, the elements of a new humanism are new awareness of selfhood, historical consciousness, community, and an orientation to the "beyond." An existence open to these dimensions is sometimes called "genuine humanism" or "open humanism." Some of these dimensions are conspicuously absent in the traditional cultures and religions, at least in their doctrines. But today, consequent to the impact of Western ideologies and movements which are directly or indirectly inspired by the gospel, there is a search for a new humanism.

In this context, the main agenda of theological reflection is the relation between this concern for humanity and the gospel. How does Thomas define the relation? The answer is dependent on how he interprets new humanity in Christ, that is, his Christology. Of course, Thomas has not attempted a full-fledged treatise in Christology along the lines laid down by classical works on the subject. An essential task for him is to interpret the meaning of the person and work of Christ as a response to the revolution in modern religion and society.

Thomas describes Christ's humanity as "cruciform humanity." This is his interpretation of the cross, the humanity that is exemplified in the suffering love of Christ. The message of the cross "when posited against human self-justification" can release men and women for a new existence:

> The cross of Jesus is also the answer to the human problem of justification of human existence. Responding in faith to the free Divine forgiveness and acceptances offered by the crucified Christ, man is released from the necessity to seek security and justification by his own spirituality and moral or social idealism. But the release from the anxiety from the search of means for self-justification is a release for self-giving love of God and neighbour, which the Cross itself reveals as the destiny of man.[27]

Salvation as Humanization

Perhaps Thomas's most provocative interpretation of Christ's reality is his proposal regarding salvation as humanization. His theology can be summed up in this. His booklet *Salvation and Humanization* was the outcome of his search for the "point of contact" and perhaps represents his most mature thinking on the issue. He found the concept to be a valuable guide for interreligious dialogue as well as dialogue with secular movements.

> It is my conviction that the relation between salvation and humanization i.e. between the ultimate destiny of man and his historical destiny which we saw as fundamental in Christian re-thinking is also the fundamental issue debated within all religions and secular movements of India. Only the language of discourse varies from one movement to another. My thesis therefore is the theme of humanization which provides the most relevant point of entry for any Christian dialogue with these movements—at spiritual and theological depth.[28]

He introduced the concept of the "Christ-centred secular fellowship outside the church" as a *koinonia* "which was the manifestation of the new reality of the Kingdom at work in the world of men in world history." He argues that "salvation itself could be defined as humanization in a total and eschatological sense." Thomas agrees that salvation is the victory of Christ over sin. But both salvation and sin should be understood in corporate terms: "Sin has its corporate expression in the dehumanising spiritual forces of corporate life, the demons of principalities and powers; and the victory of Christ should mean victory over them and salvation in Christ must find its manifestation in power over these forces, as power for the humanization of our structures of collective existence."[29]

The relationship between salvation and humanization is defined this way: "Salvation is the spiritual inwardness of true humanization and humanization is inherent in the message of salvation in Christ." In the interpretation of salvation lies the relation of God and human, eternal and historical. The traditional pattern has been to start with the ultimate, the *Divinium*, and come to humankind's historical destiny. But Thomas says it should be possible to start where humankind is. Anthropology could be "the point of entry for the understanding of man's ultimate destiny in the purpose of God, i.e. his eternal salvation. . . . The question is not where you enter, but whether you reach a point where you are aware of the interrelation of the historical and the eternal—of the reality of the historical and the human in the eternal, and the presence of the eternal in the historical and the human."[30]

Thomas is not identifying salvation with a process of humanization, but he wants to affirm the interrelatedness of the two. In his dialogue with Hendrikus Berkhof, the Dutch theologian, on this issue, Thomas says, "I am not denying . . . that the unique gospel comes in the first instance as a judgment on the quest of modern man. I am only emphasising the other side, namely, the quest of modern man for his fuller humanity comes often as a judgment on our lopsided apprehension of Gospel and gets corrected by it."[31]

If salvation is linked to a process of humanization, then it follows that the church is not the only body through which Christ is mediated in the world. The whole process of history, secular ideologies, and religious movements work as God's agents. The church, of course, has a clearer perception of Christ's work: "The mission of the church is the revealing of what is hidden, a revealing which is not gnosis, but redemption involving victory over evil and transformation of the world."[32]

Some who are otherwise sympathetic to finding Christ active in history hesitate to put the situation in just the way Thomas does because of their propensity for viewing the church as the sole field of the activity of Christ. The various schemes for potentially including others within the church, even though they don't know it, which have appeared in the history of Christian thought have been intended in large part to somehow retain the church as the field of Christ's activity, while at the same time extending far beyond the known church. But this seems an unbiblical way of explaining Christ's activity—by confining it to the church, widely and vaguely defined. Frequently the New Testament relates Christ's direction directly to the world, rather than to the church, or through the church in the world.

Thomas also argues for a cultural syncretism as distinct from a religious syncretism or a "Christ-centred syncretism." Thomas says that a major concern of theological reflection should be "the development of a common cultural ethos expressing the idea of a social humanism which can provide motive and dynamics for the new structures." This can be done only in partnership between people of many religions and secular faiths. But it is not a syncretic faith that is envisaged. Thomas writes, "Religious syncretism should be avoided, not only for the sake of the purity of the Gospel, but also for the sake of a new culture. But religious syncretism should not be confused with cultural syncretism which cannot be avoided in our contemporary struggles for a new cultural ethos conducive to modernisation."[33] Thomas gives a practical suggestion: the church should help in "building up a Christ-centred fellowship of faith within society, culture and religion in which [people] live, transforming their structures and values from within."

Christian Witness in Society

What is the character of Christian witness in the midst of social, political, and cultural changes? Thomas's immediate answer is: it is to participate in the tasks of building new structures of political, economic, and social life and the cultural foundations for them.

One of Thomas's most significant contributions is on Christian participation in politics. Convinced that the gospel offers the dynamics for Christian engagement in politics, he has written about the political responsibility of Christians with a clarity and commitment rarely matched. He articulated these reflections in his WSCF days from the "encounter between Christian attitudes born in the context of pre-independent Asia with those born in the context of post-war Europe moving into the era of Cold War. . . . For me it was a stage in the process of my thinking on the roots of politics in the realm of personal existence founded on the gospel of Christ and the tension between power, justice and love in politics."[34] Thomas maintains that:

1. Christ is present and active in the world of history.
2. Christians have been called by God to fulfill a mission in the world and obedience to this call means full participation in the life of the world.
3. Biblical understanding of God's action in history belies the thesis that Christians should have nothing to do with politics.
4. The New Testament does not give political answers to present problems but it does require the child of God to grapple with the neighbour's problems, which include the political.
5. There are many Christians and churches who like to engage themselves in prophetic criticism. But only participants earn the right to be prophets: "The call of God to speak the word of judgment comes only to those who have affirmed their solidarity with the people under God and stood where they stood. It is only such prophetic word that is understood, whether it is accepted or rejected. We tend to reverse the order of God's calls."[35]

Thomas says: "Loyalty and obedience to God, the Lord of history and love of neighbour are of the essence of Christian social and personal ethics." He says that a wholehearted commitment to both these principles "would thrust a Christian headlong into politics, in its widest sense."[36] He quotes J. H. Oldham, who used to insist that a return to God should mean a return to politics, "that a recovery of the mission of the Church requires a concern for identification with the peoples who are involved in the revolutionary struggles to change existing power structures so that they can express their human dignity through real participation in the total life of society."[37]

Thomas was always conscious of the ethical dilemmas of political decisions, compromises that are needed in the active engagement in politics, and the ambiguities and pitfalls in the exercise of power. But there is also a certain "holiness" in his politics. Peter Hinchcleffe once described holiness in politics as follows: "Such a dimension would lead to a greater sensitivity to actions and motives, to a deeper understanding of situations, to self-criticism and a diminished tendency to identify one's judgements too simply with the will of God and therefore to a greater forbearance with opponents while still opposing them."[38]

In discharging the political task, how do we find the word of God for today? We read the signs of the times by discernment. To quote Thomas, "For a church which acknowledges the lordship of Christ over the whole world and of all history, it is necessary to discern Christ working in the world so that we may witness to what he is doing and be with him as he acts." The WCC Church and Society Conference in 1966 put it this way: "Holy Scriptures, history of the church, contemporary Christian experience and the insights from social sciences and other secular disciplines do inform the situation. In their light, the Christian is called to be obedient to his understanding of God's will in his particular situation."[39]

Thomas was always convinced that discernment comes with information, and therefore meticulous study is a hallmark of his political responses. Vision and ecstasy may be the source of symbolic actions, but discernment is achieved by putting one's understanding of human life, drawn ultimately from the biblical witness to Jesus Christ, alongside a diagnosis of what is going on today. As Preston notes, "To exercise the quality of discernment we need information—our own experience, the perspective of those in the struggle, experts—in the end we will have to judge the experts."[40] Therefore, Thomas wrote, "In the modern world it is impossible to conceive of any particular moral or Christian responsibility in politics, economics or society without involving ourselves in technical problems which are rarely simple and clear. One may go further and say that it is in the technical decisions that one is moral or immoral and Christian or non-Christian."[41]

M. M. Thomas's theological insights are yet to be fully explored. They offer a rich resource for the ecumenical movement as it faces new challenges.

CHAPTER 7

K. M. George

Metropolitan Paulos Mar Gregorios: Dimensions of Ecumenism

Paulos Mar Gregorios (formerly Paul Verghese) was born to an Orthodox Christian family on 9 August 1922 in Tripunithura, Kerala, India. Although a brilliant student at school, he could not afford to go to college because his father, a schoolteacher, had only modest means to support the family. Paul's mother became seriously ill when he was 13. He completed his high school and turned to freelance journalism, contributing articles and reports to various newspapers in the then-kingdoms of Kochi and Malabar. Later he joined the Indian Post and Telegraph Department in 1942. By sheer chance he was offered a teacher's position in Ethiopia in 1947. He came to the attention of Haile Selassie I, emperor of Ethiopia, because of the proficiency he had acquired in a short time in the Amharic language. The relationship that developed between them led young Paul to important appointments at various educational institutions in Ethiopia. Later, he went to the United States to advance his education, and undertook undergraduate studies at Goshen College. In 1954, he returned to India with a master's degree in theology, and worked as the associate director of the Fellowship House in Aluva and as visiting lecturer at the Union Christian

College, Aluva. He also served as the general secretary of the Orthodox Students Christian Movement. During the visit of the emperor Hailie Selassie to India in 1956, Verghese was persuaded by the emperor to return to Ethiopia. There he assumed a prestigious position as the emperor's personal aide and advisor. After three years he left his imperial assignment and pursued advanced studies at Princeton and Yale universities in the United States. In 1959, he returned to India and was ordained priest. While doing his doctoral studies in Oxford he was invited to conduct five Bible studies at the New Delhi assembly of the World Council of Churches (WCC) in 1961 and later to join the WCC staff in Geneva as its associate general secretary. In 1967 he left Geneva, returned to India, and became the principal of the Orthodox Theological Seminary at Kottayam, Kerala. In 1975, Father Paul Varghese was consecrated bishop with the name Paulos Mar Gregorios, and was assigned the newly formed diocese of Delhi of the Malankara Orthodox Syrian Church, a position he held until his death in November 1996.

This article deals with only some aspects of the "ecumenical" involvement of Mar Gregorios, a stunningly multifaceted personality.

Bible Study and the Ecumenical Movement

As noted above, the stage for the formal entry of Metropolitan Paulos Mar Gregorios into the ecumenical movement was the New Delhi assembly of the World Council of Churches in 1961. He was then a 39-year-old newly ordained priest of the Malankara Orthodox Syrian Church in India, a founding-member church of the WCC. A doctoral research student at Oxford, Verghese was invited to be one of the Bible study leaders at the assembly together with Martin Niemoeller from Germany and Paul Minear from Yale University. His five Bible studies in one section of the assembly became legendary. It is said that with every passing day his audience swelled as many people left their previously assigned places of Bible study in the two other sections. Archbishop Michael Ramsay of Canterbury attended all of Verghese's Bible studies, and they became lifelong friends.[1]

In fact, one of Verghese's major contributions to the ecumenical movement, particularly in the gatherings of the WCC, was precisely the Bible studies he conducted. He continued to be one of the most distinguished Bible study leaders until his practical withdrawal from the active service of the WCC at the Canberra assembly in 1991. In fact, he was always passionate about the study of the Bible long before he had received any formal theological training. While a teacher in Ethiopia in the 1940s he conducted regular Bible studies for his Ethiopian students.[2] He gratefully traced the source of his passion for Bible learning to the training he received as a young boy in the Orthodox spiritual and liturgical tradition in his home parish in Kerala. His approach and his interpretation of the scripture always exuded a discreet patristic-liturgical flavour coupled with his prodigious intelligence and insight into the contemporary reality of the world. This is probably what set his Bible studies apart from the regular staple people usually received in ecumenical and confessional church circles in the form of sermons and homilies. Once he had his formal theological education he would use the original languages of the Bible—Greek and Hebrew—for his exegetical Bible studies. On special occasions, he would make his own translation for the Bible passage from the original languages. The dimensions of meaning of the text and the freshness of insights he brought to the listener have always been incomparable. In his unfinished autobiography he remembers how, as a rather new theology graduate from the United States, he was tested by the saintly Catholicos Baselios Geevarghese II, head of the Malankara Orthodox Church, on his knowledge of Bible and the Orthodox tradition. It had been rumoured that a layman called Paul Verghese was teaching American Protestant views to Indian Orthodox students. He was summoned by the Catholicos, reputed for his spiritual insights into scripture and liturgy. Verghese had to undergo an unusually long interview. He was asked some 64 questions on the Bible and he answered 62 to the great satisfaction of the Catholicos. Verghese was given laudable approbation and permission to teach in the church.[3]

Early Search for Unity

Most of the Eastern and Oriental Orthodox Churches became members of the WCC at the New Delhi assembly. Prior to the assembly, Verghese, together with Father K. Philipose, Central Committee delegate from the Malankara Orthodox Church, wrote to the delegates from these churches regarding the possibility of an informal meeting of Eastern and Oriental Orthodox Church delegates to discuss the old christological issues which had divided them at the Council of Chalcedon in 451 CE and to explore the possibilities of restoring communion.[4] This was one of the first initiatives that later culminated in the informal series of theological conversations between the two families of Orthodox churches. The churches in both families accepted the findings and agreed upon statements from the informal conversations between 1964 and 1971, and they set up an official joint commission to facilitate the path to unity and eucharistic communion.[5]

Some of the Eastern and Oriental Orthodox delegates to the New Delhi assembly visited Kerala for the first time on the invitation of the Malankara Orthodox Church to discover the ancient church of India that remained faithful to the apostolic tradition of St Thomas, the apostle of Christ, down through the centuries. On their meeting with the Catholicos the delegates requested that Father Verghese be permitted to join the staff of the World Council of Churches in Geneva.[6] He had already been invited by the general secretary to assume an important position on the staff. The Catholicos gave him permission, and Verghese became the associate general secretary in charge of the Division of Ecumenical Action, the first Orthodox and the first Asian African to hold such a top position in the WCC.

On the Staff of the WCC

From the very beginning of his work as a staffperson he was both devoted to and critical of the WCC with regard to its self-understanding and policy orientation. He repeatedly affirmed his conviction that the ecumenical movement was nothing new but that it was born with the Pentecost, and was as old as the gospel itself since the commission to the apostles to be witnesses of Jesus Christ to the end of the earth was integral to the gospel of Christ. [7]

He held that the WCC was only one of the many instruments, perhaps a privileged one, useful to foster the unity of the body of Christ. He was an ecumenical visionary and his vision transcended the frame of a bureaucratic organization created and sustained mainly by the white Western Protestant churches. He was very sensitive to the fact that "the two-thirds world" (Mar Gregorios detested the expression "third world") was only nominally represented on the council at the time he joined it. Mar Gregorios was, however, very positive in affirming the fundamental significance of the ecumenical movement: "I want to argue first that Christians cannot question the ecumenical movement itself without putting the fundamentals of their own faith in question."[8]

As early as 1983, as part of his reflections on the Vancouver assembly, he made "some bold proposals" for the proper orientation of the ecumenical movement which should include, according to him, "the four fundamental families of Christendom," namely, the mainline churches of the Reformation, the evangelicals in their associations and sects, the Roman Catholic Church, and the Eastern/Oriental Orthodox.[9] He proposed the creation of a body which he called "the Communion of the Churches of Reformation" as a means to forge a more genuine ecumenical relationship with the other great streams of Christianity.[10] In his overwhelming concern to transform the WCC into an authentic instrument of genuine ecumenism he always raised the question, "Can the WCC continue under a predominantly Western Protestant leadership and still remain the privileged instrument of the ecumenical movement?"[11] The WCC today has certainly made a great leap toward the vision of embracing people of all colours and confessional beliefs, including the Pentecostal/Evangelical stream.

Mar Gregorios even had a blueprint for the style of life and work of the staff in Geneva. For example, he visualized the staff members living as one community in a mode of sharing and participation in the life of families rather than as individuals working in a bureaucratic setup just like in any business office. He would also recommend regular, intensified Bible studies for the staff. The study of the Bible was not to tear up the body of Christ using divisive assumptions and prejudices but to build it up, even while using the best academic scholarship.[12] This, he hoped, would make the witness of the WCC more authentic. He was concerned that with the passing of the first-generation pioneers, who were passionate ecumenists, the great cause of ecumenism should not be compromised by any routine bureaucracy.

Church, Society and the Ecumenical Calling

As moderator of the WCC subunit on Church and Society, Mar Gregorios made a lasting contribution to the ecumenical movement. His versatile mind and his broad intellectual-spiritual interests singularly equipped him for a highly competent dialogue with science, technology, socioeconomic and political structures, and with the secular society at large. He provoked a new debate regarding the ethical-philosophical dimensions of scientific research and the calling of theology and theologians to engage the secular world in a close-knit and creative conversation. His outstanding ability to comprehend the broad strokes and the orientation of research and debates in any discipline made him a confident interlocutor between the world of faith and the complex world of science and technology, philosophy, and ideologies like Marxism. He was convinced that "the world-ward orientation of the church is just as important as the God-ward orientation."[13] Mar Gregorios preferred the phrase "church and humanity" rather than church and society because he felt that the broader dimensions of humanity were not always captured by the word *society*, a human social construct.

The world conference on "Faith, Science and the Future," held at the Massachusetts Institute of Technology (MIT) in August 1979, involving some top scientists, philosophers, theologians and social scientists together with the delegated representatives of churches, brought together some one thousand persons.[14] One may hardly find anything comparable to this event in the history of the World Council of Churches in terms of the quality and breadth of a breakthrough dialogue between theology and sciences, between church and the secular society. Mar Gregorios moderated the whole conference while also presenting a keynote address on science and faith, and delivered a brilliant homily to conclude the conference. Paul Abrecht, director of the Church and Society subunit, chief organizer of the MIT conference, and longtime colleague and friend of Mar Gregorios, said:

> In 1976 by action of the central committee, Gregorios was made moderator of the working committee on Church and Society and thus leader of the preparations for the world conference on "Faith, Science and Future", convened at the Massachusetts Institute of Technology in 1979. With more than 400 official participants and an additional 500 press and invited guests, this was undoubtedly one of the most significant WCC sponsored encounters of the 1970's, and the metropolitan responded to the challenge brilliantly: as chairman of the conference he captivated the assembled scientists and technologists and the MIT community by his understanding of the social ethical problems in their disciplines. Undoubtedly it was one of his greatest contributions to the life and work of the WCC and to the witness of the ecumenical movement in the contemporary world.[15]

Mar Gregorios challenged both theologians and scientists to reexamine their conventional paradigms in the light of newly evolved perceptions in both religion and science. He called on theologians to awaken "to the fact that space, time and causality are themselves doubtful constructs of our human consciousness and that we cannot creditably discharge our task by providing theologies which explain the universe and man as sequentially 'caused' by a creator who is temporally prior to the universe and spatially distinct from it."[16]

Similarly, he challenged the scientists to see if "our present paradigm is too fragmentary and incoherent—clusters of theories in various disciplines without any single coordinating scheme for a holistic approach to reality."[17] Mar Gregorios envisioned a new scientific paradigm which would provide at least four things: (a) a framework for coordinating the central theoretical insights of various scientific disciplines; (b) a meaningful pattern in which perceptions such as religious, mystical, paranormal, and other nonordinary phenomena can also be incorporated and not arbitrarily ruled out simply because they do not fit into present theory; (c) provide some indication of ways of transcending the paradoxes in current theory; and (d) provide for the emerging fact that human beings and universe are inextricably interrelated and that the subject–object, knower–known dichotomy is ultimately untenable.[18]

Mar Gregorios did not simply bypass conceptual knowledge in favour of any nonconceptual perception. He pleaded for a passage through the problems of science and its paradoxes, through "taught ignorance" (*docta ignorantia*) that goes beyond conceptual knowledge in a silent adoration. Science and faith through respectful collaboration and self-criticism can work for a new perception of truth for humanity.

Peace, Disarmament, and Social Justice

Mar Gregorios dedicated a major part of his time, energy, and talents to the cause of nuclear disarmament and peace with justice in the international arena. In association with the World Peace Council he moderated several roundtable discussions held in Moscow during the Cold War period.[19] His understanding of ecumenism was so broad-based that he always placed the unity of humankind and the emergence of an international community rooted in peace and justice as a real target of a genuine ecumenism. He often challenged the assumptions of the ecumenical movement to the embarrassment and provocation of some leaders who couldn't see the issue of unity beyond a certain denominational get-together and the fostering of missionary work abroad.

Mar Gregorios moved with great ease and confidence in the two worlds separated by the Iron Curtain. Well respected in the countries of Eastern Europe for his critical candour and his bold vision of a new humanity, he was equally opposed to the capitalist market economy and to totalitarian regimes that oppressed people. He openly declared his allegiance and commitment to a socialist order of society where human freedom, dignity, justice, and peace are afoot. The discreet archetype that inspired his vision of socialism was the kingdom of God as taught by Jesus Christ.

Interfaith Dimension of Ecumenism

It was after he left the council staff position in 1967 and returned to India that he began to take serious interest in the study of other religions and interfaith dialogue. Over the years, he deepened his understanding of the Indian tradition of the Advaita Vedanta in the Hindu heritage as well as the Buddhist and Jain philosophical-spiritual traditions. He got involved in regular philosophical forums and became the president of the Indian philosophical congress.[20] In New Delhi, as bishop of the Malankara Orthodox Church, he found a very congenial climate for deeper spiritual and intellectual exchanges with leaders like the Dalai Lama, Karan Singh, Baba Virsa Singh, and others.[21] He was sought after by professors and students of social sciences from Delhi University and Jawaharlal Nehru University.

It was a rare privilege for an Indian Christian bishop to address the 100th anniversary of the World Parliament of Religions in Chicago in 1993 where, a century before, the great Indian sage Vivekananda made a historic speech and captivated the Western audience.[22] In his own residence in Delhi, the bishop envisaged a *Sarva Dharma Nilaya*—a house for all religions—and a *Niti Shanthi Kendra*—a centre for justice and peace. These reflected Bishop Gregorios' abiding concern and his view of an inclusive ecumenism, of which he always dreamt while working in Geneva and struggling with an array of international issues. He was able to enrich the dialogue between Christian faith and Asian religions with a philosophical and Eastern Christian patristic dimension in a unique way. He thought that Christian theology itself would gain much if some of the Christian theological issues were accosted from the perspective of ancient Asian religions. The gospel of John, for example, could be read in a new and deeper way if we properly understood the idea of enlightenment central to the Buddhist tradition.

Despite his Western education and long years of dealing with the international community, Mar Gregorios always remained an Indian to the core. He once said that he could have become a Mennonite in Goshen or a Presbyterian in Princeton, but he chose to remain faithful to his origin and identity as Indian and Orthodox Christian. This is probably the source of a lot of conflicts he faced in his relationship with self-assuming Western-educated Indians as well as some Western intellectuals. It is remarkable, however, that in his relationship with great sages and committed scholars in any religion he showed an unusual humility and openness to learn from and dialogue with them. While some of his critics at times considered Mar Gregorios to be an arrogant intellectual, his relationship with saintly people, with true seekers of knowledge, and with little children revealed a totally different dimension of his personality that was extremely humble, and willing to be challenged spiritually and intellectually. In his personal dialogue with members of other religions he genuinely experienced great spiritual delight without any inhibitions, any hidden or ulterior motives of converting the other, or overwhelming the dialogue partner with an air of superiority. He always thought this experience of delight was the fruit and reward of a genuine dialogue.

Education and Ecumenism

While Mar Gregorios was on the staff of the WCC, he initiated the new department of education, as he strongly believed that education was key to the shaping of a solid ecumenical vision.[23] He led an important delegation of the Council to UNESCO, where the distinguished Indian educator Malcolm Adiseshaiah was heading the department. On his return to India from Geneva, he was appointed as the principal of the Orthodox Theological Seminary at Kottayam, where he started some important initiatives for the theological education of laymen and women in addition to the regular theological education of the candidates for priesthood. He conceived a broad curriculum for the religious education of the Oriental Orthodox Churches and got it approved at the historic meeting of the heads of Oriental Orthodox Churches hosted by Emperor Haile Selassie in Addis Ababa in 1965. He believed that through a common curriculum of education the unity of these ancient Oriental churches of one faith and one eucharistic communion could be made alive. An office was set up in India for this purpose, and a team of educators drawn from the Oriental Orthodox Churches produced some common textbooks for instruction in Sunday schools of these churches. However, political and ecclesiastical conflicts prevented the full flowering of the project, to the disappointment of Mar Gregorios.

In India, he played a key role in the formation of the All India Association for Christian Higher Education (AIACHE) in the 1970s, which still continues as an important educational facilitator and coordinates Christian university colleges in India for a value-based and excellence-aiming higher education.

Orthodox Unity as Ecumenical Expression

One of the major breakthroughs in the modern ecumenical movement was the starting of an intense and successful theological dialogue, first at the informal level and then taken up officially, between the family of Eastern Orthodox Churches in communion with the Patriarchate of Constantinople, on the one hand, and the family of ancient Oriental Orthodox Churches of Egypt (Coptic), Syria, Armenia, Ethiopia, and India (Malankara), on the other. Father Paul Verghese, associate general secretary of the WCC, and Nikos Nissiotis, Greek Orthodox lay theologian, then associate director of the Bossey Ecumenical Institute, fruitfully collaborated under the auspices of the WCC Faith and Order department to hold the first unofficial meeting of theologians from both families in Aarhus, Denmark, in 1964. The Aarhus consultation was followed up in three successive meetings in Bristol, Geneva, and Addis Ababa. They were to reexamine the christological positions of both families, which had broken communion ever since the Council of Chalcedon in 451. The conclusion of the unofficial conversations was that the two families had in fact maintained the same apostolic faith and spiritual-liturgical ethos of the undivided church, though in the christological formulation in the fifth century some terminological disagreements coupled with political and cultural factors in the Byzantine imperial context created the unfortunate division. The unofficial consultations could reach agreed-upon statements on those issues that had divided the two families 1,500 years ago. The findings were submitted to the churches on both sides, and the churches formally took up the dialogue by creating an official joint commission to follow up the theological agreements into canonical and pastoral actions to restore eucharistic communion. From the Oriental Orthodox side, Verghese and Father V. C. Samuel, his colleague in the Malankara Orthodox Church in India and an expert on early Chalcedonian christological debate, played a decisive role. Mar Gregorios was passionate about the possibility of reunion of these ancient church families as a witness of Orthodoxy to the ecumenical movement. He truly believed that a sincere desire for full unity along with compassionate, mutually respecting, and informed dialogue could overcome long centuries of conflict and alienation in the life of Christian churches. The formation of the Church of South India in 1947 was greatly celebrated as an expression of the ecumenical spirit on the Protestant side. In fact, the coming together of the Eastern and Oriental Orthodox churches, though not consummated yet in eucharistic communion, is something to be celebrated as Orthodoxy's sincere witness to the unity of the body of Christ as willed by Jesus Christ. Although communion is not formally restored, the principle of economy is exercised in some metropolitan centres as well as in some countries in the Middle East where eucharistic communion is practiced, for example, between the two families of the Orthodox Churches in the Patriarchate of Antioch.

In the World Council of Churches the two Orthodox families always stand together in all theological and policy matters. The enormous personal contributions Mar Gregorios made, and the passion and sincerity he demonstrated in order to bring about this historic change, are not all recorded, but known to his close associates.

The many critical comments Mar Gregorios made in the early days of his association with the ecumenical movement and the WCC with regard to the marginalization of the Orthodox constituency and the domination of Western Protestant agenda, however, bore fruit much later, for example, in such initiatives as the creation of the Special Commission for the Participation of the Orthodox in the World Council of Churches and the Permanent Committee now afoot to watch over the just participation of all churches in the council.

Roman Catholic Church and Ecumenism

Mar Gregorios had a special interest in the life and tradition of the Roman Catholic Church. He had genuine respect for the spirituality of various monastic orders in the Catholic Church and for the bold position taken by the

Roman Catholic Church with regard to moral-ethical issues in a fast-changing, secularized West. Though he was staunchly critical of some of the theological positions of the Roman Church, like those on primacy and authority, and the uncharitable proselytism perpetrated by Uniate (Oriental Catholic) churches against the Orthodox churches, and so forth, Mar Gregorios always stood in favour of the participation of the Roman Catholic Church in the life of the WCC, and he believed that the Protestant tradition, in spite of its many great contributions, had rejected some of the fundamental doctrinal positions held by the undivided church. This position of Mar Gregorios had often provoked his colleagues from the Reformation tradition, but he held on to it as an important point at issue in the process of the reunion of churches, and not simply out of any prejudiced and parochial opposition to the Reformation tradition, which he respected in many other ways.

Mar Gregorios was a delegated observer at the Second Vatican Council. His theological inputs were seriously considered by the council theologians, particularly on questions of authority and collegiality. Together with his Orthodox colleagues he took a proactive position to bring the best Orthodox insights into the council discussion and decrees. He always considered Pope John XXIII as a truly Spirit-inspired and saintly personality.

Mar Gregorios' vast experience with the Roman Catholic Church, its spiritual-monastic tradition, and its theological position were brought to bear on the historic *Pro Oriente* Consultations between the Roman Catholic Church and the Oriental Orthodox Churches initiated by Cardinal Archbishop Koenig of Vienna. Some of the best theologians from the Oriental Orthodox Churches sat with distinguished Roman Catholic theologians to sort out a rather broad spectrum of theological, doctrinal, and canonical matters that divided the Western and Oriental churches. From the Indian side, Mar Gregorios and Father Samuel again played a key role in the formulation of agreed statements.

The legendary speech of Mar Gregorios at the Canberra assembly in 1991, publicly challenging the keynote speaker Bob Hawke, prime minister of Australia, to his face on the issue of justice to the aboriginal people of Australia, shook the assembly as the audience literally stood up and applauded him at every sentence. Several Western leaders and part of the WCC leadership were embarrassed at the provocative and splendidly moving way in which Mar Gregorios challenged the prime minister, though most of the people gathered there—delegates, observers, and guests—expressed their full solidarity with the speaker and the cause for which he spoke with such incredible brilliance.

Conclusion

Paulos Mar Gregorios was not obviously a person who would easily fit into ecclesiastical or ecumenical straitjackets. Endowed with a rare form of holistic intelligence and broad intellectual curiosity of a polymath, with a sincere quest for a new and just order of the world and deep compassion to the least ones, he was always tormented by intellectual puzzles and internal spiritual conflicts. He was impatient with any shallow interpretation of ecumenism as some sort of a social get-together of churches and their simple do-goodism. Deeply sensitive to any trace of chauvinism on the part of people assuming the leverage of authority or racial or academic superiority, he sometimes reacted with bitter irony and sarcasm, which created for him lifelong enemies. On such occasions it was hard for many people to sense the real humility of his heart and his internal wounds, which he frankly shared with some of his close associates. He was most joyous in the company of small children, and always reminded his students of Jesus' words that the guardian angels of those children were beholding the face of God. It seemed that the enormous time he took to play with and teach children was probably some form of self-imposed penitential reparation for his many angry moods with haughty and powerful men.

Mar Gregorios' intellectually sophisticated and out-of-the-ordinary interpretation of ecumenism was not easily digestible to many. His deeply insightful philosophical and theological writings on dialogue with Asian religions, for example, are rarely referred to even by Asian students in their theological dissertations on interfaith dialogue. Probably they are never exposed to them by their own teachers or they are unable to grasp the depth and the integral character of his arguments.

In his *Last Will and Testament*, Mar Gregorios summarized his "ecumenical" vision in the following words:

> Christ's love is for all humankind, not just for Christians. It is for the whole of humanity that he has died, not just for Christians alone. He lives for the human race, and he is the lover and Saviour as well as Lord of the whole race of humankind. How can I then draw any limits to my love and compassion, or deny it to any group of human beings? Even those who regard themselves as my enemies I am not to hate or exclude from Christ's love and compassions. That has been the basis of my approach to all sorts of groups, people of other religions, Communists, Moonies . . .

Christ is for me much more than a great teacher of humanity. . . . In him everything holds together, and in him shall the whole creation, purged of all evil, be finally harmonised. This, I believe, and I have no reason to hide my faith, though I do not talk about it all the time. I live by this faith. This is the source-spring of my actions. This is the hope that keeps me from despair and despondency, even when everything looks so bleak and gloomy in God's world.[24]

CHAPTER 8

S. Wesley Ariarajah

The Pioneering Ministry of Stanley J. Samartha

Stanley Samartha is one of the most important figures from India who made a significant difference to the ecumenical movement by playing a central role at one of the most crucial moments of its programmatic history. Christian relationship to people of other religious traditions had been a much-debated subject since the birth of the modern ecumenical movement, commonly identified with the first World Missionary Conference in Edinburgh in 1910. The controversy over the issue peaked at the third World Missionary Conference in Tambaram (1938). Eventually, the newly constituted World Council of Churches (WCC) and the International Missionary Council (IMC) jointly set up a worldwide study process entitled "The Word of God and the Living Faiths of Men" to continue to explore the "Tambaram Controversy" over what should be the Christian approach to other religious traditions. The findings of this study process, which was done through study centres around the world, were pulled together at an important meeting in Kandy, Sri Lanka (1967). The WCC then began to look for someone who would take the new openings, impulses, and moves made at the Kandy conference forward by giving a new focus and life to the divisive issue. The invitation to join the WCC staff to accomplish this challenge was extended to Stanley J. Samartha in 1968.

Preparation for the Ecumenical Ministry

Samartha was born on 7 October 1920 in Karkala, in the Karnataka state in India. His father was a pastor with the Basel Evangelical Mission and his mother was a primary schoolteacher. Samartha had gradually obtained the educational qualifications that enabled him to take up the appointment at the WCC. Having done his B.A. degree at St Aloysius College, affiliated then to the University of Madras, and his B.D. at the United Theological College (UTC), Bangalore, Samartha obtained his S.T.M. at the Union Theological Seminary, New York, studying with Paul Tillich and Reinhold Niebuhr, and his PhD at the Hartford Seminary Foundation. Before he returned to India he spent a period of time in Basel, Switzerland, at the invitation of the Basel Mission, attending lectures and seminars of Karl Barth and meeting Hendrik Kraemer, then the director of the Ecumenical Institute at Bossey. In so doing, he had had the opportunity to encounter and learn directly from the two persons whose theologies on other religious traditions were at the heart of the Tambaram controversy.

On his return to India in 1952 he was appointed principal of the Basel Evangelical Mission Theological Seminary (now Karnataka Theological College), which was followed by distinguished teaching and leadership careers at the United Theological College, Bangalore, and Serampore College, Calcutta. While deeply rooted in the Christian faith and committed to the church and its ministry, Samartha concentrated on Hinduism, especially the Advaitic tradition, for his graduate work. His dissertation was on the Hindu understanding of history. His abiding interest both in Christian theology, Hinduism, and in the history and philosophy of religions had prepared him well for the work he was called to do at the WCC.

Contribution to the Ecumenical Movement

During his 12 years at the WCC, Samartha was instrumental in preparing, shaping, and implementing a new approach of the ecumenical movement to peoples of other religious traditions. Soon after his appointment, he did a critical evaluation of the ecumenical approaches to other religions and realized that one needed to move from the study and assessment of other religions to actual relationships and dialogue and that the emphasis should be on people and not on systems of belief. With this new framework in mind, within a year of his arrival, in 1969, he got the consent of the Central Committee and organized the first WCC-sponsored interfaith dialogue event in Ajaltoun, Lebanon (1970). The meeting, which constituted Hindus, Buddhists, Christians, and Muslims, not only reflected on the purpose, nature, and limits of interreligious dialogue, but also facilitated actual dialogue. Two months later, he called a consultation in Zurich, which evaluated theologically the experience of dialogue in Ajaltoun and produced a report, the *Zurich Aide-Memoire*, that became the fundamental document on the basis of which the WCC Central Committee, meeting in Addis Ababa in 1971, created a new programme subunit on Dialogue with People of Living Faiths and Ideologies, with Samartha as its first director.

Within a short period he had succeeded in enabling an important leap forward in an ecumenical approach to other religions despite the strong stream within the WCC that emphasized world mission and evangelism as the ecumenical priority. He was able to achieve this partly because of the respect and admiration he had earned from his colleagues and the leadership of the council, both on the staff and in the decision-making bodies. He placed integrity above many other virtues and had meticulous personal and professional disciplines: he weighed every word he spoke or wrote for its appropriateness, precision, and effect, and paid much attention to how it would be heard and received. He also had a good sense of strategy and never pushed an issue before it was, at least in his judgment, mature for reception. He was also much respected and admitted by the dialogue partners of other religious traditions, who considered him completely trustworthy, fair, and clear and open about his intentions. Samartha's personal traits and qualities contributed a great deal in removing some of the initial hesitations many Hindus had about Christians wanting suddenly to engage in dialogue with them. He did much to remove the prejudice among Hindus and Buddhists that dialogue is yet another tool in Christian zeal for evangelism.

Samartha's skill and intellectual acumen was put to severe test at the fifth assembly of the WCC in Nairobi (1975). He had got the consent of the Central Committee to have a section at the assembly devoted to interfaith relations and dialogue under the title "Seeking Community: The Common Search of Peoples of Various Faiths, Cultures and Ideologies." More interestingly, he had also persuaded the executive committee to approve an invitation to five guests of other faith traditions who could speak at the assembly only if invited by the moderator to do so, but with the right to participate fully in the section discussions, which dealt with interfaith relations and dialogue. The tradition of inviting guests of other faiths to the assembly, which he initiated at Nairobi, continues to this day. It is of interest to note, from his later writings, what he had in mind in seeking their participation:

> The presence of guests of five major world faiths at a world Christian assembly was more than a matter of a splash of colours—a turban and a saffron robe in the midst of Episcopal robes and patriarchal gowns. Although these guests constituted a tiny minority in the vast gathering with no right to speak in the assembly, their presence had a symbolic significance larger than their number suggests though not sufficiently recognized then or even now. What their visible presence brought was a touch of reality, a reminder of the fact of the *plurality* of faiths in the global community, not in an abstract way for theological discussions but in a personal way through the presence of *people* of living faiths.[1]

Since the newly constituted dialogue programme was for the first time reporting to an assembly, some difficult discussions were anticipated; the assembly included persons with strong commitment to world evangelization. But Samartha was taken aback when the acrimonious debate on floor of the assembly moved in the direction of challenging the very concept of dialogue and the need for it. The section report on "Seeking Community," which he had guided, was sent back to the drafting group. The arguments presented were that dialogue betrays the missionary mandate, compromises the uniqueness and finality of Christ, and would lead to syncretism. The report was accepted later, after an addition of a preamble that emphasized the missionary mandate, but Samartha had to quickly come up with a proposal that would save the immediate and long-term future of the subunit on dialogue.

The strategy he developed with the leadership was to propose a major consultation after the assembly that included the assenting and dissenting voices at Nairobi to take up and clarify the questions and issues raised by those who opposed the programme. Organizing this strategic conference, which was held in Chiang Mai, Thailand, in 1977, with the right mix of people, with adequate preparatory work, skilled leadership, excellent drafters, and in an atmosphere of mutual listening and learning is a telling testimony to Samartha's leadership skills and strategic thinking. While responding directly to some of the questions at Nairobi, and by framing the most difficult issues as "Questions that need further study and reflection," he managed to extract sufficient agreement among the participants to be able to draft a statement on "Dialogue in Community," which formed the basis for the fully spelt out "Guidelines for Dialogue with People of Living Faiths and Ideologies" (1979), a document that became the basis for many guidelines on dialogue that were drawn up by member churches. Even though Chiang Mai did not fully respond to all the issues, it was one of the historic meetings of the WCC, which eliminated the threat the dialogue programme itself was facing at Nairobi. Thus, Samartha should be given most of the credit not only for the establishment of the dialogue programme but also for ensuring its future within the WCC.

After 12 years of ministry with the WCC, and having celebrated his 60th birthday, Samartha returned to Bangalore, India, in October 1980. Although he had earlier been a professor at the United Theological College in Bangalore for many years, the return to India after a long period did present some challenges. Reflecting on this initial experience he wrote:

> I quickly discovered that old land marks had disappeared or were distorted beyond recognition. Priorities in national politics and church life had changed. New signposts were not yet visible—at least I was not yet sufficiently sensitive to recognize them clearly. From being a spectator-participant of life in India from a distance I had now suddenly become a "participant-spectator" in its contemporary history. I had to develop quickly a sense of discernment between the trivial and the substantial, between events of temporary and enduring significance in the life of the nation. I had to get my bearings and make inner adjustments to the change of the character and rhythm of life in my own country.[2]

To ecumenical friends who visited him in Bangalore it was clear that what disappointed him most was the lack of vital interest in interfaith relations and dialogue among the churches in India. He, however, became a productive contributor in retirement by agreeing to be a consultant to the Christian Institute for the Study of Religion and Society (CISRS), a visiting professor at the

United Theological College, and an advisor and supervisor of a number of doctoral students who were doing postgraduate work under the South Asia Theological Research Institute (SATHRI). He also continued his theological reflections, especially on Christology, and wrote an important volume, *Between Cultures: Ecumenical Ministry in a Pluralist World*,[3] that reflected on his life and especially his ecumenical journey. After struggling with bone cancer during the last months of his life, and having celebrated his 80th birthday, he passed away in July 2001.

Contribution to Ecumenical Thought on Interfaith Relations

There are three dimensions to his ecumenical ministry at the WCC. First, as described above, is the central role he played in establishing dialogue as an ecumenical concern and giving it an institutional standing within the WCC. The second was the relationships he built with persons of other religious traditions through bilateral and multilateral dialogue events and through personal contacts. By the time Samartha left the WCC, the organization had a considerable number of scholars and religious leaders of high repute in other religious traditions that had become part of the WCC network of relationships. He also secured a place for the WCC as an important partner in international interfaith organizations like the World Conference on Religion and Peace (WCRP), World Council of Faiths (WCF), International Association for Religious Freedom (IARF), and others.

But perhaps the most significant relationship he established was with the parallel dialogue programme of the Roman Catholic Church, the Vatican Secretariat for Non-Christians (later renamed the Pontifical Council for Interreligious Dialogue). The then-Secretary of the Vatican Secretariat, Monsignor Rossano, and Samartha established the best possible personal and professional relationships, which was extended to the relationship between the two programme units of the Vatican and the WCC. The WCC and the Vatican had established a Joint Working Group (JWG) in 1965 to discuss issues of common interest and to promote cooperation between the WCC and the Roman Catholic Church. The JWG met every year to enable this process but much of the attempts at cooperation had been tentative or short-lived. The only exception was the relationship in the area of interfaith relations. The programme subunit on dialogue and the secretariat had annual joint staff meetings, alternating between Geneva and the Vatican, and they initiated joint studies on such questions like interfaith prayer, interreligious marriages, conversion, and the like. The level of cooperation and collaboration Samartha was able to get from the Vatican was a matter of envy for other WCC programmes. The collaboration he fostered was sustained by his successors and continues to this day.

The third is the significant theological input he made, which remains a vital contribution to continuing ecumenical thought on interfaith dialogue and relationship. Samartha's theological contribution can be divided into three categories. The first is on Hinduism and Indian philosophy, which were his primary preoccupation during his postgraduate studies. He summarized the findings of his PhD dissertation on *The Modern Hindu View of History according to Representative Thinkers* (1958) into a booklet, *The Hindu View of History: Classical and Modern*, with a clear exposition of the Hindu understandings of history and how it can be enriched by an encounter with the gospel.[4] But perhaps the most important contribution during this period is his volume *The Hindu Response to the Unbound Christ*, a revised and enlarged version of a series of lectures he had given at UTC on the responses of selected Hindu thinkers to Jesus and his teachings.[5] There is every reason to believe that this study rekindled and reconfirmed Samartha's interest in interfaith dialogue and the need to have a fresh understanding of Jesus Christ in the context of religious plurality. This also played an important role in his desire to formulate a "revised Christology"—a monumental task he undertook toward the end of his ministry.

The second area relates to his theological insights on religious plurality, the theological bases for interfaith dialogue, and the related concern for an adequate theology of religions. And the third is his theological explorations on the doctrine of God, Christology, pneumatology, and missiology. It is important to look in some detail at the second and third categories of his theological contribution.

Religious Plurality, Interfaith Dialogue, and the Theology of Religions

At the time Samartha was concluding his ministry with the WCC, a selection of eleven essays which constituted some of the important articles he had written and speeches he had given during his tenure at the WCC were put together into a volume, *Courage for Dialogue: Ecumenical Issues in Interfaith Relationships*.[6] The first eight chapters of the volume deal with the concept and practice of dialogue and the theological issues related to them. Samartha is well known for some pithy phrases he had coined to encapsulate the meaning of dialogue. The most important among them was "commitment and openness"; based on this he also gave the most popular definition of dialogue as "an encounter of commitments." As mentioned earlier, he was instrumental in bringing the focus on "people" of living faiths over against the classical ecumenical approach to other religions as belief systems. As a result, for him, the primary purpose of interreligious dialogue was to build "community"—a "community of heart and mind." It is by first building community that one can go "beyond community"—another phrase he coined—to mutually enrich, correct, and learn from one another. This rootedness in the life of the people informed all his thinking. "It should be kept in mind," he maintained, "that neither 'religious pluralism' nor 'human community' can be discussed as concepts that can be detached from the throbbings of surrounding life and held up for intellectual examination as hardened crystals under the microscope. They are part of the texture of human life, touching the conscience and emotions of people deeply."[7]

Behind these words also stands Samartha's convictions of the kind of discernment, openness, and humility needed in those who want to understand other religious traditions, and more specifically, to enter into dialogue with people of other faith convictions. He would not separate persons from their beliefs. For this reason, in a consideration of Samartha's theology as well, it is difficult to separate the person from his thoughts, the writings from his experience, and his theology from the ministry performed in and for the dialogue concern of the WCC.

Since the principles of dialogue which he helped to formulate in the WCC documents on dialogue and in his writings are well known, I would give below ten basic convictions about dialogue that he enunciated in his writings:

1. There can be no dialogue between religions; dialogue can take place only between people of living faiths. While concepts and ideas are important, the first step in real dialogue is to realize that religion is much more than its creeds formulated in particular categories.[8]

2. Dialogue is much more than a "talking" activity; it involves larger relationships of living together and working together. Informed understanding,

critical appreciation, and balanced judgment—these cannot arise except where people meet in trust, openness, and commitment.[9]

3. Interreligious dialogue should not lead to syncretism, a kind of "fruit salad of religions." Syncretism is an uncritical mixture of different religions. It leads to spiritual poverty, theological confusion, and ethical impotence. It would be foolish to eliminate fundamental differences between religions in the interest of shallow friendliness.[10]

4. Interreligious dialogue should not be used by any of the participants as a subtle "tool for mission," that is, to promote the interests of one particular faith community to the detriment of others.[11]

5. In many situations of dialogue there is an authentic and inescapable commitment to share and to witness. However, it should not amount to a unilateral self-projection, but lead to open hospitality whereby each may share in what is most precious to the other.[12]

6. Dialogue has as its basis the commitment of all partners to their respective faiths and their openness to the insights of the others. The integrity of particular religions must be recognized.[13]

7. Dialogue does not lead to a superficial consensus, or a dilution of convictions, or false harmony. It must lead to the enrichment of all in the discovery of new dimensions of truth.[14]

8. Dialogue should not be limited to academic discussions of conceptual ideas. The other aspects of religion, such as, the meaning of ritual, the significance of symbols, the experiences of devotion, and the ongoing dialogue in day-to-day life should not be ignored.[15]

9. Even though dialogue sometimes begins with specially delegated people, it should spread into wider circles involving larger number of peoples and communities and help to shed their fear and distrust of each other in order to build up mutual trust and confidence.[16]

10. Dialogue should lead to the discovery of deeper dimensions of one's own faith, and to the reexamining and furthering of one's own understanding of one's faith and practice.[17]

In Samartha's view, it is difficult to speak of principles of dialogue because, in the final analysis, one is dealing with the dynamics of human relationships;

persons, relationships, and interactions cannot be reduced to pen and paper. This section is best concluded with Samartha's own description of the interaction of persons of four different faiths as they met in dialogue at Ajaltoun, Lebanon, which captures some of his basic convictions about dialogue and an illustration of the wealth of imagery he often used in his writings to illustrate his points:

> It was not a group session of jelly fishes where the line of demarcation is so blurred that it is difficult to see where one ends and the other begins. Nor was it a battle between porcupines rushing out of their caves to push some quills into the bodies of the opponents, with painful consequence to all concerned. It was a meeting of people who were deeply committed to their respective faiths but who were also ready to enter into dialogue with others. For dialogue is more than just an encounter of commitments. Commitment involves both an assent and a question within oneself. The area between "I" and "Thou", between "we" and "they", is an area of personal relationships between people, sharing the burden and joy of existence, where genuine dialogue demands humility and love. Dialogue, therefore, is both an expression of faith and a sign of hope.[18]

This sentiment also coloured his understanding and approach to religious plurality. He refused to consider plurality as a concept to be discussed or an issue to be dealt with. For him, plurality is a reality; it is the stuff of life; it is lived experience; one cannot run away from it. The only question is, "How do we relate to it?" The answer to this question obviously involves a theology of religions, a theological assessment of other faith convictions in relation to one's own which informs the way one relates to the other.

Here it is important to point out that anyone who attempts to pin Samartha down on theological questions is dealing with a moving target. Even though Samartha always applied intellectual and academic rigour to what he said and wrote, he did not engage in theology as a purely academic or intellectual activity, but as a response to the reality in which he, the church, and the ecumenical movement were living. Throughout his life, he was on a dialogical journey and a theological pilgrimage. His experiences and reflections kept his theology moving. His commitment to people of other religious traditions and to dialogue pulled him forward into new theological horizons; at the same time, his deep personal faith, commitment to the church, and pastoral concerns placed restraints on what he said and did. As a result, he does not fall into any clearly defined positions on the theology of religions. He was a pluralist, but some see him more as an inclusivist. However, he felt that any theology of religions that begins with the question, "Is there salvation in other religions?" was on the wrong track:

> To ask the question such as: "Is there salvation in other religions?" is theologically illegitimate in a pluralistic neighborhood. The whole debate is vitiated by the unexamined assumption that there is only one way of experiencing salvation and expressing it, and that is one's own way. How can such a question be valid when the predicaments from which salvation is sought in different cultural situations are so different and the state of being saved is experienced and expressed in so many different ways?[19]

In a thorough study of Samartha's ideas on interreligious dialogue and theology of religions, Eeuwout Klootwijk shows why his theology of religions falls outside the traditional typologies and charts an entirely new trajectory:

> [I]n Samartha's thinking theological reflections on religions and interreligious relationships are interwoven. In adopting a personalistic and dialogical stance towards religions, he links theology of religions and human relationships. For this reason, no theology of religions can be developed without first taking into account the insights of other religious traditions gained through the actual experiences of interreligious dialogue. While Samartha develops a *Christian* theology of religions which is based upon Christology, this is done in the constant awareness of other interpretations of reality. Therefore he is in a search of a larger framework in which we can deal with the different answers which are given to questions of Ultimate Reality.[20]

As Klootwijk points out, in Samartha's view, such a fresh approach to doing the theology of religions would call for some radical rethinking of five areas of Christian faith: scripture, history, theology, community, and mission. What does it mean to speak of the Bible as the "true" scripture in a multiscriptural context? What place does one assign to other histories while giving importance to the history of the Jewish people and of the church? Would it not be arrogant to reduce theology to Christian theology when others have significant insights to offer on God? Can mission be a one-way process when peoples of other faith traditions also have stories to tell?[21]

What Samartha was attempting to do was to combine a thoroughly theocentric approach to religious plurality with a christocentric entrypoint for Christians to relate to it. What he was searching for was a Christian theology of religions that would, rather than seeking to accommodate the reality of other religious traditions, integrate the wealth of the experience other religions has on ultimate questions into the Christian experience of God in Jesus Christ. It is no wonder that he found that it cannot be easily achieved without rethinking some of the basic doctrines of the church. Therefore, he spent his theological energy, especially in the latter part of his life, in rethinking the doctrine of God, exploring the question of "truth," seeking to work on a revised Christology, and to explore its implications for reconceiving "mission" in a religiously plural world. All these, he realized, would also call for a new biblical hermeneutics.

God, Truth, and Christ

Samartha's knowledge of Hinduism and especially his attraction to the Advaitic thought is evident in his approach to the questions of God and truth. The bedrock of his approach to God is the sense of mystery, and his perception of truth is that no one religious experience can exhaust or grasp the fullness of truth. Therefore all religious peoples are co-pilgrims, all have stories and experiences to share about God, and all have their own experiences of the truth. Interfaith dialogue, for him, therefore, is a "dialogue into truth."[22] This, however, does not mean that Christians themselves have nothing to offer to this dialogue into truth. Samartha holds that the Christian experience of God as Trinity and their experience of God in Jesus Christ are inalienable aspects of what they bring to the exploration of the mystery of God.

He also extends the sense of mystery to creation, to the kingdom, God, and to life itself, and is critical of the Christian anxiety to know and explain everything. The greater sense of mystery would give the necessary theological humility to the Christians to be open to the insights offered by others. He encapsulated this overall approach to theology in a presentation on the "Holy Spirit and People of Various Faiths, Cultures and Ideologies" in 1974:

> What we need today is a theology that is not less but more true to God by being generous and open, a theology not less but more loving toward the neighbour by being friendly and willing to listen, a theology that does not separate us from our fellow human beings but supports us in our common struggles and hopes. As we live together with our neighbours, what we need today is a theology that refuses to be impregnable, but which, in the spirit of Christ, is both ready and willing to be vulnerable.[23]

Revised Christology

Samartha was convinced that such theological humility, which leads to a firm commitment to Christ and a radical openness to others, can come only from a renewed emphasis on the Holy Spirit and a revised Christology, to which he devoted much of the latter part of his life. His Christology moves away from all the classical formulations about the person and work of Christ. Committed to a Christology "from below," he makes a sharp distinction between what he calls the "Helicopter Christology" "from above" and the "Bullock-Cart Christology" that begins with Jesus and arises out of people's experiences of him.[24] The Hindu responses to Jesus he expounded in his volume, *The Hindu Responses to the Unbound Christ* (1997), continued to influence him and gave the conviction that each culture should make its response to Christ from within its culture. While everything in cultures is not accepted, uncritical rejection of cultural and religious insights would result in an impoverished Christology. Samartha does not deny the uniqueness and decisiveness of Christ, but insists that it should be only for the Christians. He seeks to maintain a christocentrism for Christians and a theocentrism when Christians relate to religious plurality.

Samartha was aware that his Christology (not fully explored here for lack of space) left some loose ends. But he was not discouraged because he was convinced that the life, death, and resurrection are also profound mysteries that cannot be fully grasped within any culture. Therefore he saw his explorations as "tentative," although confident about the directions in which he was moving.

What of Missions?

Knowing the enormous sensitivities involved in the discussion of missions, and having had the experience of the controversy at Nairobi, Samartha made fine distinctions on what he affirmed and rejected in the traditional understanding on mission and evangelism. The document on "Dialogue in Community," drafted in Chiang Mai, and the guidelines that came from it, affirmed the place of "authentic witness" in all dialogue situations. Samartha affirmed that there is place in Christian relationships to other religious traditions for both dialogue and witness. This is based on his firm belief that in the life, death, and resurrection of Jesus Christ Christians have important insights into the mystery of God that they can readily share with people of other religious traditions. This right, however, is conditional; for him, this includes the equal right of others to share their own insights as well. He coined the phrase "mutual witness" to undergird this principle.

He was, however, very clear on what he rejected, especially in the kind of mission during the colonial era:

> The abuse of mission and the doubtful methods used to "gain converts" have been criticized so much recently that one need not refer to them again here. Perhaps much more serious is the attitude implied by some of the words used to describe evangelistic work. It contradicts a dialogue relationship and should be given up. Terms such as "evangelistic campaign", "missionary strategy", "campus crusade", "occupying non Christian areas", a "blitzkrieg" of missionaries, "sending reinforcements" and the like sound more appropriate to military enterprises than to Christian witness to God's redeeming love in Jesus Christ. The statistical approach implied in the words "the unreached two billions" is derogatory to our neighbours of other faiths. Unreached by whom?[25]

He saw this understanding of mission as shaped in the colonial era, with its Europe-dominated history, church-centred theology, and unexamined assumptions of Western superiority in race, culture, and religion. At the same time, he was sensitively aware of the problems of those who see a real danger to mission when it is only presented as witness in the dialogue approach. He was also not willing to move to a position that doing good works and collaborating with others on issues of justice, peace, human rights, and so forth, necessary as they are, constituted the totality of the church's mission. Rather, he claimed that it was the Christian approaches and assumptions that have gone with the traditional concept of mission that has caused confusion. He put the dilemma of the church's concern for witness in these words:

> The Church must humbly acknowledge the dilemma it faces when proclaiming to the whole world the Gospel of Jesus Christ "to the end that all men may believe in Him and be saved". This dilemma becomes particularly obvious in the light of the claims made by other religions in their traditional and renascent forms. Necessity is laid upon the Church to proclaim the Gospel at all times, in season and out of season; but within the Church there is confusion and disarray as to what, in essence, constitutes the Gospel and how it should be communicated. The Church professes to enter into dialogue with men of other faiths, but all too often stands talking to itself on the threshold of their homes, lacking the desire or the courage to enter in, even when graciously invited.

The hesitation, in his view, has to do with not connecting the gospel message with the actual questions that are being asked because of the churches' refusal to listen. He continues:

> It professes to have the answer to man's quest for salvation, but in its frequent failure to understand what questions are being asked, it tends to give the right answer to the wrong questions. It rightly points to salvation, but cannot establish the need for and the credibility of the Saviour. It claims to have a universal message, but hesitates to shed its inhibiting particularity. It seeks to share the message with others in all humility, but pride is not altogether absent from the corridors of its power.[26]

Samartha put his finger on the dilemma that the church faces in the midst of religious pluralism. On the one hand, it is not willing to give up mission. On the other, a unilateral proclamation of a "uniquely saving truth," far from making a contribution toward true community, is more likely to be misunderstood as the arrogance borne out of an apparent claim to monopolistic possession of truth. Admitting that to avoid the dilemma would be irresponsible, he asked, "Is it possible to go beyond it?"[27]

He thinks we can. There needs to be a serious rethinking of the theology and practice of mission in the total context of human history. The theology of mission should take seriously "the persistent fact of religious pluralism" and the "need to be sensitive to the integrity of other faiths." The theology of mission should take seriously "the persistent fact of religious pluralism" and the "need to be sensitive to the integrity of other faiths." Crucial to the new concept is the question, "Is the Christian 'mission' the only mission of God in all the world at all times?" Samartha refused to believe that the church's mission is God's only mission. He felt that the missionary theology has had the effect of limiting the activity of God. "One cannot limit the extent or the mode of God's redeeming work, because it is as universal as His love which embraces all humankind at all times." Thus, we need also to recognize God's saving work in "areas outside the hedges of the Church."[28]

An Ecumenical Pioneer

The dialogue concern has flourished and moved in many directions since Samartha's time, and theological reflections on the dialogue, religious pluralism, theology of religions, and the rethinking of the Christian theology for religious plurality have also moved forward. But many who see the advances in interfaith relations these days would take it for granted and not realize what a herculean task it was to move the ecumenical movement and the churches to adopt dialogue as a way of life with our neighbours and to be at home with religious plurality. Only those who had been part of the history would know the faith, faithfulness, courage, and wisdom that Samartha had brought in to make this difficult transition possible. Samartha's involvement in the ecumenical movement at the global level happened at a crucial time in its history. There is every sense in which it can be said that by some divine providence "We had the right man, in the right place at the right time." India has every reason to be proud of the ministry of this ecumenical pioneer who has left an indelible mark on ecumenical history.

CHAPTER 9

J. Jayakiran Sebastian

"Only Christ and No Formulation of Christ Can Determine the Frontier": J. Russell Chandran's Ongoing Challenges to Christian Ecumenism

The Ecumenical Man

While primarily known for his long association with the United Theological College (UTC), Bangalore (as a student, a faculty member from 1950, as principal from 1954 to 1983, and later as visiting professor),[1] Rev. Dr J. Russell Chandran (1918–2000) was also associated with a variety of ecumenical institutions and initiatives both in India and abroad.[2] These include: the Senate of Serampore College from which he was awarded the degree of Doctor of Divinity (*honoris causa*) in 1962 and of which he was the president between 1970 and 1971; the Ecumenical Association of Third World Theologians, of which he was a founder and first president from 1975 to 1981; the World Council of Churches (WCC), of which he was the vice moderator of the Central Committee from 1966 to 1968 and an active participant for several decades in the

Faith and Order Commission; the Church of South India, of which he was the convenor of the Union Negotiations Committee; the Joint Council of the Church of North India, Church of South India, and the Mar Thoma Church, of which he was the first secretary; the Pacific Theological College, Suva, Fiji; as well as being the founder-president of the Christian Union of India. He was also deeply associated with the Christian Peace Conference.

For Chandran, along with many of the pioneers of constructive and engaged ecumenical interaction and sensitive and committed interreligious dialogue of his generation, faithfulness to the mission mandate involved both an uncompromised commitment to Christ, as well as the openness to the variety and diversity of the revelation of God in the lives of human beings. For him, the mission and ministry of the church involved bringing about liberation and rehumanization of both the oppressed and the oppressor, constantly looking for open doors, rather than being preoccupied with closed doors and dead ends. In discussing the understanding of the word *evangelical*, Chandran protested against a narrow understanding of the term and argued against the privatization of this concept. He believed that in concentrating on the peripheral questions, or what he called "side dishes," the main course—the centrality of the gospel of Jesus Christ—was being ignored, and that only Christ, and no formulation of Christ, could determine the frontier of Christian life and witness. Chandran affirms that liberation is not something that can be given, but is, rather, to be understood as a process—a process of transformation and reconciliation, including the areas of class struggle and the fight against caste-based oppression.

As a lifelong proponent of interreligious dialogue, he argued that we cannot absolutize our manner of practicing our commitment as the only possibility for the commitment of others. He asserted that in dialogue one has to be open to a combination of God's self-revelation and human wisdom, leading to the possibility of accepting the diversity of religious faiths as contributing to the beauty and richness of the complex spirituality of the human race, and to the greatness of national as well as global cultures.

Chandran did not ignore the social dimension of the mission imperative. He lamented that this has become weakened because of a lack of concern for the here and now in preference to the hereafter. He posed a challenge to the churches by asking as to whether those who claim to be concerned about the struggles of underprivileged and marginalized sections of society also reflect on whether the practice of justice in the church offers a model for the ecumenical movement and the wider society to emulate.[3]

Chandran and Mission

> May I ask one question? When you think of the Mission of the Church today, whether in the larger context of the nation and the world or in the limited context of your local congregation, do you think primarily of new opportunities or new difficulties? . . . Are we fully aware of the open doors or are we preoccupied with closed doors? Or are we so preoccupied with our problems within the church that we have no time to think of any doors at all, closed or open?[4]

Chandran's powerful and challenging questions continue to resonate today and enliven the missiological and ecumenical task of the church. Indeed, these are questions that remain relevant, questions that are uncomfortable, questions that are probing in their clarity, questions that demand our response. What is mission supposed to achieve? Chandran poses a challenge:

> . . . accepting the legitimacy of plurality of religious faiths does not mean that we abandon the evangelistic outreach, proclaiming the good news of salvation through Jesus Christ and inviting people to believe in Christ. There are situations where people live in marginalized and dehumanised conditions, oppressed and exploited by the upper caste people, and also enslaved to all kinds of superstitions and fear of demonic forces. The Gospel of Jesus Christ has to be proclaimed to the people of these areas bringing liberation and re-humanization to both the oppressed and the oppressors.[5]

Mission here is seen as a mission of liberation leading to the process of the reappropriation of that which makes us human. Chandran affirms that liberation is not something that can be given but, rather, is to be understood as a process, a process of transformation and reconciliation. In this sense "[t]heological reflection on the meaning of the Gospel in India should take into account the need to recognise the significance of the class struggle for overcoming oppression and exploitation."[6]

We need to note that the sources for the richness of Chandran's understanding of mission came from various quarters. Apart from the issues he confronted in his work as a theological teacher and a churchperson, he was active in the ecumenical movement and in organizations, both religious and secular, working for justice and peace in society. In addition, a little-explored facet is his unpublished Oxford thesis on "Christian Apologetics in Relation to Vivekananda in the Light of Origen, *Contra Celsum*," a work which combined the principle of reaching back to the early church in order to gain insights for dialogue with a range of important contemporary Indian philosophical thinking.[7]

Apart from the promise that such approaches to the understanding of mission holds for both the oppressor and the oppressed, Chandran also indicates what mission means when one takes into consideration both Christians and those belonging to other living faith traditions:

> . . . the polarisation brought about by the Christian mission is not that between Christians and non-Christians. The polarisation is between those who accept the concern of Jesus Christ for the liberation of [hu]man[s] from everything which enslaves and distorts human dignity as the basis for forging new structures of social and political existence and will promote movements which seek such liberation as part of their religious commitment and those who interpret their religion in a way which make them knowingly and unknowingly support the structures of economic and political life which continue to enslave men [and women] and distort their human dignity.[8]

It is this aspect relating to the dignity and worth of the human person that Chandran brings to the fore. Such a perception is possible because of his understanding and acceptance of the co-existence of many religions. Hence, he notes that "[i]n religious faith . . . there is a combination of God's self-revelation and human wisdom. Is it not possible to accept the diversity of religious faiths as contributing to the beauty and richness of the complex spirituality of the human race, and to the greatness of national as well as global cultures?"[9] This level of empathy is made possible because of his recognition of the transient and partial nature of mission we practice. Chandran comments: "The good news is Jesus and his mission acknowledged as God's saving work and not any particular formulation of it. Our religious commitment itself has not reached any finality. We have not reached the goal, we are only on the way, pilgrims pressing on towards the goal. Therefore we cannot absolutise our pattern of commitment as the key for the commitment of others."[10]

Chandran and Social Realities

> While considering questions about the struggles of Dalits and women in India today we also need to reflect on whether within the Church we practice a pattern of justice which the secular society can emulate. Widening the frontiers of theology has the objective of renewal of the Church as well as Society.[11]

How is it that such a concern has not been taken seriously by significant segments of the church? Chandran attributes this to a mistaken attitude to life on earth and life in heaven: "One reason for the lack of concern for social problems is the belief that the social and political life is too much of this world to be included in the sphere of religion. Many have unwittingly accepted different forms or shades of the Marcionite heresy by adopting an altogether other-worldly concept of Christianity. This has to be remedied by sound preaching and teaching."[12]

In addition, he did not shy away from addressing the evil of casteism that seemed to trump other forms of identity in the Christian church, bluntly and self-reflectively saying:

> The Church seems to be the weakest instrument to break caste solidarity. . . . It suddenly dawns on you that you have thought of a particular thing or taken a decision because unconsciously caste consideration was still dominant in you. I am not excluding myself from this phenomenon. . . . Christians [need to] be weaned out of the sense of caste solidarity, so that Christ and his universal humanity, his universal concern, will become more determinative for their outlooks, policies and social attitudes than caste of any other limiting solidarity.[13]

One of his pet themes was the question of secularization and what this meant for human dignity. Echoing Bonhoeffer in a lecture delivered at the Union Theological Seminary in New York, he pushes the meaning of what the gospel and evangelization could culminate in, by pointing out that a new vision that would transcend the present social realities in India would involve the following recognition:

> In India people are also seeking religious foundation for the new secularism that is developing. This is a secularism which seeks the liberation of [hu]man [beings] from fears and superstitions, but at the same time it also seeks to be open to the concepts of human dignity held by religious beliefs. It may be described as an open secularism or revolutionary secularism. . . . How far is it possible for the Indian Church to produce a theology of secularism or a theology of religionless Christianity as part of the dialogue with [people] of other faiths?[14]

Chandran and Ecumenism

Throughout his life, career, and in his various writings, including comments on current events in the *Guardian*, which included updates on national and international ecumenical events, Chandran maintained a passionate conviction that the way ahead for the church was to inculcate and internalize the vision of the unity of the church and to harvest the fruits from the seeds that the pioneers of ecumenical thinking and praxis from the early and mid-20th century had planted. For him, "the renewal of the Church through the ecumenical movement includes a dimension of renewal which takes place through a fresh understanding of the social, economic and political implications of the good news of Jesus Christ."[15]

He recognized that "no doctrinal formulation is true and relevant for all times and places. Our orthodoxy has to be affirmed in terms of reflection on orthopraxis in our different situations, based on our discernment of our being with God in Christ who is in solidarity with the people for their liberation and humanization."[16] This awareness, gleaned from the opportunities and challenges of his participation in meetings and conversations at various levels of bilateral, multilateral, and interdenominational ecumenical encounters, challenged what seemed to be a given and something taken for granted. It shaped him to be an activist-thinker and a thinking-activist with a profound and lasting impact on the shaping of some of the most pressing issues that the ecumenical undertaking confronted, including the question of interreligious dialogue and peace with justice.

Chandran's involvement with the Church of South India, of which he was an ordained presbyter, spanned his entire working life, not least in his untiring zest to broaden the vision of unity that gave birth to that church. Thus, he took active leadership in bringing about greater manifestations of this unity through his work with the Joint Council of the Church of South India, the Church of North India, and the Mar Thoma Church. He contributed and participated in discussions regarding a proposed common name, and brought his rich patristic, ecumenical, and international knowledge to bear on various models of unity, including conciliar fellowship, intercommunion, organic oneness, and organic union, and patiently explored the ramifications of various models, especially at the level of the local congregation. The Joint Council, formed in 1978, has from 2004 been known as the Communion of Churches in India (CCI), and although the goal of one united church has proved elusive, nevertheless, the vision for active and practical unity remains alive and vibrant.[17]

Chandran's robust optimism that such conversations could only continue the actualization of Jesus' plea "that they may all be one" (John 17:21) was not confined to the three denominations mentioned above. This passion was manifest in his role within the Church of South India and Lutheran dialogues, and he introduced the agreed statements from these exchanges, which took place from the late 1940s to the end of the 1950s. These theological astute and ecumenically hospitable conversations reveal so much of the promise and potential of the best of what the ecumenical movement was all about. One can only regret that the baton has not been taken up with such intensity and determination by succeeding generations. In his introduction, Chandran not only traces the history of this decade-long conversation, but notes that the "remarkable thing" that came through this was that "agreed statements have been produced on questions over which the churches had originally thought that there would be irreconcilable divergences."[18] The question lingers, however: To what did this assurance of "substantial doctrinal unity" lead?

Chandran and Evangelization

Chandran wrote in the heyday of what seemed to be a clash of ideologies between the so-called ecumenicals and the so-called evangelicals. He did not hesitate to address the question of what he considered to be the appropriate meaning of evangelization head on, writing: "In the New Testament the frontier is not between Christianity as a religion and other religions. The goal of evangelism was to call people to believe in Jesus Christ and not to make people simply to give up their religion and adopt Christianity as a religion."[19] For him, it was clear that the proclamation of good news could never be a one-way street, and wrote that "[w]e need to develop sensitivity to cultural and socio-political transformation taking place through the mission of God witnessed to by the Church. This may be taking place not exclusively by those who call themselves Christians but also through others."[20]

In discussing the understanding of the word *evangelical*, Chandran protests against a narrow understanding of the term and argues against the privatization of this concept, asserting that the

> distortion comes through wrong notions of the authority of the Bible, based on the concept of verbal inspiration of Scripture, and absolutising of doctrines such as penal substitution theories of the atonement, etc. Certainly some of their concerns such as personal holiness and acceptance of Jesus Christ as personal Saviour are important. But they have to be recognized as frills rather than the main body, or side dishes, rather than the main dish.[21]

A related idea is echoed in the words of another perceptive commentator on the theological scene, George Lindbeck, writing from a completely different context: "Theology should . . . resist the clamor of the religiously interested public for what is currently fashionable and immediately intelligible. It should instead prepare for a future when continuing dechristianization will make greater Christian authenticity communally possible."[22]

Chandran and Baptism

The understanding and practice of baptism was a major preoccupation with Chandran and a lifelong concern. He sets out the issues to be considered with passionate intensity:

> Rightly understood, the sacrament of baptism gives a new and radical form of self-identity for the baptised person and the community of the baptised. The traditional image of separation which has created the impression of the "baptised" being a loss to his [or her] original Hindu or Muslim family or community needs radical re-thinking. Separation can only be from sin and not necessarily from one's community. Baptism seeks to bring unity and not disunity. Separation from one's community will be necessary only if by

> belonging to that community the person lives in sin or participates in evil. . . . Baptism challenges us to identify ourselves more radically with the whole Indian community. Without such radical identity and involvement with the Indian community, transcending everything that is divisive—including the divisiveness of Christianity as a religion—we cannot claim to move on to belong to the larger humanity and the world community which is also ours in Christ.[23]

Even in his last communication as principal with the alumni of the United Theological College, he returned to this theme:

> How can the church be transformed from the present state of institutional structures with rigidly defined boundaries of membership into a movement towards the realization of the "one new humanity"? Is it possible to understand the Church of Jesus Christ as an open, non-communal fellowship, having within it a community of the baptised, a community committed for the mission of Jesus Christ, committed to work for the removal of all barriers contrary to the mind of Christ?[24]

This understanding has missiological consequences at the level of the local congregation that is rooted in the local community, in that "[p]articipation in Christ's mission is the key to both the congregation's worship and the agenda for its Church meeting. Authentic participation is only possible if the congregation is sensitive to the different forms of brokenness present in the local community and seeks ways of meeting the needs, bearing in mind the limitations of the congregation's resources."[25]

Conclusion

Chandran's legacy continues to be of value, and his contributions intersect with varied fields of inquiry. One such example is found in a major book by his former student and prominent scholar of postcolonial theology and theory, R. S. Sugirtharajah, where, in talking about the implications of postcolonial theory for the field of Bible translation, Sugirtharajah turns to Chandran to question the use of the title "Lord" as a translation of *kurios* in some of the English translations of the Bible, including the New Revised Standard Version

(NRSV). Referring to Chandran's plea to avoid the use of the word *Lord* in speaking about Jesus in Asia, especially since the word carries with it the baggage of Western colonialism, imperialism, and aggression, Sugirtharajah says that "Faced with this uneasiness, Indian theologian Russell Chandran, advocated a softer, gentler image of Christ . . . ," and goes on to argue the case for translating *kurios* as "master" or "sir."[26]

There is no doubt that Chandran's multifaceted contributions not only had an impact on the local and global church of his time, but that his legacy, directly and indirectly, endures in the forward march of the ecumenical dreams and hopes in the 21st century. A re-reading of his writings and a frank appraisal of his contributions will reward anyone who is seeking insights from the giddy excitement that the ecumenical movement generated in the latter part of the 20th century, an excitement that was rooted in reading the Bible with fresh eyes. And so, let us recall the words of Paul, relating to the reality of the God testified to by Jesus, words that Chandran chose as the text for the first sermon[27] he preached as principal of the United Theological College: "Anyone who claims to know something does not yet have the necessary knowledge; but anyone who loves God is known by him" (1 Cor. 8:2-3).[28]

CHAPTER 10

George Zachariah

Poulose Mar Poulose: An Activist of Alternative Ecumenism

> This great humanist, Bishop Dr Poulose Mar Poulose, was a spiritual sword, moral shield, and material militant who often reminded me of Gilbert Murray's burning words about Mahatma Gandhi: "Be careful in dealing with a man who cares nothing for sensual pleasures, nothing for comfort, or praise or promotion, but is simply determined to do what he believes to be right. He is dangerous and an uncomfortable enemy because his body which you can always conquer gives you little purchase over his soul."[1]

This tribute from Justice V. R. Krishna Iyer, a former judge of the Supreme Court of India, is a true testimony of the life and witness of a Christian theologian and bishop who lived out the politics of Jesus Christ through his radical involvement in the struggles for justice, and challenged the church and the ecumenical movement to continue the spirit of nonconformism in our public witnessing. This article is an attempt to re-read the life and witness of Bishop Poulose Mar Poulose,[2] focusing on his contributions to ecumenism.

Poulose Mar Poulose: A Biographical Sketch

K. A. Paul was born on 14 September 1941 in Thrissur, Kerala, the youngest child of Konikkara Anthony and Kochu Marium. Born and brought up in a devout Christian family belonging to the Chaldean Syrian Church, Paul did his school education at the Chaldean Syrian High School, Thrissur, and, later, his university education at the St Thomas College, Thrissur. Discerning his call to serve his church as an ordained priest, Mar Poulose was sent by the church to do his Bachelor of Divinity programme at the Serampore College, West Bengal. He was ordained as a priest on 13 June 1965. Recognizing his academic interests, the church sent him to the United States of America to pursue his advanced studies in theology. After completing his Th.M. at the Princeton Theological Seminary, Mar Poulose joined the Graduate Theological Union, Berkeley, California, and earned his Ph.D. His doctoral dissertation was titled "A Bonhofferian Corrective of Karl Marx's Critique of Religion."

The Chaldean Syrian Church, also known as the Church of the East, traces its origin in India back to the apostle Thomas. Paul was consecrated as Episcopa in the Chaldean Syrian Church on 13 August 1968 with the name Poulose Mar Poulose. He was only 27 years old and still a theological student when he was consecrated as bishop. His active participation in the student protests in Berkeley against the Vietnam War, demanding the withdrawal of US troops from Vietnam, provided Mar Poulose the opportunity to articulate his faith contextually, taking inspiration from both Dietrich Bonhoffer and Karl Marx. Right from his student days, Mar Poulose was a theologian who lived out his faith through his involvement in the political movements for radical social transformation.

On completion of his doctoral studies, Mar Poulose returned to India, filled with the revolutionary commitment to engage in praxiological ministry. During that time, India was under the political emergency imposed by Prime Minister Indira Gandhi. Democratic rights of the people were crushed. Censorship was enforced on media. Critics were arrested and imprisoned without trial. It was India's encounter with fascism camouflaged as democracy. The Christian community and the ecumenical movements in India, in general, sang praises to the authoritarian regime and legitimized the violation of human rights in the name of national interest. However, there was a remnant within the Indian church who dared to respond to tyranny through their underground activism and public campaigns. M. M. Thomas and Metropolitan Juhanon Mar Thoma were the prominent Christians who led this movement. Coming from the student protests in Berkeley, the Indian experience of emergency was a new rite of passage for Mar Poulose to enter the complex arena of Christian political witness in India.[3]

Bishop Poulose Mar Poulose was an active presence in Kerala society for the next two decades. He transgressed the time-honoured images and ministries of a bishop through his creative and prophetic interventions in the everyday realities of the common people. He converted street corners, seashores, college campuses, and marketplaces into sanctuaries to proclaim the good news and to engage in the ministry of confrontation, liberation, and community building. Liberation theology created its ripples in the Indian society during the second half of the 1970s, and inspired by Christian faith, a host of social-action groups and peoples' movements began to emerge in different parts of the country. The Kerala Independent Fish Workers' Federation and the social-action groups associated with the Program for Social Action were among them. There were also attempts in different churches to transform them from within through reform movements. The Faith Movement for Liberation in the Church of South India Madhya Kerala Diocese was unique, as it exposed the casteist nature of the church. Mar Poulose was an active associate of these movements and the social-action groups.

Even though Christianity is a microscopic minority in India, in Kerala the church has tremendous influence thanks to its economic, social, and political capital. The Kerala churches have always used their minority card politically to protect its assets, institutions, and vested interests. The Kerala church has a long history of being in unholy alliance with the powers that be, betraying the hopes and aspirations of the common people. Kerala, as the state that voted into power a communist government for the first time in history, has always been open to communist ideology and party politics. But the Kerala church has a history of condemning and subverting progressive initiatives of the communist governments as atheistic. Mar Poulose played a significant role in exposing the communal and right-wing politics of the church, and initiated dialogue between Christians and secular humanists, including Marxists, for the transformation of Kerala society. M. M. Thomas and Metropolitan Paulos Mar Gregorios were also part of such initiatives.

The politics and spirituality of Mar Poulose, which defied the official position of the churches, irritated many and he was branded as a Marxist and atheist. His cotton saffron cassocks symbolized his commitment to contextualize his faith and ministry. In the ecumenical youth student movements he was known as the "Bishop in Blue Jeans," which was his unique attempt not only to identify with the young generation, but also to sanitize the ecumenical youth student movements from ecclesiastical power and domination. Even though Mar Poulose believed and worked for Christian-Marxist dialogue and cooperation, he never supported the abuse of human rights under communist regimes. Mar Poulose happened to be in China when the Tiananmen Square protest took place in the spring of 1989, and he publicly condemned the suppression of that peaceful protest and challenged the communist party to engage in genuine introspection.

The Student Christian Movement in Kerala (Kerala SCM) is known for its revolutionary witness in Kerala society, challenging the church and the dominant social norms and systems, informed and inspired by Christian faith. Mar Poulose was a close associate of Kerala SCM and served as its president. His ecumenical journey began from his involvement in the Kerala SCM, and he served the World Student Christian Federation, Asia Pacific Region (1984–1986) and the World Student Christian Federation (1986–1990) as chairperson. He mentored several generations of SCMers all over the world and influenced significantly the mission of ecumenical youth student movements. He was also actively associated with the Christian Peace Conference (CPC). He also served as the chairperson of the Program for Social Action (PSA). He returned to Mother Earth on 24 March 1998, at the age of 57.

The Ecumenical Formation of Mar Poulose

Born and raised in an Eastern church, deeply influenced by the richness of its doctrines and rituals, the theological studies at the Serampore College was the first exposure for Mar Poulose to live and learn together with people belonging to different liturgical and doctrinal traditions. His advanced theological studies at Princeton and Berkeley provided him sufficient opportunity to develop theological foundations for a new ecumenical outlook and radical engagement. His participation in the student protests in Berkeley widened his understanding of public witness and ecumenical engagement that transcend even religious boundaries. Mar Poulose's academic engagement with Marx challenged him to reimagine his ecumenical vision by extending the ecumenical tent to all people of goodwill, whether they believed in God or not, who were committed to humanize the dehumanized world. His fascination with the life and theology of Dietrich Bonhoeffer inspired him to choose the prophetic vocation of confronting systemic evils and the socioeconomic and political structures that perpetuate those evils.

Mar Poulose returned to India with this vision and commitment, and he was welcomed by two trajectories of ecumenism. While the dominant model, represented by the mainstream ecumenical movements, provided theological legitimization to the fascist regime of Prime Minister Indira Gandhi, the secular *koinonia* of ecumenism, represented by Christians, socialists, Gandhians, Marxists, and people from other faith traditions were involved in challenging the political emergency and providing support for the families of political prisoners. Mar Poulose naturally opted to join the wider ecumenical movement of protest and compassionate justice, defying the ecclesiastical and societal expectations to enroll in the mainstream ecumenical trajectory perpetuating the prevailing order. This was a theological and political choice that he made, and he was welcomed by a host of movements in Kerala. Among them, it was the Kerala SCM that Mar Poulose opted as his mother home for an alternative ecumenical journey.

The history of Kerala SCM is the story of a different type of faith formation and nurturing which inspired several generations of young people to reimagine Christian discipleship and to engage in radical forms of public witnessing in church and society. Christian faith is more than memorizing and internalizing Christian doctrines and moral teachings, interpreted by the churches as universal and eternal truths. Rather, Kerala SCM encouraged students to rediscover afresh the meaning and demands of Christian faith discerning the signs of the times. Said differently, the faith formation that Kerala SCM initiated always began with a deeper understanding of the world. SCM was not a prefabricated mould which produced a generation of loyal and faithful followers. Rather, SCM was a community that facilitated the discernment process of young people by enabling them to come out of their indoctrinated faith understanding and to journey into diverse avenues of Christian witnessing. Mar Poulose always considered Kerala SCM as his mother home where he could be nourished by the intense theological debates and radical societal engagement. As a comrade, he accompanied the SCMers in their journey of rediscovering the meaning of Christian faith and discipleship through their radical engagement in the university, society, and church.

Realizing the reality that the students came to SCM after their homes and churches had initiated them into a rigorous process of Christian nurturing and doctrinal formation, Mar Poulose insisted that SCM help the students in their unlearning process. He believed that social concern without deeper social analysis and social consciousness would not help the young people to understand the sinfulness of the prevailing social order. He further exposed how our songs, liturgies, and prayers inculcated in the new generation a spirituality that legitimized the status quo. Hence, Mar Poulose encouraged SCMers to have the courage to shatter their inherited faith and doctrinal understandings for a faith that turns the world upside down. He gave leadership to this process of *metanoia* through his inspiring Bible studies and lectures which enabled the students to have alternative experiences of epiphany, experiencing God as a living presence in the struggles of the sinned against.

The 1980s and early 1990s witnessed the emergence of a host of new social movements in Kerala which challenged the dominant ways of understanding society, and initiated alternative political practices informed by the lived experiences of the subaltern communities. Some of these movements were inspired by the liberative gospel of Jesus Christ. M. M. Thomas and Mar Poulose provided profound theological insights to inspire young people to participate in the struggles of the marginalized communities as an expression of their faith in God. Mar Poulose articulated convincingly the spirituality of struggle, drawing from M. M. Thomas's concept of "spirituality for combat." According to Mar Poulose, "The source of my faith is my understanding of God as I experienced him [*sic*] in my life and in the community. My faith compels me to work both within myself and within the community towards the affirmation of life to all people spiritually, politically, economically and socially."[4] As a result, participation in the struggles of the subaltern communities such as traditional fisherpeople, Dalits, Adivasis, and women was a new baptismal experience for most of the SCMers. They discerned a new sense of "call": a call to serve God through their involvement in social movements.

Mar Poulose and the Global Ecumenical Youth Student Movements

Who speaks for the church? Who holds the authority to represent the ecumenical movement in the public sphere? Who authors the theology of the church and the social statements of the ecumenical movement? There is a speaking church and a speaking ecumenical movement; they speak categorically, with authority, on behalf of all of us. But how are they informed? Is the church also a listening church? Does the ecumenical movement have the humility to listen? We see this creative tension between speaking for the church and speaking to the church in Paul's epistle to Galatians. While the pillars of the church, Peter, John, and James, were speaking *as* the church, Paul spoke *to* the church, informed by the experiences of the Gentiles. As Barbara Rossing observes, when the church humbled itself to be in the listening and learning mode, it was informed by people "who were considered the least, those who had the face and the wounds of Jesus."[5] Mar Poulose, as chairperson of the World Student Christian Federation, both at the Asia-Pacific regional level and at the global level, contributed significantly to change the social location and politics of the ecumenical youth student movements. To understand his vision of ecumenical youth student movements, it is important to place him in the long history of the critical and transformative involvement of youth and students in the ecumenical movement.

The origin of the modern ecumenical movement can be traced back to the student and lay movements which inspired Spirit-filled young people to reclaim the apostolic praxis of "turning the world upside down" through public witness. Realizing the danger of the church becoming imperial, they committed themselves to become "rebels within the church until it becomes what it ought to be." Ecumenism, for them, was an unwavering expression of collective resilience against all contemporary expressions of empire. It was manifested in different parts of the world where Christian faith and ecumenical vision inspired young people to reject the state theology of the church (the theological justification of the status quo with its casteism, racism, capitalism, and totalitarianism by misusing theological concepts and biblical texts for its own political purposes), and to join the protest movements in the public sphere against such structural sins. Asian ecumenical youth student movements, particularly in the Philippines and Korea, demonstrated this system-threatening faith in their prophetic and daring political witness.

The mainstream ecumenical movements have gradually become new empires, however. Here we need to take seriously Barbara Rossing's exposition of the term *oikoumene*.[6] *Oikoumene* was essentially an imperial trajectory of Rome to unite the whole inhabited earth for imperial plunder and conquest. Constantine convened ecumenical councils to sort out and settle differences and dissent within the *oikoumene*. In the biblical tradition, the unity that *oikoumene* represented was not the unity of the whole inhabited earth; rather, it was the imperial plot to suppress differences to facilitate the imperial agenda of conquest and enclosure. This discernment inspired the youths and students to raise uncomfortable questions to the dominant ecumenical movement and to experiment with alternative models of being ecumenical in the world.

The fourth World Conference of Christian Youth, held in Lausanne in 1960, raised the question: "Are there no revolutionaries here, people who do not want to improve or modify the structures and institutions of our Christian life, but who are ready to break out of these prisons? . . . who want to avoid one of the major ecumenical sins—that of being 'churchy'?"[7] Over the years, this "ecumenical sin" has become the greatest ecumenical virtue as far as the mainstream ecumenical movements are concerned. As a result, prophetic theology has been replaced by a theology of consensus and political correctness so as not to hurt the traditions and faith practices of the member churches.

Mar Poulose served the World Student Christian Federation in the 1980s when SCMers all over the world were engaged in the vocation of radical witnessing, contesting the theologies and ministries of churches and dominant ecumenical movements. Chris Tremewan, a colleague of Mar Poulose in the Asian ecumenical youth student movements, articulates the story of the emerging ecumenical youth student movements in his celebrated work *Teatime at the Revolution*.[8] This book provides us the context in which Mar Poulose started his ecumenical journey at the global level with the World Student Christian Federation. According to Tremewan, church youth work, both denominational and ecumenical, degenerated into "a recruitment technique to draft young people into the activities and consciousness of conventional religion." Young people began to reject such youth movements, whose main mission was "to co-opt and undermine surges of the human spirit among young people because it destines them to become juvenile imitations of their religious mentors." As a result, "instead of going forward to the Promised Land, youth were herded back to the fleshpots of Egypt."[9]

The betrayal of this ecumenical vision can be summed up as "the corruption of the faith and the co-option of young people to its service." Tremewan further observes that "youth work needs to build into its programmes a vigorous critique of ecclesiastical polity which goes hand in hand with sustained involvement in political movements whose aim is a radical transformation of the economic and social relations of contemporary society. . . . Are youth inducted into the slavery of supporting alienating religious structures, thus becoming indentured labourers tilling soil which will bring forth a harvest of weeds?"[10] Even in our times, these questions are relevant. Ecumenism has become a lucrative career for many, and ecumenical leadership has the potential to become imperial and exclusive. Ecumenical documents and statements have become archival materials for research and publications without any influence on the mission and witness of the member churches. With the co-option of the ecumenical movements by the churches and the powerful lobbies, ecumenical involvement has become a stepping stone for ecumenical empire building. Today we have lost the politics of the reign of God. We are all infected by the politics of ecumenical career building.

It is in this context that the Asia Youth Assembly, jointly organized by the World Student Christian Federation (WSCF), Asia Pacific Region, and the Christian Conference of Asia (CCA) Youth, at the St Stephens College, Delhi, in 1984 becomes important, as it envisioned a different type of ecumenical youth student engagement. "The great promise of the Asian ecumenical youth movement is that it might get completely out of control. *Out of control* of church leaders and the ecumenical mafia, *out of control* of funding agencies and project networks, *out of control* of compromised church-state relationships and corrupt elitist theology."[11] The call to get out of control was also resonated in Bishop Poulose Mar Poulose's opening address of the WSCF Asia Pacific Region:

> In this situation what shall be the role of Christian youth? I would say that they should be a dissenting minority; they should be non-conformists. If we learn lessons from the life style of Jesus and the community life of early Christians, we will be compelled to stand as the community of Jesus, as a dynamic force within the society, acting as a dissenting minority. To live as a dissenting minority is never the same as the present tendency to foster minority consciousness among Asian Christians. Rather it means to involve ourselves with the aspirations of the people of the land for a better future, to raise a dissenting voice against the oppressive forces of our time.[12]

This brief historical scan has placed Mar Poulose in the nonconformist tradition of the ecumenical youth student movements. Christine Ledger, who served as Mar Poulose's colleague in the WSCF as its co-secretary general observes the following in her tribute to him: "He did not regard his Chairperson's responsibility as a mere formality; but engaged fully in the debates and issues of the Federation. Some of these debates were difficult, even painful, ones—revolving around the visions and structures of WSCF as it approached its centenary. . . . Students were inspired and intrigued by Poulose's radical politics and his ability to bring sharp critical thought to the issues of the day."[13] For Ledger, Mar Poulose was a visionary who not only challenged the mission and vision of the WSCF, but also mentored generations of young people from all over the world in their search for meaning in life. "The 1980s for WSCF was a period of active interest in rediscovering the Bible, and Poulose provided important leadership in this area. He demonstrated how Bible is a living document, alive to each generation in its own way."[14]

Alternative Ecumenism: The Vision of Mar Poulose

Poulose Mar Poulose, through his Bible studies, lectures, and writings, consistently challenged the ecumenical youth student movements to become prophetic and relevant by reimagining their identity and mission, informed by their organic engagement with the struggles of the people. One of Mar Poulose's lasting contributions to the WSCF was his consistent and creative efforts to develop a profound theological foundation for the Federation. For Mar Poulose, theology did not mean just *talking* theology; rather, he was committed to *doing* theology. "God is in the midst of the struggles of the people in realising their aspirations for the future, and doing theology means standing with God in the midst of these struggles. Doing theology should not be pretentious."[15] Mar Poulose further encouraged the SCMers to understand the great commandment to "go and make disciples of the world" as a mandate to engage in mission differently. It is to "stand with the people in their struggle for the realisation of the 'good news of liberation' from oppression and dehumanisation. It is not just to preach the Gospel to the people but to be together with them. The SCM should insist on a radical way of life to demonstrate total commitment to missionary activity. To do this, the SCM should join hands with all who are working for a just society, regardless of ideology or religion."[16] What we find here is an earnest effort to enable the ecumenical youth to re-read the biblical texts and to reimagine basic Christian doctrines theologically and politically to witness God relevantly in our contexts.

WSCF has always been in the forefront of exposing the sinfulness of patriarchy and challenging SCMers to participate actively in the campaigns for gender justice. In spite of his church's doctrinal positions and practices on women's space and role in the total life of the church, Mar Poulose was categorical in his theological positions on gender justice, and he motivated the ecumenical youth to be eternally vigilant against patriarchal forces and practices. "For too long women have been denied the right of participating in the church and society and given paternal protection in return for unquestioning obedience. The women's struggle is not for women alone, but for the liberation of the entire humanity. Paying attention to the women's struggle is not a token gesture. It is a total concern of the WSCF in its stand for justice and humanity."[17]

Mar Poulose was the first bishop to be elected as the chairperson of the WSCF. There has always been a love–hate relationship between the church and the SCM. Addressing a meeting of Kerala SCM in 1939, M. M. Thomas succinctly articulated this tension:

> We youths have to create division in the Church, for redeeming the Church that it may be a fitting weapon in the hands of the Master for redeeming the world around. . . . What is real Church history? It is not the history of its Popes and Archbishops—no, not at all. It is the history of people who filled with the vision of a redeemed Church, created strife and division within the Church—it is the history of Luthers and Abraham Malpans—of its heretics excommunicated, of its infidels martyred, for causing revolution in the Church. If we are to be worthy of that heritage let us make quarrels and more quarrels for the sake of its redemption.[18]

Kerala SCM continued this legacy, and it was banned in some of the church-owned colleges for identifying with the struggles of the Dalits within the church.

Mar Poulose continued this legacy of critical solidarity with the church in his writings and public life as well. As Christine Ledger recollects, the tenure of Mar Poulose as chairperson of the WSCF was a time of bridge building: "Through his presence and leadership, the WSCF engaged with the institutional church and ecclesiastical expressions of ecumenism in a new way. . . .

Thus, the decision to elect Poulose, and all that he represented, as Chairperson was an important step and symbol for WSCF in the '80s as it endeavored to build bridges with the churches."[19] While affirming the need to maintain a cordial relationship with the church "as it is still an important tool to bring about change," Mar Poulose challenged the SCMers to be "a relevant, dissenting minority."[20]

Mar Poulose's lasting contribution to ecumenism was his untiring campaign to transform the ecumenical movements to be the agents of radical social transformation through participating in the struggles of the masses. He developed a theology of struggles, articulating the ongoing struggles of the marginalized as faith imperative for all Christians, and challenged Christians to involve themselves in the struggles as expressions of their public witnessing. Quoting Bertolt Brecht, Mar Poulose reminded the SCMers that

> we must change the world, and then change the changed world. . . . We, as a community of Christians have hopes and aspirations, but do these aspirations reconcile with the aspirations of the vast masses of people suffering from oppression and deprivation? . . . The death of millions from hunger/deprivation is not a possibility of the future, but a horrible reality of today. We have to struggle hard against this suffering because there seems to be no alternative to acting thus.

The SCMers confronted him with questions about the use of violence in the struggles, and he was categorical in his theological response:

> A false call for non-violence or peace in the sense of giving up the struggle against injustice would amount to a betrayal of our own hopes and aspirations. For Christians to remain neutral in this context would be sin. Not participating in the struggles of people for justice and peace is the greatest sin of our time. Remaining neutral would amount to condoning the violence inherent in the existing unjust structures of exploitation, oppression and marginalization.[21]

In his message to the SCM of India on the occasion of its platinum jubilee celebrations in 1987, he reminded SCM that "it is not enough that we send some token representatives to peace demonstrations and protest march, but we must also see that our forms of life and worship as Student Christian

Movement show people clearly that we exist not to keep ourselves spiritually and intellectually cozy, but to witness and minister to the people, particularly to the students, and to give them a new vision."[22] Addressing the SCMers in the Asia Pacific Region, Mar Poulose shared his vision of SCM:

> We should recognize that our work should perpetuate life in its abundance (John 10:10) and we should not permit structures of society to continue degrading and destroying all of humanity. We should work for true humanization of societies within our regions and the whole earth. This however would not be possible if we isolate ourselves from the realities of life—the experiences, pains and problems of the masses. It is our role to effect change in all of life's situation from control to liberation, from oppression to self-determination and from inequality to equality. We must bear the "cross of consequences" involved in this, even until death. And only through this could we say that we have done our prophetic role in our present context.[23]

Bishop Poulose Mar Poulose was a prophet who followed Jesus the Christ as his model, and he always insisted that SCM should become a Christ-centred movement as it strives to bear witness in our context. "Only if we experience the condemnation of the existing order by the standards of the gospel, and go through a proper *metanoia* by participating in the sufferings of God in the secular life, will we be able to change the existing order."[24] In our times, the ecumenical movements have lost their movement ethos, and have become monuments. Co-option by the mainstream ecumenical movements and the temptation of ecumenical tourism and career building are the biggest ecumenical sins today that prevent SCMers from committing themselves to experience the "condemnation of the existing order." Does it mean that the life and witness of people like Mar Poulose was in vain? Not at all!

Bishop Poulose Mar Poulose's life was short; but he still lives in the ecumenical youth student movements as they continue to remain *out of control*, challenging the ecumenical mafia and the pharisaic church. We hear this voice of nonconformism from the dissenting minority, gathered in Manila, the Philippines, for the Asia Pacific Students and Youth Gathering 2013:

> We challenge our churches and encourage them to come out from their comfort zones of conservatism and reactionary tendencies and go out to the streets where the people struggle for life and dignity. We invite them to join

> the commitment of the youth to re-imagine the Church of Christ as a *Basileia* community. We call upon the ecumenical movements to undergo a genuine experience of introspection and new baptism to rise again as a vibrant prophetic movement of Christ's disciples. We invite the ecumenical students and youth movements in the region to liberate themselves from the control of powers that be, and to be filled by the spirit of God proclaiming the reign of justice and peace now! We, as the Asia-Pacific youth, students, and young workers, affirm our role in reshaping our unfolding history. Our active participation in the people's movements in consciously transforming the world—to be the new ecclesia and the new *oikoumene*—is therefore our offering.

We see here the birthing of an alternative ecumenical movement, and we hope and pray that they will be blessed with enough courage and divine foolishness to remain *out of control*!

CHAPTER 11

D. Preman Niles

Ninan Koshy: An Ecumenical Voice in the World of Nations

Political thinker and activist, expert on foreign affairs, social analyst, theologian—these are some of the epithets that have been used to describe Ninan Koshy. He read widely, wrote copiously in English and Malayalam, and even ran for the Indian Parliament (Lok Sabha) as a Left Democratic Front candidate in 1999 and lost narrowly. He was ecumenically involved locally, regionally, and globally. This essay is no more than a brief account of the versatility of the man and the ecumenical contributions he has made.

Ninan Koshy belongs to a respected Indian tradition of lay theologians who did not go through formal theological training, though in the case of some a veneer of formal theology was added at the end of their careers. Unhampered by the constraints of theological training, this breed of men and women had the freedom to think theologically, beginning with the secular. For these, social and political engagement was primary. To pick a few names: M. M. Thomas (1916–1996), C. I. Itty (1927–2005), and now Ninan Koshy; Pandita Ramabai (1858–1922), Sarah Chakko (1905–1954), and now Aruna Gnanadason. In brief, the world with its people, especially those on the margins of society for whom God specially cares, was the starting point for their ecumenical engagement and theological ruminations. These were "secular" theologians in the best sense of the word.

My intention is, first, to give a biographical sketch of Ninan Koshy (from now on referred to as Ninan) up to the time he joined the staff of the World Council of Churches (WCC) as a framework for describing his ecumenical formation. Second, I will recount some of the areas in which he made a significant ecumenical contribution as a staff member and then director during his long period of work (1974–1991) in the Churches' Commission on International Affairs (CCIA) at the WCC. Third, I will mention some of the important contributions he is continuing to make since leaving the WCC. Finally, I end with a personal note on him that shows his character.

A Biographical Sketch: The Ecumenical Formation of Ninan Koshy

Ninan was born in 1934, and had his education in colleges in the state of Kerala. He received a master's degree in English Literature at St John's College, Agra, and worked as a tutor in English at St Berchman's College, Changanacherry, from 1956 to 1958.

Ninan was attracted to politics and particularly to the leftist movement during his college years at a time when the Communist Party began to be influential in college campuses in Kerala. He was also active in the church founded by the Church Missionary Society (Anglican), which later became part of the Church of South India (CSI). Consequently, he found it difficult to cope with the tension between his faith and politics. He was introduced to M. M. Thomas, who helped him to perceive the political dynamics in the gospel that called for ideological choices. Thomas himself had gone through this process. From then on, Thomas, who had perceived Ninan's potential, became his mentor and played an active role in guiding him in his ecumenical career.

Ninan was active in the youth movement of the Central Kerala Diocese of the CSI and became its president at the age of 21. He also edited the diocesan youth magazine. In 1962, at the age of 28, he was elected to the council and executive committee of the synod of the CSI. During this period he served as the head of the English department at the Bishop Moore College and in 1964 became the vice principal of the college.

From 1960 to 1964, he was a columnist on politics and international affairs in *Malayala Manorama*, a Malayalam mass-circulation daily. Ninan says, "With little background of history or politics in my education, I did a lot of reading. That was how I became a 'specialist' in international affairs."

Involvement in the study of politics continued when Thomas asked him to write a book in Malayalam on the relationship between church and state. This book was a big undertaking. He spent a few weeks in Bangalore reading extensively on the subject in the libraries at the Christian Institute for the Study of Religion and Society (CISRS) and the United Theological College Bangalore. It was a matter of some pride for him that his first book was in Malayalam and would serve the churches in Kerala.

Thomas, who was then the director of CISRS, asked him in 1966 to do a sociological study with a theological commentary on the caste system that prevailed in the churches in Kerala. With the help of a small team he made a survey with a select number of questions on the issue, followed by a few seminars with sociologists and theologians. Published in 1968 under the title *Caste in the Kerala Churches*, it is a groundbreaking study on the impact that caste has on the churches and exposes the lack of fellowship in the churches as a result of discrimination against those who come to the church from outcaste or Dalit communities. It also surfaces vested interests in perpetuating the caste system in the churches. It is one of the most cited of Ninan's books, and was digitalized by some universities in the USA, including the University of California and the University of Michigan in 2007, as it seems to be the only study of its kind. There are plans to publish a new edition of the book with a postscript on the contemporary situation. This was his initial foray into the discipline of sociology.

Thomas prevailed on him to give up his comfortable teaching position at Bishop Moore College and membership in the Kerala University Senate. With some hesitation he left this security to enter the risky arena of ecumenical work full-time as general secretary of the Student Christian Movement (SCM) of India in 1968. At that time Latin American liberation theology held sway at the World Student Christian Federation (WSCF), and there was heavy pressure for all local SCMs to embrace that theological and ideological stance. In response, Ninan wrote to the leadership of the WSCF that theological and ideological diversity in the national SCMs is inevitable given the variety of ideological positions in the various nations of the world. It would be disastrous for the WSCF leadership to universalize one contextual perception from a particular region and assume that the others are at a lower level of understanding. If the Federation has to exist as a federation, argued Ninan, political and ideological diversity needs to be accepted and respected. This was not just a theoretical position, because at that time "the Asian Revolution" was the main topic of discussion in the East Asia Christian Conference (later the Christian Conference of Asia); and the theme of the triennial conference of the Indian and Ceylon SCMs was "Students in the Asian Revolution." To be politically involved, because God loves the whole world and not just parts of it, meant respecting diversity without taking fixed positions—something that he carried into his work in the CCIA. At this time Ninan was also involved in a seminar on China, which the Indian SCM organized for the WSCF. It had experts on China from India and abroad, and helped Ninan take a continuing interest in that country. During this period, Ninan also served on the executive and working committees of the National Council of Churches of India. Continuing as a member of governing bodies of the CSI, he was sent as one of its delegates to the Uppsala assembly of the WCC in 1968. He was one of the youngest delegates at that assembly.

Besides his responsibilities as general secretary of the Indian national SCM, Ninan wrote a column every week commenting on current affairs in *The Guardian: A Christian Weekly on Political Affairs*, of which Thomas was the general editor. In the absence of other similar journals, this weekly publication was influential in shaping public opinion on current events both local and international.

In 1973, Ninan left the SCM and joined the staff of the Ecumenical Christian Centre at Whitefield in Bangalore and served first as its associate director and then as director-in-charge. The Centre was founded by M. A. Thomas, a visionary ecumenist who encouraged interaction between the church and society and promoted interreligious dialogue.

He left the Centre in July 1974 and joined the staff of CCIA of the WCC. All the experiences gained and skills acquired in many fields of study with a clear theological perspective flowed into his work in the CCIA, of which he became director from 1981 to 1991.

Ninan's Time at the CCIA: Significant Ecumenical Contributions

When Ninan joined the CCIA, Leopoldo Niilus, an Argentinian lawyer originally from Estonia, was director. Leopoldo had previously worked in other organizations on several facets of international affairs. He carried this broad approach into his directorship. Consequently, during his time there were no strict region-wise or issue-wise divisions of responsibilities. Everybody was responsible for everything! In a word, all the staff were "specialists." This style of work encouraged collaboration. It also discouraged specialists from other Western Christian organizations from needlessly intruding into the work of CCIA staff and lecturing them. Ninan recounts an incident when a specialist on Asia from the USA was visiting the CCIA. Leopoldo said to Ninan, "He will assume that as an Indian you will be responsible for Asia. Say that you have Africa as your area of responsibility!" While such a response would be off-putting, it would not be totally false. Ninan was engaged with other WCC staff members in addressing the problems apartheid was creating in South Africa and the rest of that continent. Allergic to so-called specialists and their supposed superior knowledge, Leopoldo once remarked, "Do not assume that the Intelligence Services are necessarily intelligent!" A healthy dose of skepticism ensured that CCIA staff carried a critical inquiring mind into their work and were not easily seduced by so-called expert opinions.

By the time Ninan became director, changes had already begun to take place in staffing responsibilties. Of particular importance in this matter was the role that Philip Potter, general secretary of the WCC, played. His guidance, support, and encouragement both to Ninan and other CCIA staff was immense. Potter was extremely knowledgeable on international affairs, followed developments closely, and provided for Ninan the framework for analysis, policy making, and action.

With the stress on analysis leading to clear action, specializing both in terms of issues and geographical areas was necessary. The world was becoming a more complex place. Greater scrutiny and analysis were needed if what the CCIA said and did were to be credible. Also, allowance had to be made for relationships both with churches and with outside organizations such as the various UN departments. However, while there was a "lead" staff member who specialized in a particular region or issue, actions were always taken in consultation with other staff colleagues and under the leadership of the director. On some very important issues, as we shall see below, there was joint effort, involving a degree of specialization for all on the team. In effect, it was a combination of specialization and collaboration.

Ninan's main contribution within CCIA's set-up was in the analyses he had to carry out of critical international situations, in developing theological and conceptual clarity in the area of international affairs, and exploring possibilities for what may be called "ecumenical diplomacy." In practical terms this meant contributions in five specific areas, among others: (1) clarifying the role of the WCC in international affairs; (2) the drafting of public statements leading to action; (3) disarmament and militarism; (4) facilitating the entry of the China Christian Council into the fellowship of the World Council of Churches, which it had abandoned shortly after the Amsterdam Assembly (1948); and (5) bringing about a rapproachment between Christians in South Korea and North Korea.

The role of the WCC in international affairs

Following WCC practice that documents commended to member churches should not carry the name of the staffperson or persons responsible, the document "The Role of the World Council of Churches in International Affairs" does not go under Ninan's name. But, in fact, he was the person who crafted and drafted it, so I am personalizing its authorship.[1] The document brings together all his skills as a historian and political thinker together with his theological nous.

From its very inception, the WCC had to concern itself with international affairs, raising questions such as, Why is the WCC involved in international affairs? How does it perform its function in the area? What are the criteria for selection of issues for actions? What special contribution has a body like the WCC in this field?

There is a *theological dimension* to the role that the CCIA played on behalf of the WCC. Formed in the aftermath of the Second World War, the WCC was particularly concerned with the loss that people especially in Europe suffered, the displacement of those people, and the Cold War that followed, which was a sustained political and military tension between the West (America and Western Europe) and the Union of Soviet Socialist Republics (USSR) with its satellites in Eastern Europe. One of the functions of the WCC, according to its constitution, is "to express the common concern of the churches in the service of human need, the breaking down of barriers between people, and the promotion of the human family in justice and peace."

After the end of the Second World War and during the Cold-War period, ecumenical social thought, which translated theological principles into ethical models for social and political engagement, operated with the model of the "responsible society." It was particularly suited for churches in the West on how to live and act responsibly in any society using the principle of "middle axioms," which bridged the demands of the values of the kingdom of God with the realities of the world. With the entry of churches from the so-called "third world," ecumenical social thought moved from the model of the responsible society to the model of the "just, participatory, and sustainable society," which brought in for ecumenical consideration a wider set of issues.[2] At the Vancouver assembly of the WCC (1983), issues of justice and peace were seen as inextricably linked. In almost apocalyptic language, the assembly described a world situation that calls for concerted ecumenical action:

> Humanity is now living in the dark shadow of an arms race more intense, and of systems of injustice more widespread, more dangerous and more costly than the world has ever known. Never before has the human race been as close as it is now to total destruction. Never before have so many lived in the grip of deprivation and oppression.
>
> The peoples of the world stand in need of peace and justice. Peace is not just the absence of war. Peace cannot be built on foundations of injustice. Peace requires a new international order based on justice for and within all nations, and respect for the God-given humanity and dignity of every person. Peace is, as the Prophet Isaiah has taught us, the effect of righteousness.
>
> The churches today are called to confess anew their faith, and to repent for the times when Christians have remained silent in the face of injustice or threats to peace. The biblical vision of peace with justice for all, of wholeness, of unity for all God's people is not one of several options for the followers of Christ. It is an imperative in our times.[3]

This emphasis was enshrined in a request that the assembly made: "To engage member churches in a conciliar process of mutual commitment (covenant) to justice, peace and the integrity of creation should be a priority for World Council programmes."[4]

In the document on the role of the WCC in international affairs, Ninan takes account of this changing mood and emphasis for ecumenical involvement and action. He combs through the various WCC assembly statements and the statements from the assemblies of other units, especially the Commissions on World Mission and Evangelism (CWME), on Faith and Order, and on Church and Society, to show how the expectation enshrined in the constitution was developed. It was important to do such a survey because, as Ninan argues, there was not, and could not be, a

> clear set of universally valid rules which provide an immediate answer to these dilemmas [changing human predicaments], nor can the solutions be found through a simple application of abstract principles to concrete situations. But Holy Scripture, Christian history, contemporary Christian experience and the insights of the social sciences and other secular disciplines do inform the situation, and in their light Christians and churches are called to be obedient to the understanding of God's will in the particular situation.[5]

In brief, concerning oneself with international affairs in the world which God loves is not only a matter of analysis but also a matter of *confessing the faith*. It is a call to action. The report of the World Conference of CWME in Melbourne, Australia (1980), with the theme, "Your Kingdom Come," succinctly states:

> There is a need for the churches to awaken to their prophetic task in the many human struggles—to say "yes" to that which conforms to the Kingdom of God as revealed to humankind in the life of Jesus Christ and say "no" to that which distorts the dignity and freedom of human beings and all that is alive. . . . As Christ has come not for a part but for the whole of humanity, the churches must be a means of reconciliation in the midst of human struggles: this will make it necessary to take very specific stands in struggles and conflicts.[6]

As Ninan rightly points out, in the end it is the churches themselves who are the primary actors in the arena of international affairs. Taking specific stands is not simply a matter of churches and Christians standing on the sidelines shouting "foul" or "fair." They need to be a "means of reconciliation." Consequently, there is also a *pastoral dimension* with its ramifications—when to speak, when not to speak, when to organize pastoral visits, and so on. Sometimes there is ambiguity in how the WCC should respond when it hears conflicting voices from member churches in a particular national situation. For instance, when the then-prime minister of India, Indira Gandhi, persuaded the president of India to declare a state of emergency in 1975 so that she could rule by decree to curb social unrest in the interest of development, some Christians supported what she did and others opposed this measure as the beginning of the end of democratic rights of people. The WCC had to make a judgment. At other times, a pastoral visit with quiet representations to governments would be more appropriate. And still other times, a WCC team visit to member churches facing difficulties would instill hope that they were not alone.

Without going into details in this brief article, it would be better to show how the ideas that Ninan amplifies in the document find expression in specific actions.

Analysis and public statements: the case of South Africa

Almost from the time he joined the staff of CCIA and certainly from 1979 onwards, Ninan drafted the public statements of the WCC on international affairs. This meant that he was actively involved in policy making on public issues. A good example is the involvement of the WCC in South Africa during the apartheid period.

While the programmatic responsibility regarding South Africa was with the Programme to Combat Racism (PCR), the CCIA was continuously involved in the analysis of the situation, maintaining contacts with liberation movements and the South African Council of Churches. The CCIA under Ninan's leadership followed each new development inside and outside South Africa. The CCIA also maintained active contact with the United Nations and diplomats from several Western countries—especially the Nordic countries—on the situation in South Africa. Many diplomats, and even the UN, turned to the WCC for information and analysis of developments in South Africa and Namibia.

While Ninan helped to draft most of the statements, they were all issued by the general secretary, central committee, executive committee, and assembly during the 1970s and 1980s. These called the attention of the churches to their special responsibility taking note of the violation of God-given human dignity in South Africa, and the false claim of South Africa to be a "Christian nation," premised on a faulty theology derived from a perverse reading of the creation accounts in Genesis for justifying apartheid. When Ninan joined the CCIA, there was little cooperation between the CCIA and the PCR. After he joined the staff, there was full collaboration, for a number of reasons. PCR was an excellent example of ecumenical activism, but its policy framework was sometimes not clear, though PCR had good contacts with churches on the ground. Ninan's task was to analyze the various international developments with regard to South Africa and to make policies and provide advice on the larger context, including the responses of the USA and of the Soviet Union to developments in South Africa.

From the 1960s, the WCC had taken a bold stand in supporting liberation movements in southern Africa (South Africa, Namibia, and Zimbabwe), and through the PCR set up a special fund for humanitarian aid for those in the liberation movements who were being deprived of their share of "daily bread." Greatly misundersood, WCC's involvement in southern Africa became controversial.

By supporting the liberation movements, especially the African National Congress, the WCC earned the displeasure of several Western governments, especially the USA and the United Kingdom. Margaret Thatcher, who was at that time prime minister of the United Kingdom, reflected the mood of the pro-apartheid Western governments. She branded the African National Congress "a typical terrorist organisation. . . . Anyone who thinks it is going to run the government in South Africa is living in cloud-cuckoo land."[7] Dan Rather from the USA interviewed Philip Potter in his office in Geneva for the *60 Minutes* television programme. It was an occasion not so much to let Potter explain the involvement of the WCC in southern African affairs as a scurrilous attack on the WCC as a pro-Russian organization that supported terrorists.

Despite all the calumny and pain, for the WCC to carry on undaunted was shown to be worth it when in June 1990, shortly after his release, Nelson Mandela visited Geneva and in the main hall of the WCC buildings expressed his personal thanks for the important role the WCC played in the anti-apartheid struggle. He repeated what he said at the 50th anniversary celebrations of the WCC at Harare in December 1998: "Thirty years ago you launched a programme that broke new ground and set new directions for the future. You moved beyond the affirmation of the right to resist on the part of the oppressed, to the risk of active engagement in the struggle to end oppression. Today the WCC is called upon to show that same engagement in the new and more difficult struggle for development and the entrenchment of democracy."[8]

Through the WCC and the leadership of Philip Potter, Ninan played no small part in the move from analysis and public statements to the dismantling of apartheid.

Disarmament and militarism

From the time of the Nairobi assembly (1975) the issue of the increasing militarization of nations as a way of ensuring their security has been a concern of the WCC. The Central Committee that followed (1977) endorsed plans for studies leading to an action-oriented programme on militarism and disarmament. Several consultations on militarism and disarmament followed, showing more fully the dire consequences for justice with the increasing reliance of nations on armed forces as the cornerstone of their foreign and often domestic policies.

In 1980, the Central Committee requested the WCC subunit on Church and Society and the CCIA to arrange jointly an international public hearing on the current threat to world peace, with a special focus on the increased danger of nuclear war. In November 1981, Ninan, together with Paul Abrecht, who was the director of the subunit on Church and Society, organized a public hearing on nuclear weapons. Forty witnesses from around the world, representing a wide variety of theological, political, scientific, and miltary backgrounds, together with leaders from popular peace movements gathered in Amsterdam to meet with a panel of 17 persons. Never previously had the WCC consulted with such a large group of experts and workers in the field about the threats posed by the continuing development and increasing stockpile of nuclear weapons. The complete record of the public hearing was subsequently published as a book, *Before It's Too Late: The Challenge of Nuclear Disarmament.*[9] The published report contains careful, thought-provoking analyses and spells out urgent tasks for the churches. The book was well received in UN circles, and by NGOs and peace movements.

"The Statement on Peace and Justice" of the Vancouver WCC assembly (1983) had the benefit of all the work that had been done including the results of the public hearing. It said, "The concept of deterrence, the credibility of which depends on the possible use of nuclear weapons, is to be rejected as morally unacceptable and as incapable of safeguarding peace and security in the long term." The assembly went on to say, "We believe that the time has come when the churches must unequivocally declare that the production and deployment as well as the use of nuclear weapons is a crime against humanity and such activities must be condemned on ethical and theological grounds." Over against national security based on the concept of deterrence, the assembly put forward the concept of "people's security":

> The blatant misuse of the concept of national security to justify repression, foreign intervention and spiraling of arms budget is of profound concern. No nation can pretend to be secure as long as others' legitimate rights to sovereignty and security are neglected or denied. Security can therefore be achieved only as a common enterprise of nations but security is also inseparable from justice. A concept of "common security" of nations must be reinforced by a concept of "people's security". True security for the people demands respect for human rights, including the right to self-determination, as well as social and economic justice for all within every nation and a political framework that would ensure it.[10]

The term "people's security" was picked up in other political discussions, and the United Nations began using the term from 1994 in its Human Development Report.

After the Vancouver assembly, Ninan concentrated mainly on nuclear disarmament and was considered a specialist on the issue. He participated in UN conferences and conferences of NGOs on disarmament to explain the position of the WCC.

The WCC and churches in China and Korea

Ninan writes,

> One of the memorable moments during the seventh assembly of the World Council of Churches in Canberra, Australia, in February 1991 came when the general secretaries of the National Council of Churches of Korea (Republic of Korea) and of the Korean Christian Federation (Democratic People's Republic of Korea) appeared together on the podium and embraced each other. Even more significant was the moment in the same assembly when the re-entry of the church in China, represented by the China Christian Council, was announced. . . . Most delegates in Canberra were probably unaware that both of these memorable moments at the assembly were preceded by almost a decade of patient negotiations.[11]

On the same page, Ninan rightly observes, "There were no theological or ecclesiological reasons why these two churches were absent for so long from the fellowship of the WCC." Geopolitical factors played a part in keeping these two churches away from the ecumenical fellowship of the churches. The WCC's muddled handling of geopolitical issues was also responsible.

Re-entry of the church in China into the WCC

Chinese Christians were active in the ecumenical movement through the WSCF, YMCA, and YWCA from the beginning of the twentieth century. Four member churches from China were present at the Amsterdam assembly in 1948. T. C. Chao from China was elected one of the presidents of the WCC, a position from which he resigned in disgust when at the Toronto meeting of the WCC Central Committee (July 1950) a statement was made supporting the UN's "police action" in North Korea, which was deemed the aggressor in the Korean War. It was later found that the architect of this position was John Foster Dulles, at that time special advisor to the U.S. president, Harry S. Truman, and directly involved with the Korea issue. He was mainly instrumental in changing the WCC position on Korea from "negotiation" to support for "police action." Just ten days earlier the CCIA had asked the UN to pursue the path of negotiations. There is reason to assume that Dulles wanted to use the WCC's support as a moral weapon in the propaganda war. In this matter the WCC had ignored the voices from China and North Korea.

Not quite knowing the background to the Toronto statement and the mistake made, the WCC could not quite understand the silence of the Chinese churches. The WCC never received any letter of withdrawal from them. There was no reply to the invitation extended by the WCC to the Chinese churches to the Evanston assembly (1954). The last time a Chinese church representative participated was at the Central Committee in 1956 when K. H. Ting attended as an observer. A Central Committee resolution expressed a "deep sense of satisfaction" in maintaining contacts with the Chinese church.

In 1961, CCIA made a statement calling for the admission of the People's Republic of China (PRC) to the United Nations.[12] At that time, the position was occupied by Taiwan. The WCC, through the CCIA, was one of the first international organizations to affirm that it was the PRC which should be represented at the UN. This "one China" policy became helpful in all future negotiations with the Chinese church and the Chinese government.

There was reference at the WCC Uppsala assembly (1968) to the absence of "Chinese brothers" and the great significance of bringing the PRC into the international community. An invitation was extended to Bishop K. H. Ting to the Nairobi assembly through visiting friends. He said that it was too early. It was in the beginning of the 1980s that active negotiations began with Bishop Ting and the China Christian Council about the reactivation of the membership of the Chinese church in the WCC.

Together with his colleagues Erich Weingartner and Victor Hsu, Ninan began to identify some of the issues to be dealt with in rebuilding relations with the Chinese church. They included the statement of the 1950 Central Committee on the Korean War, the fact that the original member churches of the WCC were no longer there and all of them had become part of the China Christian Council, listing Taiwan as a country in the WCC membership list, and the objection of the Taiwanese church to membership of the mainland church. The negotiations had to be careful as they involved several parties and interests. For every movement on the issue, CCIA also had to get the permission of the Chinese government. Furthermore, Bishop Ting had to proceed cautiously and overcome some resistance in the China Christian Council. He had to convince them that it was not because of his past association with WSCF and WCC and his personal friendship with Philip Potter that he wanted the Chinese church to be part of the WCC.

Regarding the statement on the Korean War, the 1989 Central Committee of the WCC admitted it was a mistake. This was made clear in North Korea as well as in China. The question was raised in some circles whether the China Christian Council could be treated as a church and as the legitimate continuation of the original member churches of the WCC from China. The WCC maintained that it was the self-understanding of the Chinese church that should decide the issue.

The Chinese government was willing to allow Chinese church delegates to attend the Vancouver assembly held in 1983. This assurance was given by a senior Chinese diplomat who visited Ninan. But this move was scuppered when the diplomat discovered in the WCC handbook that the Taiwan Presbyterian Church was listed under Taiwan as a country.

This was a difficult issue. The CCIA called representatives of the China Christian Council and the Taiwanese church to Geneva and had discussions with them on several issues, including the name of the country Taiwan, to which the China Christian Council objected. In the 1980s, to gain international recognition, Taiwan wanted to enter as many international organizations as possible. The Taiwanese government persuaded the Presbyterian church, which did not participate in any WCC meetings at that time, to activate its membership and block any attempt to readmit the church in China into the membership of the WCC.

With regard to naming Taiwan, Ninan suggested that member churches should not be listed under countries but regions. The China Christian Council and the Taiwan Presbyterian Church, the latter being the name of the church, would be listed under Asia. The formula was based on the principle that it is churches, not countries, that are members of the WCC. Ninan managed to persuade the two sides to agree to this solution after getting the agreement of the general secretary of the WCC. The formula was first introduced at the CWME meeting in San Antonio (May 1989), at which representatives from both the China Christian Council and the National Council of Churches in Taiwan were present.

The Canberra assembly in 1991 had the delegates listed under the new formula. This was also appreciated by several churches in Eastern Europe like the Estonian Lutheran Church, the Latvian Lutheran Church, and so forth, which had previously been listed under the Soviet Union, and whose countries had begun struggles for national independence.

At the Canberra assembly, representatives of the China Christian Council and the Presbyterian Church in Taiwan were present, but the Taiwanese church still kept objecting to the membership of the China Christian Council. Ninan explained that it was not a question of new membership but the "reactivation" of membership for which there could be no objection from either side. With much difficulty, the Taiwanese agreed. They had been under political pressure to object to having the church from the mainland in the WCC, and the Taiwanese press reported daily about the negotiations, adding to the pressure on the Taiwanese representatives. The Taiwanese media publicized that the WCC had recognized both the People's Republic of China and Taiwan. This naturally made it difficult for our friends from the mainland to explain their membership to their government.

The assembly had closed. The China Christian Council and the Taiwanese Presbyterian Church had "re-entered" the WCC. The story did not end there. Late that night the WCC general secretary, Emilio Castro, and Ninan were told by Bishop Ting and Han Wenzao, general secretary of the China Christian Council, that the impression these "re-entries" created was that the WCC has a two-China policy. They wanted a letter from the general secretary explaining the WCC's position. Ninan drafted the letter. The letter from the general secretary to Bishop Ting, dated 20 February 1991, said:

> Over all these years, the WCC has maintained a one-China policy in its actions and statements. The WCC through its Commission of the Churches on International Affairs, was one of the first international organizations to press for the admission of the Peoples' Republic of China in the United Nations.
>
> As you are aware, through membership the WCC related to churches and not to states. The nature of the fellowship to which we all belong demands from all of us respect for the self-understanding and integrity of all member churches. The listing of member churches therefore in no way affects our policy on China.

This appeared to be satisfactory to the Chinese authorities. Without a doubt, this was one of the most difficult cases in the area of ecumenical diplomacy.

Churches in Korea

The same trio of Ninan Koshy, Erich Weingartner, and Victor Hsu, with the support of the general secretary, Philip Potter, were involved in another important matter in the area of ecumenical diplomacy. When the Korean peninsula split into North Korea and South Korea, under a perverse interpretation of the Marxian maxim that religion is the opiate of the people, the North Korean armed forces rounded up all the ordained ministers they could find and executed them. It is also possible that these were viewed as representatives of hated Western governments. This act decimated a flourishing Christian population, especially in and around Pyongyang, the capital of North Korea. Many Christians, including the families of executed ministers, fled to South Korea. Some carried the bitterness of this experience and hated North Korea. Others, however, yearned for the reunification of the Korean peninsula, the division of which they viewed as a local manifestation of the global cold war and a blight on the yearning of the people for peace and justice. In brief, it was a specific case of national security versus people's security.

Mutual suspicion and the intransigence of both governments affected people in both countries, and any talk of reunification was taboo. In South

Korea, those who even theoretically explored possibilities for reunification were imprisoned. It was in this context that Christians in South Korea appealed to the WCC for help. Besides condemning the draconian measures of the South Korean government in the interests of national security to silence voices for the reunification of the Korean peninsula, the WCC general secretary and CCIA staff made a series of visits to both Koreas and to the People's Republic of China to explore possibilities for discussions on reunification.

From 29 October to 2 November 1984, 65 church leaders from 20 nations of Asia, Pacific, the Middle East, Latin America, North America, and West Europe gathered in Tozanso, Japan, for the ecumenical consultation on "Peace and Justice in North-East Asia: Prospects for Peaceful Resolution of Conflicts." There were no representatives from North Korea, but the consultation had received a message from the central committee of the Korean Christian Federation (KCF) "wishing all success to the consultation in every effort to realize peace and justice in the region, particularly peaceful reunification of Korea." This meeting was not the end but the beginning that came to be known as the "Tozanso Process."

In June 1985, Ninan and Erich Weingartner received an invitation to visit North Korea. It was signed jointly by the Committee for the Peaceful Reunification of the Fatherland (CPRF) and the Central Committee of the KCF. The Tozanso consultation was mentioned in the invitation. Ninan and Erich visited North Korea in November 1985. This was the first "official" visit by any church or ecumenical body to North Korea. For the first time, they could collect information, however limited, on the Christian community there, and the WCC could enter into discussions with the North Korean government on the issue of reunification and related issues.

The idea of a meeting of Christians from North and South Korea supported by KCF was favourably received by the North Korean government. Ninan, together with CCIA staff, followed this up with the South Korean churches and government. These discussions paved the way for the next significant step in the process, a seminar on the "Biblical and Theological Foundations of Christian Concern for Peace." Glion I, as the meeting came to be known, brought together for the first time representatives of churches from the North and the South in September 1986. A eucharist at this gathering in a symbolic act affirmed the role Christians could play to break down barriers, though there were major differences in ideology and socioceconomic systems between the two Koreas.

In July 1989, the WCC Central Committee meeting in Moscow, with representatives from both North and South Korea present, adopted a major policy declaration on "Peace and Reunification of Korea." The declaration begins with a confession: "The WCC confesses that it has not always dealt equitably with the Korean question. Mistakes of the past should weigh on the conscience of the ecumenical community and intensify our determination to struggle for peace and reunification of Korea." It goes on to make this momentous statement, "The Korean division is in microcosm a symbol of the division of the world. If this wound in the human community can be healed, there would emanate from Korea a hope for all humanity. We pray that the cross of the Korean people can lead to an Easter for us all."[13]

There is still a long way to go. Ninan calls this episode in the work of the CCIA "the politics of hope."[14]

After CCIA

While still at the CCIA, in 1991 Ninan was invited to the Harvard Law School to be a visiting fellow for a year. Besides becoming more deeply acquainted with international laws regarding human rights, it was a time for reflection and for putting together the ideas and themes he had been working on while at the WCC, including his book *Churches in the World of Nations* (1994). Equally important was his book *The War on Terror: Re-Ordering the World*,[15] which shows how under the pretext of combatting terrorism, the United States with its allies, principally the United Kingdom, is reordering the world into a global empire. Still well received, this book was the beginning of Ninan's continued interest and publications on economic globalization and threats to world peace.

With short notice, Ninan rescued a project on the history of the ecumenical movement in Asia. He wrote the first volume, which is a detailed account of this history beginning with Christianity in Asia from the period before 1500 CE up until now. He edited the second volume, which contains essays on different aspects of ecumenism in Asia.[16]

The book *The War on Terror* elicited an interesting response from Donald Shriver, emeritus professor of ethics and president of Union Theological Seminary in New York. He raised the question, "While the political analysis is good, where is the theology?"[17] When I asked Ninan, he said that the book was written for a secular readership. Right there is his theology: the ability to reflect his theological convictions deeply rooted in the Bible and in his spirituality nourished in the church when writing on issues that concern the world of people. In truth, these are the hallmarks of a secular theologian.[18]

A Personal Note

During the last period of Ninan's work in the CCIA, I was in charge of the ecumenical process on Justice, Peace, and the Integrity of Creation (1986–1991). Expectations had changed since the process was launched at the Vancouver assembly, and the Vatican and confessional bodies were also invited to join in the process. Ecclesiological differences brought in differing and conflicting theological approaches and viewpoints. There were also stresses and strains within the WCC offices, which made my work difficult, if not impossible. I decided to resign. I informed Ninan, who was one of those who wanted me to take on this job. He said, "Hold it till we meet for lunch outside the WCC offices." We met and Ninan said two things that not only remained with me but also showed his character: "If you leave, your story dies with you and their story remains. In the final analysis you are not accountable to people here but to the people outside who have taken heart to continue their struggles for justice, peace and the integrity of God's creation. You being here is a sign of hope for them. You should not let them down." I stayed on and finished the job, culminating in the World Convocation on Justice, Peace, and the Integrity of Creation (Seoul, March 1990). What Ninan said to me reflected his own character: the willingness to persist in struggles for justice and peace, whatever the impediment, because the cause is right.

SELECT BIBLIOGRAPHY

Abraham, K. C. *Christian Witness in Society: A Tribute to M. M. Thomas*. Bangalore: BTESSC, 1998.

______. "Globalization: A Gospel and Culture Perspective." *International Review of Mission* 85, no. 336 (January 1996): 85–92.

______. "Third World Theology: Paradigm Shift and Emerging Concerns." In *Confronting Life: Theology Out of the Context*, M. P. Joseph, ed. Delhi: ISPCK, 1995.

Abrecht, Paul. "In Memoriam: Paulos Mar Gregorios." *Ecumenical Review* 49, no. 1 (January 1997): 110.

Adiappa, E. "Writings of Russell Chandran: A Select Bibliography." In *A Vision for Man: Essays on Faith, Theology, and Society in Honour of Joshua Russell Chandran*, ed. Samuel Amirtham, 19–25. Madras: CLS, 1978.

Amirtham, Samuel. *Theology by the People*. Geneva: WCC Publications, 1986.

______, ed. *A Vision for Man: Essays on Faith, Theology and Society in Honour of Joshua Russell Chandran*. Madras: The Christian Literature Society, 1978.

______, and S. Wesley Ariarajah. *Ministerial Formation in a Multifaith Milieu: Implications of Interfaith Dialogue for Theological Education*. Geneva: WCC Publications, 1986.

Athyal, Jesudas M. "The Changing Face of the Indian Society . . . and the New Challenges for Dalit Theology." *Gurukul Journal of Theological Studies* XVI, No. 1&2; January & July (2005): 73-91.

______. "Come Holy Spirit, *Diagnose*, Heal and Reconcile: Lingering Questions from Athens." *International Review of Mission* 94, no. 375 (October 2005): 535–45.

Ayrookuzhiel, A. M. Abraham. *The Sacred in Popular Hinduism*. Madras: CLS, 1983.

Azariah, Masilamani. *A Pastor's Search for Dalit Theology*. Delhi: ISPCK, 2000.

______. *Christ and Dalit Liberation*. Madras: Dalit Liberation Education Trust, 1987.

______. *The Un-Christian Side of the Christian Church: The Plight of the Untouchable Converts*. Bangalore: Dalit Sahitya Akademy, 1985.

Baago, K. *National Christian Council of India: 1914–1964*. Nagpur: NCCI, 1965.

Balasundaran, Franklyn J. "Indian Missionary Society." In *A Dictionary of Asian Christianity*, eds. Scott W. Sunquist, David Wu Chu Sing, and John Chew Hiang Chea, 369–70. Grand Rapids: Eerdmans, 2001.

Barnabas, A. P. *Indian Politics after Nehru*. Bangalore: CISRS, 1967.

Bauman, Chad M. *Christian Identity and Dalit Religion in Hindu India, 1868–1947*. Grand Rapids: Eerdmans, 2008.

Bent, Ans J. Van Der. *Vital Ecumenical Concerns: Sixteen Documentary Surveys*. Geneva: WCC Publications, 1986.

Bird, Adrian. *M. M. Thomas and Dalit Theology*. Bangalore: BTESSC/SATHRI, 2008.

Boyd, R. H. S. *An Introduction to Indian Christian Theology*. Rev. ed. Madras: CLS, 1975.

Brown, Judith M. "Indian Christians and Nehru's Nation-State." In *India and the Indianness of Christianity: Essays on Understanding—Historical, Theological, and Bibliographical—in Honor of Robert Eric Frykenberg*, 217–34. Grand Rapids: Eerdmans, 2009.

Carr, Dhyanchand. *Sword of the Spirit: An Activist's Understanding of the Bible.* Risk book series. Geneva: WCC Publications, 1992.

Chandran, J. Russell. "Baptism—A Scandal or a Challenge?" *Religion and Society* 19, no. 1 (March 1972): 51–58.

______. "A Christian Approach to Other Religions." *Bangalore Theological Forum* 7, no. 2 (July–December 1975): 1–20.

______. "Christianity and World Religions: The Ecumenical Discussion." *The Indian Journal of Theology* 30, nos. 3–4 (July–December 1981): 186–203.

______. "Concern for Man in the Ecumenical Renewal." *Religion and Society* 15, no. 1 (March 1968): 32–38.

———. "Congregation is the Church." *National Council of Churches Review* 112, no. 3 (March 1992): 166–75.

______. "Directions of Christian Theology in India." In *For The Sake of the Gospel: Essays in Honour of Samuel Amirtham*, ed. Gnana Robinson, 16–28. Madurai: T.T.S. Publications, 1980.

______. "From an Institution-Based Mission to a People-Based Mission." *National Council of Churches Review* 111, no. 5 (May 1991): 1020–31.

______. "Mission in Today's Pluralistic Context." *National Council of Churches Review* 114, no. 5 (May–June 1994): 347–61.

______. "The Theological Task of the Church in India." *Union Seminary Quarterly Review* 20, no. 3 (March 1965): 247–59.

______. "Theologizing in the Context of the Marginalized and Oppressed." *Bangalore Theological Forum* 24, nos. 3–4 (September–December 1992): 3–15.

______. "Widening Frontiers of Christian Theology—Indian Context." In *Dalits and Women: Quest for Humanity*, ed. V. Devasahayam, 11–19. The Gurukul Summer Institute 1992. Madras: Gurukul Lutheran Theological College, 1992.

Chenchiah, Pandipeddi. *Rethinking Christianity in India.* Madras: A. N. Sudarisanam, 1938.

Chunakara, Mathews George. "A Survey of the Ecumenical Scenario in Asia: Prospects and Challenges." *CTC Bulletin* 22, no. 2 (August 2006): 61-80.

Clarke, Sathianathan. *Dalits and Christianity: Subaltern Religion and Liberation Theology in India*. New Delhi: Oxford University Press, 1999.

______, Deenabandhu Manchala, and Philip Vinod Peacock, eds. *Dalit Theology in the Twenty-First Century: Discordant Voices, Discerning Pathways*. New Delhi: Oxford University Press, 2011.

Daniel, Harry F. J. "Urban Industrial Mission in Asia." *International Review of Mission* 59, no. 234 (April 1970): 189–97.

Devanandan, P. D. *Christian Concern in Hinduism*. Bangalore: CISRS, 1961.

______. *The Concept of Maya: An Essay in Historical Survey of the Hindu Theory of the World with Special Reference to the Vedanta*. London: Lutterworth Press, 1950.

______. *The Gospel and Renascent Hinduism.* Bangalore: CISRS, 1959.

______. *I Will Lift Up Mine Eyes Unto the Hills: Sermons and Bible Studies of Paul D. Devanandan.* Ed. Stanley J. Samartha and Nalini Devanandan. Bangalore: CISRS, 1963.

______. *Our Task Today: Revision of Evangelistic Concern.* Bangalore: CISRS, 1959.

______. *Preparation for Dialogue: A Collection of Essays on Hinduism and Christianity in New India*. Ed. Nalini Devanandan and M. M. Thomas. Bangalore: CISRS, 1964.

______. *Resurgent Hinduism: Review of Modern Movements.* Bangalore: CISRS, 1958.

Devanesan, Chandran. *Rajaiah D. Paul: Layman Extraordinary.* Madras: CLS, 1982.

Devanesan, C. D. S. *The Making of the Mahatma.* Delhi: Orient Longman, 1969.

Devasahayam, V. *Frontiers of Dalit Theology*. Delhi: ISPCK, 1997.

______. *Outside the Camp: Biblical Studies in Dalit Perspective.* Madras: Gurukul Lutheran Theological College, 1994.

Diehl, Carl Gustav, and Ernest Theodore Bachmann. *Rajah Bushanam Manikam: A Biography.* Madras: CLS, 1975.

Duraisingh, Christopher. *Called to One Hope: Gospel in Diverse Cultures.* Geneva: WCC Publications, 1998.

______. "Encountering Difference in a Plural World." In *Waging Reconciliation: God's Mission in a Time of Globalization and Crisis*, ed. Ian T. Douglas, 174–75. New York: Episcopal Church, 2002.

______. "From Church-Shaped Mission to Mission-Shaped Church." *Anglican Theological Review* 92, no. 1 (Winter 2010): 7–28.

Fox, Frampton F. *Edinburgh 1910 Revisited: 'Give Us Friends!'—An India Perspective on 100 Years of Mission.* Papers from the 16th annual Centre for Mission Studies Consultation, Union Biblical Seminary, Pune. Bangalore: Center for Mission Studies/Asian Trading Corporation, 2010.

Frykenberg, Robert Eric. *Christianity in India: From Beginnings to the Present.* New York: Oxford University Press, 2008.

George, K. M. *The Silent Roots: Orthodox Perspectives on Christian Spirituality.* Geneva: WCC Publications, 1994.

Gnanadason, Aruna. "Nameless and Silenced No Longer, We Will Overcome Violence!" *In God's Image* 24, no. 1 (March 2005): 3–8.

______. "Women and Spirituality in Asia." In *Feminist Theology from the Third World: A Reader*, ed. Ursula King, 351–60. London: SPCK/Maryknoll, NY: Orbis, 1994.

Gregorios, Paulos Mar. *Cosmic Man. The Divine Presence: An Analysis of the Place and Role of the Human Race in the Cosmos, in Relation to God and the Historical World in the Thought of St. Gregory of Nyssa*. New Delhi/Kottayam: Sophia Publications, 1982.

______. "For a Nuclear Weapons Free World for the Survival of Humanity." Address given at the International Forum, Moscow, 14–16 February 1984. *The Journal of the Moscow Patriarchate*, no. 5 (1984): 52-53.

______. *The Freedom of Man*. Philadelphia: Westminster, 1972.

______. *The Human Presence: An Orthodox View of Nature*. Geneva: WCC Publications, 1978.

______. *Love's Freedom—The Grand Mystery: A Spiritual Autobiography.* Kottayam: MGF, 1997.

______. "May the Light Dawn." Address delivered at the Global Celebration of the Centenary Year of the Chicago Parliament of World Religions. *Khera* 13, no. 2 (July–December 1993): 136–31.

______. *On Ecumenism.* Ed. Fr. Dr Jacob Kurian. Kottayam: ISPCK & MGF, 2006.

______. "Science and Faith: Complementary or Contradictory?" Address delivered at WCC Conference on Faith, Science and the Future, Massachusetts Institute of Technology, Cambridge, USA, 12–24 July 1979. In *Faith and Science in an Unjust World*, ed. Roger L. Shinn, 46–58. Geneva: WCC Publications, 1980.

______. “The Scientific Temper Debate: Some Reflections and a Few Tentative Conclusions.” *Bulletin of the Indian Institute of World Culture* (May 1982): 26–35.

______. “Why the Churches Are Gathering at M.I.T.?” *One World*, no. 42 (May 1979).

______, William H. Lazareth, and Nikos A. Nissiotis, eds. *Does Chalcedon Divide or Unite?* Geneva: WCC Publications, 1981.

Harper, Susan Billington. “The Dornakal Church on the Cultural Frontier.” In *Christians, Cultural Interactions, and India's Religious Traditions*, ed. Judith Brown and R. E. Frykenberg, 183–211. Grand Rapids: Eerdmans/London: Routledge Curzon, 2002.

______. *In the Shadow of the Mahatma: Bishop V. S. Azariah and the Travails of Christianity in British India.* Grand Rapids: Eerdmans/London: Routledge Curzon, 2000.

Harris-Wilson, Susannah. “Sarah Chakko 1905–1954.” In *Ecumenical Pilgrims: Profiles of Pioneers in Christian Reconciliation*, ed. Ioan Bria and Dagmar Heller. Geneva: WCC Publications, 1995.

Hedlund, Roger E. “Theology of Mission in Historical Perspective: A Survey of Theological Trends as Traced in Major Conferences on Mission in the 20th Century in Relation to South Asia.” In *Missiology for the 21st Century: South Asian Perspectives*, ed. Roger E. Hedlund and Paul Joshua Bhakiaraj, 128-43. Delhi: ISPCK/Chennai: MIIS, 2004.

______, ed. *Christianity Is Indian: The Emergence of an Indigenous Community.* Rev. ed. New Delhi: ISPCK/Chennai: MIIS, 2004.

______, Jesudas M. Athyal, Joshua Kalapati, and Jessica Richard, eds. *The Oxford Encyclopaedia of South Asian Christianity.* 2 vols. New Delhi: Oxford University Press, 2012.

Itty, C. I. “Are We Yet Awake? The Development Debate within the Ecumenical Movement.” *Ecumenical Review* 26, no. 1 (January 1974): 6–20.

Jai Singh, Herbert, ed. *Interreligious Dialogue.* Bangalore: CISRS, 1967.

Jeyakumar, D. Arthur. "Church of South India." In *The Oxford Encyclopedia of South Asian Christianity*, vol. 1, ed. Jesudas M. Athyal, et al., 183-84. New Delhi: Oxford University Press, 2012.

Jeyasingh, J. M. "Indigenous Missionary Movements: A Critical Study." In *Christianity Is Indian: The Emergence of an Indigenous Community*, rev. ed., ed. Roger E. Hedlund, 208–220. New Delhi: ISPCK/Chennai: MIIS, 2004.

John, E. C., ed. *Lord, Let Me Share: Life and Writings of Canon Subir Biswas.* Tiruvalla: Ecumenical Christian Academy/NCCI/Christava Sahitya Samithy, 2012.

John, George M. *Youth Christian Council of Action 1938–1954: The Story of a Dynamic Movement of Christian Youth.* Bangalore: CISRS, 1972.

Kim, Sebastian C. H. "The Politics of Conversion During the British Raj: 'Mass Movements' in the 1930s and Their Impact on Indian Politics and the Church." *Dharma Deepika* (July–December 2013): 6–25.

Kinnamon, Michael. *The Ecumenical Movement: An Anthology of Key Texts and Voices.* Geneva: WCC Publications, 1997.

______. *The Vision of the Ecumenical Movement and How It Has Been Impoverished by Its Friends.* St. Louis: Chalice, 2003.

Koshy, Ninan. *Caste in the Kerala Churches.* Rev. ed. New Delhi: CISRS/ISPCK, 2014.

______. "Challenges to the Ecumenical Movement: Reflections in the Context of Globalization and the War on Terror." *Ecumenical Review* 56, no. 1 (January 2004): 40–49.

______. *Churches in the World of Nations: International Politics and the Mission and Ministry of the Church.* Geneva: WCC Publications, 1994.

______. "The Ecumenical Understanding on Religious Liberty: The Contribution of the World Council of Churches." *Journal of Church and State* 38 (Winter 1996): 137–54.

______. *A History of the Ecumenical Movement in Asia*, vol. 1. Hong Kong: WSCF AP/YMCA/CCA, 2004.

______. *Religious Freedom in a Changing World.* Geneva: WCC Publications, 1992.

______, ed. *A History of the Ecumenical Movement in Asia*, vol. 2. Hong Kong: WSCF AP/YMCA/CCA, 2004.

______, and Paul Abrecht, eds. *Before It's Too Late: The Challenge of Nuclear Disarmament.* Geneva: WCC Publications, 1983.

Kraemer, Hendrik. *The Christian Message in a Non-Christian World.* Grand Rapids: Kregel Publications, for the International Missionary Council, 1956 [1938].

Kuriakose, M. K., ed. *Orthodox Identity in India: Essays in Honour of V. C. Samuel.* Bangalore: V. C. Samuel 75th Birthday Celebration Committee, 1988.

Kurian, M. *A Quest for the Unknown: A Biography of Late Rev. Dr. M. A. Thomas, Founder Director of Ecumenical Christian Centre.* Delhi: ISPCK, 2002.

______. *Sarah Chakko: A Voice for Women in the Ecumenical Movement.* Tiruvalla: Christhava Sahitya Samithi, 1998.

Kurien, C. T. "Capitalism and Socialism: A Reconsideration." *Ecumenical Review* 43, no. 3 (July 1991): 308–317.

______. *Poverty and Development.* Madras: CLS, 1974.

Ledger, Christine. "Bishop Paulose Mar Paulose: Bishop, Activist, Brother, and Friend." *Praxis*, no. 2 (April–June 1998): 25.

Lundstrom, K. *Church Life and Theological Education in Tamil Nadu: Indian Christianity in a Hindutva State.* Uppsala: Swedish Institute of Missionary Research, 2003.

Mallampalli, Chandra. *Christians and Public Life in Colonial South India, 1863–1937: Contending Marginality.* London: Routledge Curzon, 2006.

Manchala, Deenbandhu. *Nurturing Peace: Theological Reflections on Overcoming Violence.* Risk book series. Geneva: WCC Publications, 2005.

Manikam, Rajah Bushanam. *Christianity and the Asian Revolution.* Madras: Joint East Asia Secretariat, IMC/Geneva: WCC Publications, 1954.

Mar Thoma, Juhanon. *Christianity in India and a Brief History of the Mar Thoma Church.* Rev. ed. Tiruvalla: CSS, 2011.

Massey, James. *Downtrodden: The Struggle of India's Dalits for Identity, Solidarity and Liberation.* Geneva: WCC Publications, 1997.

McPhee, Arthur G. *The Road to Delhi: J. Waskom Pickett and Missions in the Twilight of the Raj and Dawn of Nationhood.* Rev. ed. Lexington, KY: Emeth Press, 2012.

Moses, David G. "Christianity and the Non-Christian Religions," *International Review of Mission* 43 (1954): 146-54.

______. *Religious Truth and the Relation between Religions.* Madras: CLS, 1950.

Minz, Nirmal. *Mahatma Gandhi and Hindu–Christian Dialogue.* Madras: CLS, 1970.

Newbigin, Lesslie. *The Reunion of the Church: A Defense of the South India Scheme, and the Household of God.* London: SCM Press, 1953.

Nirmal, A. P., ed. *A Reader in Dalit Theology.* Madras: Gurukul Lutheran Theological College, 1991.

Oommen, George. "Challenging Identity and Crossing Borders: Unity in the Church of South India." *Word & World* 25, no. 1 (Winter 2005): 60–67.

______. "Something Different, Something Broader: Seventy-Five Years in the Life of the United Theological College." In George Oommen, *To Serve, Not to Be Served.* Bangalore: UTC, 1985.

Osthathios, Geevarghese Mar. *Sharing God and a Sharing World.* Delhi: ISPCK, 1995.

______. *Theology of a Classless Society.* Maryknoll, NY: Orbis, 1984.

______. *The Sin of Being Rich in a Poor Society.* Madras: CLS, 1983.

Pachuau, Lalsangkima, and Knud Jørgensen, eds. *Witnessing to Christ in a Pluralistic Age: Christian Mission among Other Faiths.* Oxford: Regnum Books International, 2011.

Parmar, Samuel L. *The Church in North India.* New Delhi: Christian Book Depot, 1969.

Paul, K. T. *The British Connection with India.* London: SCM Press, 1967.

Paul, Rajaiah D. *Ecumenism in Action: A Historical Survey of the Church of South India.* Madras: CLS, 1972.

Philip, T. V. *Ecumenism in Asia.* Delhi: ISPCK, 1994.

______. *Edinburgh to Salvador: Twentieth Century Ecumenical Missiology: A Historical Study of the Ecumenical Discussions on Mission.* Tiruvalla: CSS & ISPCK, 1999.

Pickett, J. Waskom. *Christian Mass Movements in India.* Lucknow: Lucknow Pub. House, 1933.

Poulose, Poulose Mar. *Church's Mission: Struggle for Justice and Involvement in Political Struggles.* Bombay: BUILD, 1978.

______. "Discipleship as Identification with the Sufferings and Presence in the Struggles of the People." In *People's Struggle Continues: Peoples Forum '91.* Hong Kong: Christian Conference of Asia, 1991.

______. *Encounter in Humanization.* Tiruvalla: CSS, 2003.

______. *Inter Church Dialogue*. Delhi: ISPCK/MGF, 2010.

______. *Spirituality for Struggle*. Tiruvalla: CSS, 1999.

Ram, Eric, ed. *Transforming Health: Christian Approaches to Healing and Wholeness*. Monrovia, CA: MARC Publications, 1995.

Ram, Augustine Ralla. "Evangelism in Changing India." *NMI* 42, no. 8 (October 1948): 89.

______. "Organic Church Unity: A Comment From India." *Ecumenical Review* 8 (1956): 243–48.

______, ed. *The Church of Christ in India: Essays on Indian Missions*. Allahabad: Student Christian Movement, 1937.

______, E. L. King, and Vere W. Abbey. *Putting Fresh Meaning into the Words Indian Christian.* Madras: Methodist Publishing House, 1929.

Rolston, M. A. Z. "A New Frontier For the Church in India." *International Review of Mission* 54, no. 214 (April 1965): 184–88.

______. "The Roles of National Councils in Relation to Missionary Agencies." *International Review of Mission* 58, no. 231 (July 1969): 270–77.

Sail, Rajendra K., and Ajit Muricken, eds. *Transcending Boundaries: Essays in Honour of George Ninan.* Raipur: RCDRC & VAK, 1995.

Samartha, Stanley J. *Between Two Cultures: Ecumenical Ministry in a Pluralist World.* Geneva: WCC Publications, 1996.

______. *Courage for Dialogue: Ecumenical Issues in Inter-Religious Relationships*. Geneva: WCC Publications, 1982.

______. "Dialogue as a Continuing Christian Concern." *Ecumenical Review* 23, no. 2 (April 1971): 129–42.

______. "Dialogue: Significant Issues in the Continuing Debate." *Ecumenical Review* 24, no. 3, (July 1972): 327–40.

______. "Guidelines on Dialogue." *Ecumenical Review* 31, no. 2 (April 1979): 155–62.

______. *The Hindu Response to the Unbound Christ.* Madras: CLS, 1974.

______. *The Hindu View of History: Classical and Modern.* Bangalore: CISRS, 1959.

______. "The Kingdom of God in a Religiously Plural World." Address delivered at the seventeenth session of the Synod of the Church of South India, 11 January 1980, Tambaram, Madras. *Ecumenical Review* 32, no. 2 (April 1980): 152–65.

______. *The Lordship of Christ and Religious Pluralism.* Madras: CLS, 1981.

______. "More than an Encounter of Commitments." *International Review of Mission* 59, no. 236 (October 1970): 392–403.

______. *One Christ—Many Religions: Toward a Revised Christology.* Maryknoll, NY: Orbis, 1991.

______. *The Other Side of the River: Some Reflections on the Theme of the Vancouver Assembly.* Madras: CLS, 1983.

______. "Partners in Community: Some Reflections on Hindu-Christian Relations Today." *Occasional Bulletin of Missionary Research* 4, no. 2 (April 1980): 78-82.

______. "The Quest for Salvation and the Dialogue between Religions." *International Review of Mission* 57, no. 228 (October 1968): 424–32.

______. "Reflections on a Multi-lateral Dialogue." *Ecumenical Review* 26, no. 4 (October 1974): 637–46.

______. "Religions in the Quest for World Peace," paper presented to the World Conference of Religious Workers for Peace, Disarmament and Just Relations among Nations, Moscow, 6-10 June 1977. Published in German: "Religionen auf der Suchenachdem, Weltffieden," Evangelische Monatsschrift, Heft 8 (August 1977): 205-207.

______. "The World Council of Churches and Men of Other Faiths and Ideologies," *Ecumenical Review* 22 (July 1970): 190–98.

______, ed. *Dialogue between Men of Living Faiths: Papers Presented at a Consultation Held at Ajaltoun, Lebanon, March, 1970*. Geneva: WCC Publications, 1971.

______, ed. *Faith in the Midst of Faith: Reflections on Dialogue in Community.* Geneva: WCC Publications, 1977.

______, ed. *Living Faiths and the Ecumenical Movement.* Geneva: WCC Publications, 1971.

______, ed. *Living Faith and Ultimate Goals: Salvation and World Religions.* Geneva: WCC Publications, 1974.

______, and Lynn A. de Silva, eds. *Man in Nature: Guest or Engineer? A Preliminary Enquiry by Christians and Buddhists into the Religious Dimensions in Humanity's Relation to Nature.* Colombo: EISD/Geneva: WCC Publications, 1979.

______, and J. B. Taylor, eds. *Christian–Muslim Dialogue: Papers Presented at the Broumana Consultation, 12–18 July 1972.* Geneva: WCC Publications, 1973.

Scovel, Myra. *I Must Speak: The Biography of Augustine Ralla Ram.* Allahabad: North India Christian Literature Society, 1961.

Sebastian, J. Jayakiran. "Baptism and the Unity of the Church in India Today." In *Baptism and the Unity of the Church*, ed. Michael Root and Risto Saarinen, 196–207. Grand Rapids: Eerdmans/Geneva: WCC Publications, 1998.

______. "Only Christ and No Formulation of Christ Can Determine the Frontier: Chandran's Challenges to Christian Mission." *National Council of Churches Review* 122, no. 5 (June 2002): 493–500.

Selvanayagam, Israel. *Samuel Amirtham's Living Theology.* Bangalore: BTESSC/SATHRI, 2007.

Shimray, Shimreingam, et. al (eds). *Tribal Theology: A Reader*. Jorhat: Tribal Study Centre, 2003.

Slater, Mary Louis. *Future Maker in India: The Story of Sarah Chakko*. New York: Friendship Press, 1958.

Srisang, Koson, Annie Kunzli, Maitet Diokno, and Clarence Dias, eds. *An Ecumenical Black Gem: Life and Work of C. I. Itty*. Bangkok: Friends of C. I. Itty, 1994.

Stanley, Brian. *The World Missionary Conference, Edinburgh 1910.* Grand Rapids: Eerdmans, 2009.

Swart, Ignatius. *The Churches and the Development Debate: Perspectives on a Fourth Generation Approach.* Stellenbosch: African Sun Media, 2006.

Thomas, T. Jacob, ed. *M. M. Thomas Reader: Selected Texts on Theology, Religion and Society*. Tiruvalla: CSS, 2002.

Thomas, M. C., ed. *Decoding Mission Beyond Edinburgh: Revisiting Mission and Ecumenism Today*. Tiruvalla: Commission on Ecumenical Relations of the Mar Thoma Syrian Church, 2011.

Thomas, M. M. "The Absoluteness of Jesus Christ and Christ-centred Syncretism." *Ecumenical Review* 37, no. 4 (1985): 387–97.

______. *The Acknowledged Christ of the Indian Renaissance.* 3rd ed. I. T. L. series no. 4. Madras: CLS, 1991.

______. "The Asian Churches and the Study of Rapid Social Change." *Ecumenical Review* 37, no. 1 (January 1985): 17–25.

______. "An Assessment of Tambaram's Contribution to the Search of the Asian Churches for an Authentic Selfhood." *International Review of Mission* 78 (1988): 390–97.

______. "The Christian Gospel of Redemption as the Formulation of a True Secular Humanism." *Student World*, 2nd quarter (1953): 135-40.

______. *The Christian Response to the Asian Revolution.* London: SCM Press, 1966.

______. *The Church's Mission and Post-Modern Humanism: Collection of Essays and Talks, 1992–1996*. Delhi: ISPCK, 1996.

______. *A Diaconal Approach to Indian Ecclesiology.* Rome: Centre for Indian and Inter-Religious Studies, 1995.

______. "The Gospel and the Quest for Modern Asia." *Union Seminary Quarterly* 22, no. 3 (March 1967): 230–31.

______. *Ideological Commitment within Christian Commitment.* Madras: CLS/ Bangalore: CISRS, 1983.

______. *Man and the Universe of Faiths*. Bangalore: CISRS, 1975.

______. *My Ecumenical Journey.* Trivandrum: Ecumenical Publishing Centre, 1990.

______. *Religion and the Revolt of the Oppressed.* Delhi: ISPCK, 1981.

______. *Response to Tyranny*. New Delhi: Forum for Christian Concern for People's Struggles, 1979.

______. *Risking Christ for Christ's Sake: Towards an Ecumenical Theology of Pluralism*. Geneva: WCC Publications, 1987.

______. *Salvation and Humanization: Some Crucial Issues in Contemporary India.* Bangalore: CISRS, 1971.

______. *The Secular Ideologies of India and Secular Meaning of Christianity*. Madras: CLS, 1976.

______. "Significance of the Ecumenical Study of the Humanum for the Church in India." *National Christian Council Review* 90, no. 11 (November 1970): 451-52.

______. *Some Theological Dialogues*. Bangalore: CISRS, 1977.

______. "A Spirituality for Combat." *The Princeton Seminary Bulletin* 5, no. 2 (1984): 144–47.

______. "Towards a Christian Social Philosophy." *Student Outlook* (February–March 1946).

______. *Towards a Theology of Contemporary Ecumenism*. Madras: CLS/ Geneva: WCC Publications, 1978.

______, Emilio Castro, and Willem Adolph Visser't Hooft. *Christian Action in the Asian Struggle*. Singapore: Christian Conference of Asia, 1973.

______, and P. D. Devanandan. *Christian Participation in Nation Building*. Bangalore: NCCI & CISRS, 1960.

______, and P. T. Thomas. *Towards an Indian Christian Theology: Life and Thought of Some Pioneers*. Tiruvalla: CSS, 1998.

Thomas, Pradip, ed. *An Ecumenical Wordsmith: The Writings of T. K. Thomas*. Tiruvalla: CSS, 2002.

Webster, John C. B. *The Dalit Christians: A History*. Delhi: ISPCK, 1994.

______. "Gandhi and the Christians: Dialogue in the Nationalist Era." In *Hindu Christian Dialogue: Perspectives and Encounters*, ed. Harold Coward, 80–99. Maryknoll, NY: Orbis, 1989.

Wietzke, Joachim, *Theologie im Modernen Indien: Paul David Devanandan*. Bern: Herbert Lang, 1975.

Wolters, Heilke T. *Theology of Prophetic Participation: M. M. Thomas's Concept of Salvation and the Collective Struggle for Fuller Humanity in India.* Delhi: ISPCK/UTC, 1996.

Young, Richard Fox, ed. *India and the Indianness of Christianity: Essays on Understanding—Historical, Theological, and Bibliographical—in Honor of Robert Eric Frykenberg.* Grand Rapids: Eerdmans, 2009.

Zachariah, George. *Alternatives Unincorporated: Earth Ethics from the Grassroots.* London: Equinox, 2011.

Zachariah, Mathai. *The Christian Presence in India: Editorials in the N.C.C. Review.* Madras: CLS, 1981.

______. *The Church: A People's Movement.* Nagpur: NCCI, 1975.

______. *The Indian Church: Identity and Fulfilment.* Madras: CLS, 1971.

NOTES

Introduction

1. Brian Stanley, *The World Missionary Conference, Edinburgh 1910* (Grand Rapids: Eerdmans, 2009), 129.

2. For a comprehensive discussion of the Asian ecumenical movement, see Ninan Koshy, *A History of the Ecumenical Movement in Asia*, 2 vols. (Hong Kong: WSCF AP/YMCA/CCA, 2004) (note: Koshy authored the first volume, and served as editor of the second).

3. The work of the World Student Christian Fellowship (WSCF)/SCM during this period broadly overlapped with that of the churches and therefore is considered in this discussion.

Chapter 1: The Indian Ecumenical Symphony

1. Ninan Koshy, *A History of the Ecumenical Movement in Asia*, vol. 1 (Hong Kong: WSCF AP/YMCA/CCA, 2004), 90.

2. See ch. 1 in this volume on V. S. Azariah.

3. George Oommen, "Challenging Identity and Crossing Borders: Unity in the Church of South India." *Word & World* 25, no. 1 (2005): 60–67.

4. D. Arthur Jeyakumar, "Church of South India" in Roger E. Hedlund, et al., eds., *The Oxford Encyclopaedia of South Asian Christianity*, vol. 1 (New Delhi: Oxford University Press, 2012), 184.

5. Koshy, *History of the Ecumenical Movement*, 91.

6. For a systematic study of the ecclesiology behind the Church of South India, see Lesslie Newbigin's *The Reunion of the Church: A Defense of the South India Scheme, and The Household of God* (London: SCM Press, 1953). For a

detailed discussion on united churches see G. B. Firth, *An Introduction to Indian Christian History* (Madras: CLS, 1961); Michael Kinnamon, ed., *Unity: In Each Place . . . In All Places: United Churches and the Christian World Communions* (Geneva: WCC Publications, 1983); T. V. Philip, *Ecumenism in Asia* (Delhi: ISPCK, 1994); and M. M. Thomas and P. T. Thomas, *Towards an Indian Christian Theology: Life and Thought of Some Pioneers* (Tiruvalla: CSS, 1998).

7. David G. Moses participated also in the Whitby (1947) and Willingen (1952) conferences of the International Missionary Council (IMC) and served as a vice chairman of IMC. He is considered as one of the architects of the integration of IMC with WCC and, in recognition of his services, was elected at the New Delhi Assembly as a WCC president. He had also served as a president of NCCI. His writings include "Christianity and the Non-Christian Religions," *International Review of Mission* 45 (1954): 146–54; *Religious Truth and the Relation between Religions* (Madras: CLS, 1950); and, "The Problem of Truth in Religion," in *Authority of Faith*, Madras series, vol. 1 (London: IMC, 1939). See also Jesudas M. Athyal, "Moses, David G.," in Roger E. Hedlund, et al., eds. *The Oxford Encyclopedia of South Asian Christianity*, vol. 2 (New Delhi: Oxford University Press, 2012), 460–61.

8. Koshy, *History of the Ecumenical Movement*, 1:102.

9. Juhanon Mar Thoma was the Metropolitan of the Mar Thoma Church from 1947 to 1976, and played an important role in ushering the Indian church to the ecumenical movement. He frequently commented on social and political developments in his home state of Kerala and in India. At the Evanston assembly (1954), he was elected as a WCC president. His books include *Christianity in India and a Brief History of the Mar Thoma Church*, rev. ed. (Tiruvalla: CSS, 2011); and *Basic Christian Beliefs* (Tiruvalla: CSS, 2008).

10. Mar Thoma, *Christianity in India*, 73–74.

11. "The Communion of Churches in India," http://communionofchurchesinindia.org/index.php/component/content/?view=featured.

12. For a discussion on the contributions of J. Russell Chandran for church unity—particularly in the Church of South India, the Joint Council of the Church of South India, the Church of North India, and the Mar Thoma Church (the Communion of Churches in India) and the Church of South India and Lutheran dialogues—see ch. 9 on Chandran in this volume.

13. Michael Kinnamon, "United and Uniting Churches," in Nicholas Lossky, et al., eds., *Dictionary of the Ecumenical Movement* (Geneva: WCC, 1991), 1033.

14. M. M. Thomas, *The Nagas Towards A.D. 2000* (Madras: CReNIEO, 1992), 136.

15. T. V. Philip, *Edinburgh to Salvador: Twentieth Century Ecumenical Missiology: A Historical Study of the Ecumenical Discussions on Mission* (Tiruvalla: CSS & ISPCK, 1999), 6.

16. K. Baago, *National Christian Council of India: 1914–1964* (Nagpur: NCCI, 1965), 28.

17. Ibid., 37. Until 1936, P. O. Philip, an Indian Christian layman, was the only Indian staffperson in the NCCI.

18. John C. B. Webster, "Gandhi and the Christians: Dialogue in the Nationalist Era," in Harold Coward, ed., *Hindu–Christian Dialogue: Perspectives and Encounters* (Maryknoll, NY: Orbis, 1989), 83.

19. Ibid., 87.

20. Mathews George Chunakara is the director of the WCC Commission of the Churches on International Affairs (CCIA). He had earlier served as the Asia Secretary of WCC and as the executive secretary of the Christian Conference of Asia (CCA), in charge of International Affairs. He is a member of the Mar Thoma Church.

21. Mathews George Chunakara, "A Survey of the Ecumenical Scenario in Asia: Prospects and Challenges," *CTC Bulletin* 22, no. 2 (August 2006): 64.

22. M. M. Thomas, "An Assessment of Tambaram's Contribution to the Search of the Asian Churches for an Authentic Selfhood," in *International Review of Mission* 78 (1988): 393.

23. Philip, *Edinburgh to Salvador*, 39.

24. M. M. Thomas and P. T. Thomas, *Towards an Indian Christian Theology* (Tiruvalla: The New Day Publications of India, 1992), 125.

25. Thomas, "An Assessment of Tambaram's Contribution," 393.

26. Philip, *Edinburgh to Salvador*, 39.

27. Baago, *National Christian Council of India*, 61.

28. Rajah B. Manikam was the first Indian Lutheran bishop of the Tamil Evangelical Lutheran Church and the first Joint East Asia Secretary of the World Council of Churches and the International Missionary Council. In his capacity as the executive secretary of the Christian Council of India and Pakistan, Manikam served on the presidium of the East Asian Christian Conference (Bangkok, 1940), which has been described as the first conference of its kind to be held in East Asia. See Carl Gustav Diehl and Ernest Theodore Bachmann, *Rajah Bushanam Manikam: A Biography* (Madras: CLS, 1975);

and Jacob G. J. Sundersingh, "Manikam, Rajah B.," in, *Oxford Encyclopedia of South Asian Christianity*, 2:423. See also Manikam's writings, *Christianity and the Asian Revolution*, International Missionary Council (Madras: Joint East Asia Secretariat, IMC/Geneva: WCC Publications, 1954); and *The Christian Family in Changing East Asia* (Manila: Philippine Federation of Christian Church, 1954).

29. Baago, *National Christian Council of India*, 62.

30. Philip, *Edinburgh to Salvador*, 20.

31. In particular, see ch. 8 on Stanley J. Samartha and ch. 5 on P. D. Devanandan, below.

32. According to M. M. Thomas, K. T. Paul was the first Christian statesman of India who produced a theology of the church and the church's mission in the context of the developing nationalism of a religiously pluralistic society. See Thomas and Thomas, *Towards an Indian Christian Theology*, 113. See also Paul's writings: *Papers on India*, nos. 2, 3, and 5 (London: SCM Press, 1921); and *The British Connection with India* (London: SCM Press, 1967).

33. Thomas and Thomas, *Towards an Indian Christian Theology* (1992), 115.

34. See Hendrik Kraemer, *The Christian Message in a Non-Christian World* (Grand Rapids: Kregel Publishers, for the International Missionary Council, 1956).

35. Thomas, "An Assessment of Tambaram's Contribution," 395.

36. Thomas and Thomas, *Towards an Indian Christian Theology* (1992), 193.

37. See D. M. Devasahayam and A. N. Sudarisanam, eds., *Rethinking Christianity in India* (Madras: A. N. Sudarisanam, 1938). See also H. L. Richard, "Rethinking 'Rethinking,'" *International Journal of Theology* 45, nos. 1 & 2 (2003): 88–104, http://www.biblicalstudies.org.uk/pdf/ijt/45_088.pdf.

38. Frans Wijsen and Robert J. Schreiter, *Global Christianity: Contested Claims* (Amsterdam: Rodopi, 2007), 79.

39. Prasanna Kumari, ed., *Liberating Witness* (Gurukul: Madras, 1995), 12.

40. As a consummate editor and lay theologian, T. K. Thomas, during a long ecumenical career, served the Christian Institute for the Study of Religion and Society (CISRS), YMCA of India, Christian Conference of Asia (CCA), the World Association for Christian Communication (WACC), and WCC, as editor and publisher. See Pradip Thomas, ed., *An Ecumenical Wordsmith: The Writings of T. K. Thomas* (Tiruvalla: CSS, 2002).

41. The author's email correspondence with Pradip Thomas, 23 August 2014.

42. Chandran Devanesan was the first Indian principal of Madras Christian College, and also served as the vice chancellor of the North-Eastern Hill University. See S. V. Appasamy, "Dr. Chandran Devanesan," in R. E. Frykenberg and Chris Barrigar, eds., *Tirunelveli Evangelical Christians* (Bangalore: SAIACS, 2003); and C. D. S. Devanesan, *The Making of the Mahatma* (Delhi: Orient Longman, 1969).

43. Global Ministries, "Toward More Mutual Relationships in the Global Church," in *Missionary Herald* (January 1965), http://globalministries.org/resources/mission-study/college-of-mission/toward-more-mutual.html.

44. Ibid.

45. The story of the Indian presence in the ecumenical movement would be incomplete without reference to the work of missionaries such as Lesslie Newbigin (who was consecrated a bishop at the time when the Church of South India came into being), Stephen Neill (another Anglican bishop in India who also documented the history of the ecumenical movement), R. R. Keithan (a Gandhian who lived and died in India. He had also mentored several Indian Christian leaders), and scores of others. The contribution of the overseas missionaries in the building of the ecumenical movement was significant, but this volume will not go into a detailed discussion of that.

46. See, in this volume, ch. 5 on Devanandan, and ch. 6 on Thomas.

47. Founded in 1930, the Henry Martin Institute has a long record of teaching and research, with a wide circle of research scholars from both within the country and abroad who use the institute's facilities for master's, doctoral, and postdoctoral research.

48. M. M. Thomas, *My Ecumenical Journey* (Trivandrum: Ecumenical Publishing Centre, 1990), 366.

49. The institute's name was changed, after 1984, to the Christian Institute of Religious Studies.

50. See V. Devasahayam, *Frontiers of Dalit Theology* (Delhi: ISPCK, 1997); A. P. Nirmal, ed., *A Reader in Dalit Theology* (Madras: Gurukul Lutheran Theological College, 1991); and John C. B. Webster. *The Dalit Christians: A History* (Delhi: ISPCK, 1994).

51. See A. M. Abraham Ayrookuzhiel, *The Sacred in Popular Hinduism* (Madras: CLS, 1983).

52. See Shimray, Shimreingam, et. al (eds). *Tribal Theology: A Reader* (Jorhat: Tribal Study Centre, 2003). Also see K. Thanzauva, "Tribal/Indigenous Interpretation of the Bible: A Keynote Address" in Yangkahao Yashum, ed., *Tribal Theology and the Bible: A Search for Contextual Relevance* (Rajabai, Jorhat: Tribal Study Centre/Eastern Theological College, 2011), 13-25.

53. Samuel Amirtham was the first principal of the Tamilnadu Theological Seminary Madurai, director of the Programme on Theological Education of the WCC, and bishop of the South Kerala Diocese of the Church of South India. See Samuel Amirtham, *Theology by the People* (Geneva: WCC Publications, 1986); and Amirtham and S. Wesley Ariarajah, *Ministerial Formation in a Multifaith Milieu: Implications of Interfaith Dialogue for Theological Education* (Geneva: WCC Publications, 1986).

54. Israel Selvanayagam, *Samuel Amirtham's Living Theology* (Bangalore: BTESSC/SATHRI, 2007), 780.

55. Mathai Zachariah served as a regional secretary of SCMI and as a youth secretary and study secretary of NCCI. In the 1980s he was the general secretary of NCCI. See Aruna Gnanadason, Mathai Zachariah, M. A. Thomas, M. M. Thomas, and Eugene Loudon Stockwell, *Ecumenism, Hope in Action: Essays in Honour of Dr. Mathai Zachariah* (Nagpur: NCCI, 1990). See also Mathai Zachariah's writings, *Beyond Ecumenism: A Journey into Light* (Tiruvalla: CSS, 2002); *Inside the Indian Church* (Delhi: ISPCK, 1994); *The Christian Presence in India: Editorials in the N.C.C. Review* (Madras: CLS, 1981); *The Church: A People's Movement* (Nagpur: NCCI, 1975); and *The Indian Church: Identity and Fulfilment* (Madras: CLS, 1971).

56. "Tribute of WCC General Secretary Olav Fykse Tveit at the demise of Mathai Zachariah," 19 December 2012, http://www.oikoumene.org/en/resources/documents/general-secretary/tributes/mathai-zachariah.

57. According to Michael Kinnamon, "no ecumenical leader has articulated the integration of unity and justice more eloquently or persistently than M. M. Thomas" (Kinnamon, *Can A Renewal Movement Be Renewed? Questions for the Future of Ecumenism* [Grand Rapids: Eerdmans, 2014], 62).

58. Ignatius Swart, *The Churches and the Development Debate: Perspectives on a Fourth Generation Approach* (Stellenbosch: African Sun Media, 2006), 40.

59. Prof. Parmar was, by training, an economist and had served as professor of economics at the University of Allahabad. He was one of the staunch leaders of SCMI and had served as a vice chairperson and a member of the executive committee of WSCF. He was also closely associated with the work of

NCCI and CISRS. For a time he served on the faculty of the Bossey Ecumenical Institute and was involved in the life of the WCC. See Samuel L. Parmar, *The Church in North India* (New Delhi: Christian Book Depot, 1969).

60. Koshy, *History of the Ecumenical Movement*, 1:173.

61. Paul Abrecht, "Society," in Lossky, et al., eds., *Dictionary of the Ecumenical Movement*, 936.

62. Mark T. B. Laing, *From Crisis to Creation: Lesslie Newbigin and the Reinvention of Christian Mission* (Eugene, OR: Pickwick, 2012), 214.

63. According to M. M. Thomas, it was because of Parmar's work that the order of priorities of economic development in the WCC changed from economic growth, self-reliance, and social justice to social justice, self-reliance, and economic growth (Thomas, *My Ecumenical Journey*, 359).

64. See P. D. Devanandan and M. M. Thomas, *Christian Participation in Nation Building* (Bangalore: NCCI & CISRS, 1960).

65. Abraham Vazhayil Thomas, *Christians in Secular India* (Cranbury, NJ: Associated University Presses, 1974); and M. M. Thomas and Harry F. J. Daniel, eds., *Human Problems of Industry in Bangalore* (Bangalore: CISRS & St. Mark's Cathedral Industrial Team Service, 1964), are two books that discuss this work.

66. Harry Daniel's work was recognized globally when, in 1968, he became the first secretary of the East Asia Christian Conference/Urban Industrial Mission (EACC/UIM). During 1968–70, he served as the fulltime staffperson in charge of UIM and laid the foundation of urban and rural mission in the various Asian countries. In 1970, Daniel joined the staff of the WCC, but in the midst of many changes in the Christian Conference of Asia (CCA), he was called back from Geneva to become an associate general secretary of CCA, a position he held with distinction during 1973–79.

67. See Harry F. J. Daniel, "Urban Industrial Mission in Asia," *International Review of Mission* 59, no. 234 (April 1970): 189–97.

68. Meredith Lake, "Western Heritage, Asian Destiny: The Australian Council of Churches' Activity in Asia, 1950–1965," *Eras Journal*, 4, ftp://ftp.uic.edu/pub/library/scua/ERAS/2005.07.03.ERAS.pdf.

69. George Ninan was the executive secretary of Urban Rural Mission (URM/CCA) and the associate general secretary of CCA. In India, he had served as the bishop of the Church of North India (Nasik Diocese) and secretary of the Communion of Churches in India (CCI). See Rajendra K. Sail and

Ajit Muricken, eds., *Transcending Boundaries: Essays in Honour of George Ninan* (Raipur: RCDRC & VAK, 1995).

70. "Voices of Hope: Call to Action and Incarnation," The Anglican Church of Canada, file:///C:/Users/je/Downloads/voh_feb21story_pg43_.pdf. See also E. C. John, ed., *Lord, Let Me Share: Life and Writings of Canon Subir Biswas* (Tiruvalla: Ecumenical Christian Academy/National Council of Churches in India/Christava Sahitya Samithy, 2012).

71. M. A. Z. Rolston was one of the early leaders of Urban–Rural Mission in India. He had also served as a general secretary of NCCI and as a bishop of the Church of North India. See his writings, "A New Frontier For the Church in India," *International Review of Mission* 54, no. 214 (April 1965): 184–88; and "The Roles of National Councils in Relation to Missionary Agencies," *International Review of Mission* 58, no. 231 (July 1969): 270–77.

72. Rolston, "A New Frontier," 184. Also see Rolston, *Christian Concern in Urban Industrial Situation* (Christian Industrial Service); and idem, *Violence and Peace* (Nagpur: ISPCK, 1987).

73. Indian economist C. T. Kurien served as the director (and later, the chairman) of the Madras Institute of Development Studies, and as a professor at the Madras Christian College. He is a past president of the Indian Economic Association. Several of his books, notably, *Poverty and Development* (Madras: CLS, 1974), and *Wealth and Illfare: An Expedition into Real Life Economics* (Bangalore: Books for Change, 2012), question the value of an economic system based on the pure pursuit of profit. At the request of the WCC Central Committee, Kurien served as a member of the group that prepared a statement on economic life.

74. C. T. Kurien, "Capitalism and Socialism: A Reconsideration," *Ecumenical Review* 43, no. 3 (July 1991): 308.

75. C. I. Itty was a director (during 1970–1979) of the Commission on the Churches' Participation in Development (CCPD) of the World Council of Churches. In the WCC, he had also served the Youth and Laity Departments. In the 1950s he had worked in the SCM in India and Indonesia. "An ecumenical pioneer, C. I. Itty's vision of full humanity came from his school days in an Indian village in the state of Kerala, India. He pursued that vision through the Student Christian Movement, the YMCA's, the World Council of Churches and the United Nations" (from Koson Srisang, ed., in collaboration with Annie Kunzli, Maitet Diokno, and Clarence Dias, *An Ecumenical Black Gem: Life and Work of C. I. Itty* [Bangkok: Friends of C. I. Itty, 1994]). Also

see C. I. Itty's writings: "Are We Yet Awake? The Development Debate within the Ecumenical Movement," *The Ecumenical Review* 26, no. 1 (January 1974): 6–20; and "The Church and the Poor in Asian History," in Julio de Santa Ana, ed., *Separation Without Hope? Essays on the Relation Between the Church and the Poor During the Industrial Revolution and the Western Colonial Expansion* (Maryknoll, NY: Orbis, 1980).

76. According to Ninan Koshy (who was a close friend and colleague of C. I. Itty), "the inspiration and guidance that C. I. gave to a large number of persons engaged in justice-oriented action inside and outside the churches will be always remembered" (*CCA News*, March 2005, 32, http://cca.org.hk/home/wp-content/uploads/2013/07/05-03.pdf).

77. During the years 1980 to 1996, Samuel Isaac "served at the World Council of Churches in Geneva, mobilizing a workforce for change and progress within the one ecumenical movement, sharing resources among church-related agencies of caring both large and small. Perhaps his greatest impact came as deputy director of CICARWS, the commission on inter-church aid, refugee and world service. His critical thinking and managerial skills were crucial as the churches worked together in proclaiming the Good News while alleviating poverty, violence and suffering" (Condolence Message of Olav Fykse Tveit, WCC General Secretary on 21 August 2014, http://www.oikoumene.org/en/resources/documents/general-secretary/tributes/condolence-on-death-of-samuel-isaac/). In Asia, Sam Isaac had served as the secretary for Inter-Church Aid & Development in CCA and as the director of the Asian Christian Service (ACS) in Laos.

78. "Mr. Samuel M. Isaac former CCA Executive passes away," NCCI News, 22 August 2014, http://nccinet.blogspot.com/2014/08/mr-samuel-m-isaac-former-cca-executive.html?utm_source=feedburner&utm_medium=email&utm_campaign=Feed%3A+nccinet+%28NCCI+NEWS%29.

79. See M. M. Thomas, "A Spirituality for Combat," *The Princeton Seminary Bulletin* (1984): 144.

80. Hielke T. Wolters, *Theology of Prophetic Participation: M. M. Thomas's Concept of Salvation and the Collective Struggle for Fuller Humanity in India* (Delhi: ISPCK/UTC, 1996), 129.

81. K. C. Abraham is a leading Indian ecumenical theologian who served as the president of the Ecumenical Association of Third World Theologians (EATWOT) and the director of the South Asia Theological Research Institute (SATHRI), Bangalore. He is a presbyter of the Church of South India.

Some of his major writings include: *A Purposeful Education for All* (Bangalore: SCM, 1991); *Break Every Yoke* (Bangalore: ECC, 1983); "Globalization: A Gospel Culture Perspective," *International Review of Mission* 85, no. 336 (January 1996): 85–92; "Globalisation and Liberative Solidarity," in Dale Irvin and Akintunde Akinade, eds., *The Agitated Mind of God: The Theology of Kosuke Koyama* (Maryknoll, NY: Orbis, 1996); "Homosexuality: Some Reflections from India," *Ecumenical Review* 50 (January 1998): 22–29; and "Third World Theology: Paradigm Shift and Emerging Concerns," in M. P. Joseph, ed., *Confronting Life: Theology Out of the Context* (Delhi: ISPCK, 1995).

82. Foreword to K. C. Abraham's book, *Liberative Solidarity: Contemporary Perspectives on Mission* (Tiruvalla: CSS, 1996).

83. Christopher Duraisingh is a professor of theology at the Episcopal Divinity School, Cambridge, Massachusetts, USA. He had served as the general secretary of the Council for World Mission, the director of the Commission on World Mission and Evangelism, and the executive secretary for Gospel and Cultures of WCC. He is a presbyter of the Church of South India.

84. See the many writings of Christopher Duraisingh in this area, particularly *Called to One Hope: Gospel in Diverse Cultures* (Geneva: WCC Publications, 1998); "Encountering Difference in a Plural World," in Ian T. Douglas, ed., *Waging Reconciliation: God's Mission in a Time of Globalization and Crisis* (New York: Episcopal Church, 2002); and, "From Church-Shaped Mission to Mission-Shaped Church," *Anglican Theological Review* 92, no. 1 (Winter 2010): 7–28.

85. Eric Ram worked within the WCC's Christian Medical Commission (CMC) from 1977 to 1988, and steered the medical and health programmes of member churches worldwide. He also directed a six-continent study on the Christian understanding of health, healing, and wholeness. As the director of CMC, Ram was a consultant and advisor to both the World Health Organization and UNICEF. He was a member of the Church of North India.

86. "Dr. Eric R. Ram (1935–2006)," World Council of Churches, http://www.oikoumene.org/en/press-centre/news/dr-eric-r-ram-1935-2006.

87. See also Eric Ram, ed., *Transforming Health: Christian Approaches to Healing and Wholeness* (Monrovia, CA: MARC Publications, 1995).

88. Konrad Raiser, "Ecumenical Discussion of Ecclesiology and Ethics," *Ecumenical Review* 48, no. I (January 1996): 7.

89. Thomas., *My Ecumenical Journey*, 432.

90. M. A. Thomas was an ecumenical leader and a visionary who founded the Ecumenical Christian Centre (ECC) in Whitefield (Bangalore) with the vision of promoting "the unity of humankind as an expression of radical obedience to Christ" (http://www.eccbangalore.org/p/blog-page.html). He also launched a new, national-level human rights organization, the Vigil India Movement. Thomas was a priest of the Mar Thoma Church. See M. A. Kurien, *A Quest for the Unknown: A Biography of Late Rev. Dr. M. A. Thomas, Founder Director of Ecumenical Christian Centre* (Delhi: ISPCK, 2002).

91. WCC General Secretary Philip Potter wrote a letter to Prime Minister Indira Gandhi on 9 October 1975 that expressed the anguish of the ecumenical community at the emergency regime in India, under which freedom of expression and other democratic rights had been suspended.

92. In a statement, Metropolitan Paulos Mar Gregorios criticized the WCC general secretary's letter to Prime Minister Gandhi and wondered if "the World Council of Churches is also being used, perhaps unwillingly, to support the cause of the external elements which want either a situation of total chaos as prelude to revolution or a swing to the right which will make more secure the interests of the privileged and undemocratic minority in India." (Metropolitan Paulos Gregorios, Secretary for External Church Relations, The Orthodox Syrian Church of the East, "The National Emergency: A Preliminary Personal Evaluation from India," http://paulosmargregorios.in/English%20Articles/emergency.htm.

93. While several Indian ecclesiastical leaders supported the emergency, Metropolitan Juhanon Mar Thoma wrote a letter to Prime Minister Gandhi "advising her to withdraw the emergency in stages, to release political detainees and not to hold elections or make constitutional changes during the emergency" (M. M. Thomas, *Response to Tyranny* [New Delhi: Forum for Christian Concern for People's Struggles. 1979], 65). Another Indian leader, M. J. Joseph, resigned his job as the development secretary of NCCI and began organizing faith-based groups against the emergency regime. The Political Detainees Family Distress Relief Fund during that period also was an ecumenical response to the situation.

94. M. M. Thomas, *The Church's Mission and Post-Modern Humanism: Collection of Essays and Talks, 1992–96* (Delhi: ISPCK, 1996). Thomas further argued that while the term *koinonia* is commonly used within Christian settings, it is possible to use it outside the church context. He pointed out that the ecumenical statements also affirm that "it is possible in the light of Jesus

Christ to look at forms of caring *koinonia* outside the church as movements of the Holy Spirit gathering people to serve God in ways they may not fully understand. In humility the church may seek to point to what the Spirit is doing outside its visible boundaries, as well as within, thus witnessing to the wider work of God in the world of creation" (Thomas F. Best and Wesley Granberg-Michaelson, eds., *Koinonia and Justice, Peace and Creation: Costly Unity* [Geneva: WCC, 1993], 98), quoted in M. M. Thomas. *A Diaconal Approach to Indian Ecclesiology* (Rome: Centre for Indian and Inter-religious Studies, 1995), 14.

95. See Christie R. House, "The World Missionary Conference at Edinburgh, 1910," *New World Outlook* (January-February 2010), http://gbgm-umc.org/global_news/full_article.cfm?articleid=5620.

96. For a detailed discussion on the coordinated work between the Programme to Combat Racism (PCR) and the Churches' Commission on International Affairs (CCIA) in the WCC, see ch. 11 in this volume on Ninan Koshy.

97. Masilamani Azariah served the Church of South India as the general secretary (1982–1990) and the bishop of Madras (1990–1999). He was described as the "Dalit voice" in the nation, the church, and the ecumenical movement. He had also taught at the Gurukul Lutheran Theological College, Chennai.

98. Although Masilamani Azariah's request was not immediately acted upon, this unexpected intervention at the plenary made enough impact to cause further informal conversations in WCC circles. Later, Azariah was appointed as a consultant to the Commission of the WCC Programme to Combat Racism and, in that capacity, he hosted a meeting of the Commission in Madras in November 1989.

99. Based on Adrian Bird's discussion with Masilamani Azariah, from email correspondence with Bird on 29 June 2014.

100. Kunchala Rajaratnam was an economist, social scientist, and theologian who served as the president of NCCI, master of the Council of Serampore College (University), Asia secretary of the Lutheran World Federation, and director of the Gurukul Lutheran Theological College, Chennai. See his writings: *Development and Environmental Economics: The Relevance of Gandhi* (Chennai: CReNIEO, 1993); *Structural Crises of National and Global Economics: Relevance of Received Economic Theory Questioned* (Chennai: CReNIEO, 1981); also see Prasanna Kumari, ed., *Adventurous Faith, Bold Theological*

Vision & Commitment to Service: Dr. Kunchala Rajaratnam as Testified by Others (Chennai: UELCI, 2000).

101. V. Devasahayam, *Doing Dalit Theology in Biblical Key* (Chennai: ISPCK/Gurukul, 1997), 55. See also idem, *Outside the Camp: Biblical Studies in Dalit Perspective* (Madras: CLS, 1994).

102. James Massey, *Dalit Bible Commentary on the Gospel According to Luke* (New Delhi: Centre for Dalit/Subaltern Studies, 2007), 6. See also Monodeep Daniel, *Dalit Bible Commentary on the Gospel According to Matthew* (New Delhi: Centre for Dalit/Subaltern Studies, 2008).

103. Deenabandhu Manchala was on the staff of WCC from 2000 to 2014. From 2000 to 2005 he coordinated the WCC's Decade to Overcome Violence programme. Most recently he has served as the WCC's co-coordinator of the Just and Inclusive Communities programme. In that capacity he has overseen the theological and mission work done through five networks of marginalized people that challenge discrimination and exclusion in various regions of the world. He is a minister of the Andhra Evangelical Lutheran Church (India). In 2014, he became the Southern Asia Area Executive of the United Church of Christ. See Sathianathan Clarke, Deenabandhu Manchala, and Philip Vinod Peacock, eds., *Dalit Theology in the Twenty-First Century: Discordant Voices, Discerning Pathways* (New Delhi: Oxford University Press, 2011); and Deenbandhu Manchala, *Nurturing Peace: Theological Reflections on Overcoming Violence*, Risk book series (Geneva: WCC Publications, 2005).

104. Deenabandhu Manchala, "Expanding the Ambit: Dalit Theological Contribution to Ecumenical Social Thought," in Clarke, Manchala, and Peacock, eds., *Dalit Theology in the Twenty-First Century*, 41.

105. Quoted by Mani Chacko in his "Decoding Edinburgh—1910: Subaltern Perspective," in M. C. Thomas, ed., *Decoding Mission Beyond Edinburgh: Revisiting Mission and Ecumenism Today* (Tiruvalla: Commission on Ecumenical Relations of the Mar Thoma Syrian Church, 2011), 90.

106. Nirmal Minz is a pioneering theologian of the Adivasi (indigenous people) concerns in India. He is a bishop of the North Western Gossner Evangelical Lutheran Church and a social activist. In the 1960s, he helped produce the volume edited by M. M. Thomas and R. W. Taylor, *Tribal Awakening* (Bangalore: CISRS, 1965), one of the first publications on the theology and sociology of the indigenous people. Minz is deeply involved in the movement of the Adivasis of Jharkhand for freedom and self-rule and he theologizes in the midst of the hope and struggles there. See Minz, *Mahatma Gandhi and*

Hindu–Christian Dialogue (Madras: CLS, 1970); idem, "Survival of Adivasis in India," in Joseph Marianus Kujur and Sonajharia Minz, eds., *Pearls of Indigenous Wisdom* (New Delhi: Indian Social Institute, 2007), 85; and Jhakmak Neeraj Ekka, "Struggle for Truth and Justice: Nirmal Minz of Northern India," *Word & World* 28, no. 4 (Fall 2008): 405–412.

107. Thomas, *My Ecumenical Journey*, 226.

108. Nirmal Minz, "Mission & Evangelism in Jharkhand Context," in Jesudas M. Athyal, ed., *Mission Today: Subaltern Perspectives* (Tiruvalla: CSS, 2001), 54.

109. "Orthodox contribution to the WCC," public lecture by Rev. Dr Konrad Raiser at an international symposium on "Orthodox theology and the future of ecumenical dialogue: perspectives and problems," 3 June 2003, at Thessaloniki, Greece, at https://www.oikoumene.org/en/resources/documents/wcc-programmes/ecumenical-movement-in-the-21st-century/member-churches/special-commission-on-participation-of-orthodox-churches/orthodox-contribution-to-the-wcc.

110. See ch. 7 in this volume on Paulos Mar Greogorios.

111. Metropolitan Geevarghese Mar Osthathios was also one of the clearest voices of the Indian church on social justice. He grounded his passion for justice, equality, sharing, and love on the Christian doctrine of Holy Trinity. The Metropolitan was a member of the WCC Faith and Order Commission and a faculty member of the Orthodox Seminary in Kottayam, Kerala. His writings include: *Sharing God and a Sharing World* (Delhi: ISPCK, 1995); *Theology of a Classless Society* (Maryknoll, NY: Orbis, 1984); and *The Sin of Being Rich in a Poor Society* (Madras: CLS, 1983).

112. M. K. Kuriakose, ed., *Orthodox Identity in India: Essays in Honour of V. C. Samuel* (Bangalore: V. C. Samuel 75th Birthday Celebration Committee, 1988), 26.

113. K. M. George is director of the Sopana Orthodox Academy, Kottayam, India. He served as moderator of the WCC Programme Committee (1998–2006), executive secretary of the National Council of Churches in India, and as principal and professor at the Orthodox Theological Seminary in Kottayam, India. From 1989 to 1994 he was professor at the Bossey Ecumenical Institute, Switzerland. He is a priest of the Malankara Orthodox Syrian Church in India. His writings include: *The Silent Roots: Orthodox Perspectives on Christian Spirituality* (Geneva: WCC Publications, 1994); *Gospel and Culture*, trans. in the Finnish language, http://www.fatherkmgeorge.info/Books/gospel.htm; and several other books and articles in English and Malayalam.

114. Anglican bishop of Nagpur and the first chairman of the Commission on World Mission and Evangelism.

115. Rt. Rev. John Sadiq, "World Council History," *Episcopal Press and News 1962–2006*, Archives of the Episcopal Church, 8 January 1968, http://www.episcopalarchives.org/cgi-bin/ENS/ENSpress_release.pl?pr_number=61-8.

116. Kuriakose, ed., *Orthodox Identity in India*, 83.

117. Michael Kinnamon, *The Vision of the Ecumenical Movement and How It Has Been Impoverished by Its Friends* (St. Louis: Chalice, 2003), 78.

118. For a detailed discussion of the work of Sarah Chakko, see ch. 4 in this volume.

119. For a discussion on the early years of WCC's work on the participation of women in the life of the church and Sarah Chakko's pioneering role in this process, see Fidelis Daly, CP, "Women In The Ecumenical Movement: A Call For Deeper Unity in the Churches," *The Society For Ecumenical Studies* (1998), http://sfes.faithweb.com/98dalywomen.pdf; and Ans J. Van Der Bent, *Vital Ecumenical Concerns: Sixteen Documentary Surveys* (Geneva: WCC Publications, 1986).

120. Pauline Webb, "Women in Church and Society," in Lossky, et al., eds., *Dictionary of the Ecumenical Movement*, 1070.

121. Annamma George was an ecumenical leader with a clear social vision. In Kerala, she was one of the pioneers of the movement of Christian women for property rights and gender equality (see Sindhu Thulaseedharan, "Christian Women and Property Rights in Kerala: Gender Equality in Practice," Centre for Development Studies, Thiruvananthapuram, December 2004, http://www.cds.ac.in/krpcds/report/sindhu.pdf). As a theologian, Annamma George served as executive secretary of the Theological Literature Committee (TLC) and, under her leadership, scores of theological books were written and published in Malayalam, the language of the ordinary people. At the national level, she was a leader of the All India Council of Christian Women of the National Council of Churches in India (AICCW/NCCI) and the Association of Theologically Trained Women in India (ATTWI). She also served the Mar Thoma Church as the general secretary of the Sevika Sanghom, the Women's Fellowship of the Church.

122. From Aruna Gnanadason's obituary note at the demise of Annamma George, based on an email correspondence with Gnanadason on 24 July 2014.

123. Shanti Solomon founded the Fellowship of the Least Coin movement of prayer and action for peace and reconciliation, which has since become a global movement which supports work of women in all the continents with the

"least coins" women set aside with their prayers. She was also the leading spirit behind the formation of the AICCW and ATTWI.

124. Renuka Mukerji Somasekhar was the president of NCCI and the chairperson of SCMI. She was one of the leaders at the WCC Consultation on "Obstacles to the Cooperation of Men and Women, in Working Life, in Public Service: Implications for the Work of the Department," held at Odense, Denmark, 8–12 August 1958 (see Bent, *Vital Ecumenical Concerns*). As the principal of the Women's Christian College, Madras, Somasekhar was also at the helm of a pioneering institution of higher education that, over the decades, has trained thousands of women leaders in India.

125. Daisy Gopalaratnam was the first woman to become general secretary of the Church of South India, a position she held for almost a decade. She was also a president of the NCCI and member of the Central Committee of WCC.

126. During the 1960s, Ivy Khan served as the general secretary of the National YWCA of India. She was also one of the early ecumenical leaders of India and provided leadership at the Second World Conference of Christian Youth (Oslo, July 1947) as a daily chairperson (see Koshy, *History of the Ecumenical Movement*, 1:95).

127. Kay Lundeen, "Young Woman from India Observing YWCA in U.S.," *Eugene Register-Guard*, 6 May 1962, http://news.google.com/newspapers?nid=1310&dat=19620506&id=DRtWAAAAIBAJ&sjid=yuIDAAAAIBAJ&pg=6706,959941.

128. Aruna Gnanadason was the first Indian Christian woman to serve in a leadership role in the secretariat of World Council of Churches, when she was appointed director of the Women's Programme. In this capacity, she gave leadership to the second half of the Ecumenical Decade of the Churches in Solidarity with Women, playing a key role in the organization of ecumenical team visits to most of the member churches of the WCC. Of particular importance during her tenure is the way she raised the issue of violence against women, both in the society and in the life of the churches. See Natalie Maxson, *Journey for Justice: The Story of Women in the WCC* (Geneva: WCC Publications, 2014).

129. Aruna Gnanadason, "Women and Spirituality in Asia," in Ursula King, ed., *Feminist Theology From the Third World—A Reader* (London: SPCK/ Maryknoll, NY: Orbis, 1994), 352. For a detailed discussion of Gnanadason's ecumenical theology, see her writings, "Nameless and Silenced No Longer, We Will Overcome Violence!," *In God's Image* 24, no. 1 (March 2005): 3–8; and her "Introduction" to Aruna Gnanadason, Musimbi Kanyoro, Lucia Anna

McSpadden, eds., *Women, Violence and Non-Violent Change* (Geneva, WCC Publications, 1996), vii–xi.

130. See Hans-Ruedi Weber, "On Being Christian in the World: Reflections on the Ecumenical Discussion about the Laity," 7 May 1997, http://www.oikoumene.org/en/resources/documents/wcc-programmes/education-and-ecumenical-formation/ecumenical-lay-formation/on-being-christian-in-the-world/index.

131. Baago, *National Christian Council of India*, 8.

132. W. A. Visser't Hooft and J. H. Oldham, *The Church and Its Function in Society* (London: Willett, Clark, and Co., 1937), 117f.; and Oldham's pamphlet *The New Christian Adventure* (London, 1929).

133. WCC Assembly New Delhi Statement, http://www.wcc-coe.org/wcc/who/crete-02-e.html.

134. Rajaiah D. Paul was a government officer and a lay leader in the church who had a clear vision of the mission of the laity. For a time he served as the chairman of the Department of Laity, WCC. He had also been the general secretary of the Synod of the Church of South India. See Rajaiah D. Paul, *Ecumenism in Action: A Historical Survey of the Church of South India* (Madras: CLS, 1972); D. Arthur Jeyakumar, "Paul, Rajaiah David" in Hedlund, et al., eds., *Oxford Encyclopedia of South Asian Christianity*, 2:538); and Chandran Devanesan, *Rajaiah D. Paul: Layman Extraordinary* (Madras: CLS, 1982).

135. Cecil Hargraves, *Asian Christian Thinking* (Delhi: ISPCK, 1979), 138.

136. Baago, *National Christian Council of India*, 8.

137. For a detailed discussion on SCM, see in this volume ch. 3 on Augustine Ralla Ram, ch. 10 on Poulose Mar Poulose, and ch. 11 on Ninan Koshy.

138. Patricia Lloyd-Sidle, *Celebrating Our Call: Ordination Stories of Presbyterian Women* (Louisville: Geneva Press, 2006), 117.

139. Kinnamon, *Vision of the Ecumenical Movement*, 75.

140. See George M. John, *Youth Christian Council of Action 1938–1954: The Story of a Dynamic Movement of Christian Youth* (Bangalore: CISRS, 1972).

141. See George Zachariah, *Alternatives Unincorporated: Earth Ethics from the Grassroots* (London: Equinox, 2011).

142. Jayakiran Sebastian, "United Theological College, Bangalore," in Hedlund, et al. eds., *The Oxford Encyclopedia of South Asian Christianity*, 2:710.

143. See ch. 9 in this volume on J. Russell Chandran, the first Indian principal of the United Theological College, who served in this position from 1954

to 1983. See also G. Oommen, "Something Different, Something Broader: Seventy-Five Years in the Life of the United Theological College," in *To Serve, Not to Be Served* (Bangalore: UTC, 1985); and J. M. Razu, ed., *On the Way to Critical Praxis: Field Education as a Relevant Theological Pedagogy at the United Theological College, Bangalore* (Bangalore: UTC, 2002).

144. D. Arthur Jeyakumar, "Tamilnadu Theological Seminary," in Hedlund, et al., eds., *Oxford Encyclopedia of South Asian Christianity*, 2:679. See also Samuel Amirtham and C. R. W. David, eds., *Venturing into Life: The Story of Tamilnadu Theological Seminary* (Madurai: Tamilnadu Theological Seminary, 1990); and K. Lundstrom, *Church Life and Theological Education in Tamil Nadu: Indian Christianity in a Hindutva State* (Uppsala: Swedish Institute of Missionary Research, 2003).

145. Information on the work and theology of Samuel Amirtham is gleaned from Selvanayagam, *Samuel Amirtham's Living Theology*. This 870-page volume summarizes Amirtham's theology on numerous subjects and the ministry that went with it.

146. See Amirtham and Ariarajah, *Ministerial Formation in a Multifaith Milieu:*.

147. Dhyanchand Carr, as the secretary for Mission and Evangelism of the Christian Conference of Asia, conducted seminars on reading the Bible in the context of the poor and marginalized in a number of Asian countries. His insights, enlivened by the responses of the people, are brought together in Dhyanchand Carr, *Reading the Bible with New Eyes* (Coonoor: Creative Spirit Center, ISSU, 1971). See also Carr's book *Sword of the Spirit: An Activist's Understanding of the Bible*, Risk book series (Geneva: WCC Publications, 1992).

148. Amirtham, *Theology by the People.*

149. Consecrated as a bishop in 1953, Philipose Mar Chrysostom is one of the oldest living ecclesiastical leaders. Deeply committed to the values of Christian unity, he was a participant in the Second Vatican Council, WCC Assemblies in New Delhi and Uppsala, and was a president of NCCI. After retiring as the Metropolitan of the Mar Thoma Church in 2007, he continues to be active, at the age of 97 years at the time of this writing, as a public figure in the state of Kerala.

150. Jesudas M. Athyal and John J. Thatamanil, eds., *Metropolitan Chrysostom on Mission in the Marketplace* (Tiruvalla: CSS Books, 2002), 142.

Chapter 2: V. S. Azariah: The Forerunner of Indian Ecumenism

1. Judith M. Brown, "Indian Christians and Nehru's Nation-State," in Richard Fox Young, ed., *India and the Indianness of Christianity: Essays on Understanding—Historical, Theological, and Bibliographical—in Honor of Robert Eric Frykenberg* (Grand Rapids: Eerdmans, 2009), 219.

2. Ibid.

3. J. M. Jeyasingh, "Indigenous Missionary Movements: A Critical Study," in Roger E. Hedlund, ed., *Christianity Is Indian: The Emergence of an Indigenous Community*, rev. ed. (Delhi: ISPCK/Chennai: MIIS, 2004), 218–19.

4. Peter S. C. Pothan, "Indian Missionary Society of Tirunelveli," in Roger E. Hedlund, Jesudas M. Athyal, Joshua Kalapati, and Jessica Richard, eds., *The Oxford Encyclopaedia of South Asian Christianity*, vol. 1 (New Delhi: Oxford University Press, 2012), 333.

5. Franklyn J. Balasundaran, "Indian Missionary Society," in Scott W. Sunquist, David Wu Chu Sing and John Chew Hiang Chea, eds., *A Dictionary of Asian Christianity* (Grand Rapids: Eerdmans, 2001), 370.

6. Jeyasingh, "Indigenous Missionary Movements," 219.

7. Pothan, "Indian Missionary Society of Tirunelveli," 333.

8. Ibid.

9. Susan Billington Harper, *In the Shadow of the Mahatma: Bishop V. S. Azariah and the Travails of Christianity in British India* (Grand Rapids: Eerdmans/London: Routledge Curzon, 2000), 206.

10. Ibid.

11. Ibid., 207.

12. Ibid.

13. Jeyasingh, "Indigenous Missionary Movements," 220.

14. Ibid.

15. Harper, *In the Shadow of the Mahatma*, 235.

16. Ibid., 235–36.

17. Ibid., 237.

18. Ibid., 238, 239.

19. Ibid., 238.

20. Ibid., 247.

21. Ibid., 258.

22. J. Waskom Pickett, *Christian Mass Movements in India* (Lucknow: Lucknow Pub. House, 1933). For details of Pickett's contribution, see Arthur G. McPhee, *The Road to Delhi: J. Waskom Pickett and Missions in the Twilight of*

the Raj and Dawn of Nationhood, rev. ed. (Lexington, KY: Emeth Press, 2012), based on the author's PhD dissertation, "Pickett's Fire: The Life, Contribution, Thought, and Legacy of J. Waskom Pickett, Methodist Missionary to India," Asbury Theological Seminary, 2001.

23. Roger E. Hedlund, "Theology of Mission in Historical Perspective: A Survey of Theological Trends as Traced in Major Conferences on Mission in the 20th Century in Relation to South Asia," in Roger E. Hedlund and Paul Joshua Bhakiaraj, eds., *Missiology for the 21st Century: South Asian Perspectives* (New Delhi: ISPCK/Chennai: MIIS, 2004), 131.

24. Harper, *In the Shadow of the Mahatma*, 261.

25. Ibid., 262.

26. Ibid.

27. Ibid., 263.

28. Ibid., 280.

29. Ibid., 279.

30. Ibid., 163.

31. Ibid., 169.

32. Ibid., 170.

33. Ibid., 173.

34. Ibid., 182.

35. Ravela Joseph, "Yarraguntla, Paraiah," in Hedlund, et al., eds., *Oxford Encyclopaedia of South Asian Christianity*, 750.

36. Robert Eric Frykenberg, *Christianity in India: From Beginnings to the Present* (New York: Oxford University Press, 2008), 236.

37. Harper, *In the Shadow of the Mahatma*, 183.

38. Ibid.

39. Frykenberg, *Christianity in India*, 238.

40. Ibid., 239.

41. Harper, *In the Shadow of the Mahatma*, 187.

42. Robert Eric Frykenberg, ed., *Christians and Missionaries in India: Cross-Cultural Communication since 1500* (Grand Rapids: Eerdmans, 2003), 5.

43. Ibid., 2.

44. Ibid., 3. Originally from V. S. Azariah, "The Communal Award," *The Guardian* 10, no. 31 (8 September 1932): 368; reprinted in the *Dornakal Diocesan Magazine* 9, no. 10 (October 1932): 10–13. Quoted in Harper, *In the Shadow of the Mahatma*.

45. Frykenberg, *Christians and Missionaries*, 9.

46. Ibid., 7–8.

47. Chad M. Bauman, *Christian Identity and Dalit Religion in Hindu India, 1868—1947* (Grand Rapids: Eerdmans, 2008), 3.

48. Quoted in ibid., 2.

49. Frykenberg, *Christians and Missionaries in India*, 23.

50. Ibid., 24.

51. Bengt G. Karlsson, "Entering into the Christian Dharma: Contemporary 'Tribal' Conversions in India," in Judith M. Brown and Robert Eric Frykenberg, eds., *Christians, Cultural Interactions, and India's Religious Traditions* (Grand Rapids: Eerdmans/London: Routledge Curzon, 2002), 142.

52. Ibid., 151.

53. Andrea Palpant Dilley, "The World the Missionaries Made," *Christianity Today* 58, no. 1 (January/February 2014): 37.

54. Ibid., 38.

55. Ibid., 35.

56. Ibid., 36.

57. Ibid., 39.

58. Ibid., 41.

59. Susan Billington Harper, "The Dornakal Church on the Cultural Frontier," in Brown and Frykenberg, eds., *Christians, Cultural Interactions, and India's Religious Traditions*, 184.

60. Ibid., 185.

61. Ibid., 187.

62. Ibid.

63. Ibid.

64. Ibid.

65. Ibid., 210.

66. S. M. Michael, "Inculturation," in Hedlund, et al., eds., *The Oxford Encyclopaedia of South Asian Christianity*, 326.

67. Frykenberg, *Christianity in India*, 238–39.

68. Michael, "Inculturation," 327.

69. Sebastian C. H. Kim, "The Politics of Conversion During the British Raj: 'Mass Movements' in the 1930s and Their Impact on Indian Politics and the Church," *Dharma Deepika* (July–December 2013): 16.

70. Ibid., 17.

71. Ibid.

72. Ibid., 18.

73. Ibid., 19.

74. Ibid.

75. Ibid., 20.

76. Ibid., 21.

77. My summary of Azariah's conflict with Gandhi and political nationalism is drawn from Harper's careful reconstruction of events in her book *In the Shadow of the Mahatma*, ch. 9 (291–351).

78. Ibid., 292.

79. Ibid.

80. Ibid., 295.

81. Ibid., 297.

82. Ibid., 302.

83. Ibid., 307.

84. Ibid., 310.

85. Ibid., 315.

86. Ibid., 348.

87. Ibid., 356.

88. Ibid.

89. Ibid., 357.

90. Ibid., 359.

91. Ibid., 47.

92. Ibid., 240.

93. Ibid.

94. Brian Stanley, *The World Missionary Conference, Edinburgh 1910* (Grand Rapids: Eerdmans, 2009), 123.

95. Address by the Rev. V. S. Azariah at the World Missionary Conference, Edinburgh, 1910, from *The History and Records of the Conference*, vol. 9 (New York: Revell, 1910). The complete text of Azariah's address is available in Roger E. Hedlund, *Roots of the Great Debate in Mission: Mission in Historical and Theological Perspective* (Bangalore: Theological Book Trust, 1997), 42–48.

96. Hedlund, *Roots of the Great Debate in Mission*, 48.

97. Frampton F. Fox, ed., *Edinburgh 1910 Revisited: 'Give Us Friends!'—An India Perspective on 100 Years of Mission*, papers from the 16th annual Centre for Mission Studies Consultation, Union Biblical Seminary, Pune (Bangalore: Centre for Mission Studies/Asian Trading Corporation, 2010).

98. Harper, *In the Shadow of the Mahatma*, 351.

99. Ibid.

Chapter 3: "Lengthen Thy Cords and Strengthen Thy Stakes"

1. As quoted by Ralla Ram's daughter Sarah Shirin, "A Daughter's Reminiscences," in *Golden Jubilee Souvenir: Ralla Ram Memorial Endowment Building Dedication* (Bangalore: SCMI, 1975), 9.

2. Biography in "Finding Aid for Augustine Rall Ram Papers, 1947–1955," Missionary Research Library, Columbia University Libraries, Union Theological Seminary, New York, http://library.columbia.edu/content/dam/libraryweb/locations/burke/fa/mrl/ldpd_4492546.pdf.

3. C. S. Paul, "Augustine Ralla Ram and the SCM," in *Golden Jubilee Souvenir*, 13.

4. Chandra Mallampalli, *Christians and Public Life in Colonial South India, 1863–1937: Contending Marginality* (London: Routledge Curzon, 2006), 102–106.

5. "The Christian Messenger," January 1950, as quoted by Myra Scovel in *I Must Speak: The Biography of Augustine Ralla Ram* (Allahabad: North India Christian Literature Society, 1961), 53.

6. Scovel, *I Must Speak*, 54.

7. Ibid., 55.

8. Ibid., 4.

9. Ibid., 8.

10. Ibid., 17.

11. Ibid., 16.

12. Ibid., 20.

13. Ibid., 27.

14. Ibid., 21.

15. Shirin, "A Daughter's Reminiscences," 9.

16. Scovel, *I Must Speak*, 80–81.

17. Ibid., 87.

18. Augustine Ralla Ram, "Organic Church Unity: A Comment From India," *Ecumenical Review* 8 (1956): 243.

19. William W. Bartley III, "Horton New Dean of Divinity School," *The Harvard Crimson*, 12 April 1955, http://www.thecrimson.com/article/1955/4/12/horton-new-dean-of-divinity-school/.

20. Ralla Ram, "Organic Church Unity," 244.

21. Ibid.,

22. Scovel, *I Must Speak*, 83.

23. Augustine Ralla Ram, "Organic Church Unity," 247–48.

24. A. S. Martin, "Augustine Ralla Ram," in *Golden Jubilee Souvenir*, 13.
25. Paul, "Augustine Ralla Ram and the SCM," 12.
26. Scovel, *I Must Speak*, 33–34.
27. Ibid., 27.
28. Ibid., 56.
29. Ibid., 28.
30. Paul, "Augustine Ralla Ram and the SCM," 12.
31. Scovel, *I Must Speak*, 30.
32. Ibid., 31
33. Paul, "Augustine Ralla Ram," 12.
34. Scovel, *I Must Speak*, 25.
35. Ibid., 89.
36. Ibid., i.

Chapter 4: Sarah Chakko: A Woman Who Inspired the Ecumenical Movement

1. Susannah Harris-Wilson, "Sarah Chakko 1905–1954," in Ioan Bria and Dagmar Heller, eds., *Ecumenical Pilgrims: Profiles of Pioneers in Christian Reconciliation* (Geneva: WCC Publications, 1995), 58.
2. Nivedita Menon, based on her reading of the historical commentator Partha Chatterjee, in Menon, ed., *Introduction to Gender and Politics in India* (New Delhi: Oxford University Press, 1999), 6.
3. Ibid.
4. Dana Lee Robert, *American Women in Mission: A Social History of Their Thought and Practice* (Macon, GA: Mercer University Press, 1996), 160.
5. Mary Louis Slater, *Future Maker in India: The Story of Sarah Chakko* (New York: Friendship Press, 1958), 12; emphasis added.
6. Ibid., 29.
7. Ibid., 27.
8. M. Kurian, *Sarah Chakko: A Voice for Women in the Ecumenical Movement* (Thiruvalla: Christhava Sahitya Samithi, 1998), 23.
9. Slater, *Future Maker in India*, 10.
10. Ibid., 11–13.
11. Ibid., 40.
12. Ibid., 56.

13. From *The Indian Social Reformer, A Newspaper* 9 (7 May 1988), 282. Cited by Gouri Srivastava, *Women's Higher Education in the 19th Century* (New Delhi: Concept Pub. Co., 2000), 54.

14. Srivatsava, *Women's Higher Education*, 38.

15. Ibid.

16. Ibid.

17. Ibid.

18. See also Joy Gnanadason, *A Forgotten History: The Story of the Missionary Movement and the Liberation of People in South Travancore* (Madras: Gurukul Lutheran Theological College and Research Institute, 1994).

19. Srivatsava, *Women's Higher Education*, 38–39.

20. Slater, *Future Maker in India*, 40.

21. Ibid., 49.

22. As recorded by Harris-Wilson, "Sarah Chakko 1905–1954," 59.

23. Ibid., 55.

24. Ibid., 57.

25. Ibid., 55.

26. Susannah Herzel, *A Voice for Women: The Women's Department of the World Council of Churches* (Geneva: WCC Publications, 1981), 15.

27. As recorded by M. Kurian, *Sarah Chakko*, 96.

28. Jetty Boddert, wife of Willem Visser't Hooft, in a pamphlet entitled *Eve Where Art Thou?* written in Dutch and translated into other languages.

29. Willem Visser't Hooft, as cited by Herzel, *A Voice for Women*, 23.

30. Ibid.

31. Ibid, 98.

32. Eleni Kasselouri-Hatzivassiliadi, "'Many women were also there . . .' But Where? Challenges and Open Questions on Women's Role in the Orthodox Church (in the frame of the ecumenical movement)," in Eleni Kasselouri-Hatzivassiliadi, Fulata Mbano-Moyo, and Aikaterini Pekridou, eds., *Many Women Were Also There . . . :The Participation of Orthodox Women in the Ecumenical Movement* (Geneva: WCC Publications/Volos, Greece: Volos Academy for Theological Studies, 2010), 106.

33. Natalia Vasilevich, "The Issue of Female Ordination/Priesthood, in Ecumenical and Inter-Orthodox Discussions," in ibid., 139. See also Elisabeth Behr-Sigel and Kallistos Ware, *The Ordination of Women in the Orthodox Church* (Geneva: WCC Publications, 2000).

34. Harris-Wilson, "Sarah Chakko 1905–1954," 57.

35. Ibid.

36. Ibid.

37. Ibid.

38. Madeline Barot, cited in ibid.

39. Cynthia Wedel from the USA recalls these words of Sarah Chakko at the first meeting of the Commission on the Status and Role of Women in the Church held in Bossey, Switzerland, in 1950. As recorded by Herzel, *A Voice for Women*, 13.

40. Harris-Wilson, "Sarah Chakko 1905–1954," 57.

41. Sarah Chakko, "Reflections on Recent Travels in Europe and North America," *Ecumenical Review* 3 (October 1950–September 1951): 148–49.

42. Susannah Harris Wilson, "Sarah Chakko 1905–1954," 58.

43. Sarah Chakko, cited in ibid.

44. Ibid.

45. Ibid.

46. Kyriaki Karidoyannes FitzGerald, "Preface," in FitzGerald, ed., *Orthodox Women Speak: Discerning the "Signs of the Times"* (Geneva: WCC Publications/Brookline, MA: Holy Cross Orthodox Press, 1999).

47. M. M. Thomas, in *The Student World* 47, no. 2 (1954).

Chapter 5: P. D. Devanandan's Call to Witness

1. Where appropriate we shall adopt the terminology of Wilfred Cantwell Smith's schema, set forth in his modern classic, *The Meaning and End of Religion* (Minneapolis: Fortress Press, 1991 [1962]). Smith distinguishes between "faith" and "cumulative traditions," the inner and outer aspects of human religious life. The former is an individual's or many individuals' relationship with the divine transcendent. The latter consists in the cultural frameworks in which the life of faith has been and is expressed, the institutions, customs, laws, creeds, teachings, and theological systems of a particular community.

2. P. D. Devanandan, *The Concept of Maya: An Essay in Historical Survey of the Hindu Theory of the World with Special Reference to the Vedanta* (Cambridge: Lutterworth, 1950).

3. P. D. Devanandan, *Preparation for Dialogue: A Collection of Essays on Hinduism and Christianity in New India*, ed. Nalini Devanandan and M. M. Thomas (Bangalore: CISRS, 1964), 179ff. Devanandan's address to the WCC's New Delhi assembly probably comes closest to spelling out the main elements

of his theology of Christian witness in a pluralistic world. All quotes in the ensuing paragraphs come from this citation.

4. Among the more significant of Devanandan's works are: *Resurgent Hinduism: Review of Modern Movements* (Madras: CLS/CISRS, 1958); *The Gospel and Renascent Hinduism* (Bangalore: CISRS, 1959); *Our Task Today: Revision of Evangelistic Concern* (Bangalore: CISRS, 1959); *Christian Concern in Hinduism* (Bangalore: CISRS, 1961); *I Will Lift Up Mine Eyes Unto the Hills: Sermons and Bible Studies of Paul D. Devanandan*, ed. Stanley J. Samartha and Nalini Devanandan (Bangalore: CISRS, 1963); and *Preparation for Dialogue.*

5. M. M. Thomas, *In Memory of Devanandan* (Bangalore: CISRS, 1962); "Editorial: Life Together," *Religion and Society* (March 1964), 6.

6. Hendrik Kraemer, *The Christian Message in a Non-Christian World* (London: Edinburgh House Press, 1938).

7. D. M. Devasahayam, A. N. Sudarisanam, et al., eds., *Rethinking Christianity in India* (Madras: Hogarth Press, 1938).

8. A group of somewhat unorthodox but highly stimulating thinkers who came to be known as "The Rethinking Group," from the title of their best-selling publication *Rethinking Christianity in India* (Madras: A. N. Sudarisanam, 1938). Led by P. Chenchiah and V. Chakkarai, the group argued that the Indian Christian community could not ignore the common Hindu heritage, its culture, and traditions.

9. O. V. Jathanna, *The Decisiveness of the Christ Event and the Universality of Christianity in a World of Religious Plurality* (Berne: Peter Lang, 1981).

10. J. N. Farquhar, *The Crown of Hinduism* (London: Oxford University Press, 1920).

11. Eric Sharpe, ed., *Theology of Hogg* (Madras: CISRS/CLS, 1971), 206–22.

12. Devanandan, *Our Task Today*, 183.

13. Arend Th. van Leeuwen, *Christianity in World History: The Meeting of the Faiths of East and West* (London: Edinburgh House Press, 1964), 332.

14. *Bhagavadgita* 3:20, 3:25.

15. S. Radhakrishnan gives chapter 3 of the *Bhagavadgita* the title "*Karma Yoga* or the Method of Work," and notes that the chapter "expounds the necessity for the performance of works without the selfish attachment to results, with a view to securing the welfare of the world." S. Radhakrishnan, *The Bhagavadgita: With Introductory Essay, Sanskrit Text, English Translation and Notes* (London: George Allen & Unwin, 1948), 150.

16. Aurobindo Ghose, *The Life Divine* II (Pondicherry: Sri Aurobindo Ashram Publication Dept., 1939–1940), 684. See also P. D. Devanandan and M. M. Thomas, eds., *Christian Participation in Nation Building* (Madras: NCCI/CISRS, 1960), viii.

17. Devanandan, *Resurgent Hinduism*, 8.

18. Devanandan, *Preparation for Dialogue*, 149.

19. Dietrich Bonhoeffer, *Letters and Papers from Prison*, ed. Eberhard Bethge (New York: Macmillan, 1971), 280.

20. See van Leeuwen, *Christianity in World History*. See also Jeffrey C. Pugh, *Religionless Christianity* (London: T&T Clark, 2008).

21. Eph. 2:14-16.

22. Devanandan, *I Will Lift Up Mine Eyes*, 126.

23. Smith, *The Meaning and End of Religion*. The similarities in Devanandan's and Smith's conceptual apparati and theoretical frameworks are striking indeed, and need to be studied in greater depth.

24. Devanandan, *Preparation for Dialogue*, 114.

25. Acts 10:34-35.

26. A person who lives a life of *satyagraha* (literally "truth force" or "soul force"); Gandhi's term for a life characterized by truth, nonviolence, and self-giving love.

27. Devanandan, *Christian Concern for Hinduism*, 82.

28. Hocking played a central role in the formulation of the first major restatement on missiology in the 20th century in *Re-Thinking Missions* (New York: Harper & Bros., 1932), the Layman's Foreign Mission Enquiry report.

29. Devanandan, *Preparation for Dialogue*, 114ff.

30. William Hocking, *Living Religions and a World Faith* (New York: Macmillan, 1940).

31. William Hocking, *The Coming World Civilization* (New York: Harper & Bros., 1956).

32. R. H. S. Boyd, *An Introduction to Indian Christian Theology*, rev. ed. (Madras: CLS, 1975), 188.

Chapter 6: Explorations into Spirituality and Humanization

1. U Kyaw Than, ed., "Witness Together," in *Official Report of the Inaugural Assembly of the East Asia Christian Conference*, Kuala Lumpur Rangoon, 1959, 51.

2. M. M. Thomas, *The Christian Response to the Asian Revolution* (London: SCM Press, 1966), 29.

3. Charles West, "Ecumenical Missionary Theology," in K. C. Abraham, ed., *Christian Witness in Society: A Tribute to M. M. Thomas* (Bangalore: Board of Theological Education, Senate of Serampore College, 1998), 29.

4. See M. M. Thomas, *Response to Tyranny* (New Delhi: Forum for Christian Concern for People's Struggles, 1979).

5. M. M. Thomas, *The Acknowledged Christ of the Indian Renaissance*, 3rd ed., I.T.L series no. 4 (Madras: CLS, 1991), 29.

6. See M. M. Thomas, *Ideological Commitment within Christian Commitment* (Madras: CLS/Bangalore: CISRS, 1983).

7. Paul Abrecht, "Some Reflections on Ecumenical Social Thought," in Abraham, ed., *Christian Witness in Society*, 33.

8. M. M. Thomas, "The Politics of Social Revolution," in *Towards a Theology of Contemporary Ecumenism* (Madras: CLS/Geneva: WCC Publications, 1978), 32.

9. M. M. Thomas, "Christ the Centre of Ecumenism," in ibid., 229–30.

10. M. M. Thomas, "Peace and Radical Changes," in ibid., 142.

11. Ibid., 152.

12. Thomas, *Towards a Theology of Contemporary Ecumenism*, 63.

13. Thomas, "Peace and Radical Changes," 154.

14. Thomas, *Towards a Theology of Contemporary Ecumenism*, 69.

15. Ibid., 70.

16. "Confessing the Faith in Asia Today," statement issued by the consultation organized by the EACC, Hong Kong, 26 October–1 November 1966, 76.

17. Thomas, "Peace and Radical Change," 155.

18. Thomas, "Politics of Social Revolution," 171–72.

19. Thomas, "Christ the Centre of Ecumenism," 232.

20. Thomas, "Search for Wholeness and Unity," in *Towards a Theology of Contemporary Ecumenism*, 258.

21. Thomas, "Jesus Christ Frees and Unites," in *Towards a Theology of Contemporary Ecumenism*, 319.

22. M. M. Thomas, "Christian Action in the Asian Struggle," Christian Conference of Asia, 1973, p. 7.

23. Thomas, *Christian Response to Asian Revolution*, 267.

24. M. M. Thomas, *Man and the Universe of Faiths* (Bangalore: CISRS, 1975), 23.

25. M. M. Thomas, "Search for New Humanism as the Struggle for a Just Society," in Saral Chatterji, ed., *Political Prospects in India* (Bangalore: CISRS, 1971), 183.

26. Ibid.

27. M. M. Thomas, *The Secular Ideologies of India and Secular Meaning of Christianity* (Madras: CLS, 1976), 199.

28. M. M. Thomas, *Salvation and Humanization: Some Crucial Issues in Contemporary India*" (Bangalore: CISRS, 1971), 20.

29. Ibid., 8.

30. Ibid., 10.

31. M. M. Thomas, *Some Theological Dialogues* (Bangalore: CISRS, 1977), 20.

32. Thomas, *Secular Ideologies*, 11.

33. M. M. Thomas, "The Absoluteness of Jesus Christ and Christ-Centred Syncretism," *The Ecumenical Review* 37, no. 4 (1985): 387–97.

34. Thomas, *Some Theological Dialogues*, 21.

35. Ibid.

36. M. M. Thomas, "Christian Community in a Secular State," in A. P. Barnabas, ed., *Indian Politics After Nehru*, Social Concerns series, no. 13 (Bangalore: 1967), 176.

37. Thomas, "Politics of Social Revolution," 162.

38. Quoted by Ronald H. Preston in *Church and Society in the Late Twentieth Century*, (London: SCM Press, 1983), 120.

39. "World Conference on Church and Society: Official Report" (Geneva: WCC Publications, 1966), 111.

40. Preston, *Church and Society*, 105.

41. M. M. Thomas, *Christian Participation in Nation-Building* (Bangalore: CISRS, 1964), 297.

Chapter 7: Metropolitan Paulos Mar Gregorios: Dimensions of Ecumenism

1. Paulos Mar Gregorios, *Love's Freedom—The Grand Mystery: A Spiritual Autobiography* (Kottayam: MGF, 1997), 22.

2. Ibid., 86f.

3. Fr. Paul Verghese, "Pandithanum Parishudhanum" (Malayalam), in *HH Geevarghese II Birth Centenary Souvenir* (Kottayam, 1973), 27–29.

4. Joice Thottackad, *Prakashathilekku Oru Theerthayathra* (*A Pilgrimage to Light*) (Kottayam: Sophia Books, 1997), 237–39.

5. Paulos Gregorios, William H. Lazareth, and Nikos A. Nissiotis, eds., *Does Chalcedon Divide or Unite?* (Geneva: WCC Publications, 1981), ix–xii.

6. Gregorios, *Love's Freedom*, 23.

7. Minutes of the WCC Central Committee, New York, 1963, 20–21; Thottackad, *Prakashathilekku Oru Theerthayathra*, 255–56. Minutes of the WCC Central Committee, Paris, 7–16 August 1962, 20-21; Thottackad, *Prakashathilekku Oru Theerthayathra*, 247–49.

8. Paulos Mar Gregorios, in Fr. Dr Jacob Kurian, ed., *On Ecumenism* (Kottayam: ISPCK & MGF, 2006), 134.

9. Ibid., 131.

10. Ibid., 130.

11. Ibid.

12. Ibid.

13. Ibid., 133.

14. See Paulos Mar Gregorios, "Why the Churches Are Gathering at M.I.T.?," *One World*, no. 42 (May 1979); idem, "Report on the Conference on Faith, Science, and the Future," *Anticipation*, no. 28 (December 1980): 68–70; idem, "Science, Faith and Our Future," *The Star of the East* 1, no. 2 (April 1979): 11–20; idem, "Science and Faith: Complementary or Contradictory?," in Roger L. Shinn, ed., *Faith and Science in an Unjust World* (Geneva: WCC, 1980), 46–58; idem, "Science and Technology within the Story of Redemption" (Bible Study), in Shinn, ed., *Faith and Science in an Unjust World*, 117; idem, "Science, Faith and Our Future," *New Frontiers in Education* 9, no. 4 (October–December 1979): 1–7; idem, "An Eastern Orthodox Perspective of Nature, Man and God," *Anticipation,* no. 25 (January 1979); and idem, "Science and Faith: Complementary or Contradictory?," address delivered at WCC Conference on Faith, Science and the Future, Massachusetts Institute of Technology, Cambridge, Mass., 12–24 July 1979.

15. Paul Abrecht, "In Memoriam: Paulos Mar Gregorios," *Ecumenical Review* 49, no. 1 (January 1997): 110.

16. Paulos Mar Gregorios, "Science and Faith," in Shinn, ed., *Faith and Science*, 55.

17. Ibid., 54.

18. Ibid.

19. Paulos Mar Gregorios, "The Scientific Temper Debate: Some Reflections and Few Tentative Conclusions," *Bulletin of the Indian Institute of World Culture* (May 1982), 26–35; idem, "Space—The New Battlefield: These New Trends Should be Stopped," address delivered at the World Conference, "Religious Workers for Saving the Sacred Gift of Life from Nuclear Catastrophe," Working Presidium and Secretariat, Moscow, 3–4 January 1984; idem, "Will the Arms Race Hit Space? Some Deep Anxieties in My Mind," address delivered at seminar on "Science for Peace and Development," Indo-Soviet Cultural Society, Trivandrum, 5 February 1984; idem, "Space Without Weapons," introductory speech, International Round Table Conference of Religious Workers and Experts on Preventing the Use of Outer Space for Military Purposes, Moscow, 2–4 April 1984; idem, "For a Nuclear Weapons Free World for the Survival of Humanity," address given at the International Forum, Moscow, 14–16 February 1984, in *The Journal of the Moscow Patriarchate*, no. 5 (1984); idem, "Stop Darkness at Noon: Save Life," address delivered at International Round Table Conference of Religious Leaders and Experts on "New Dangers to the Sacred Gift of Life: Our Tasks," Moscow, 11–13 February 1985, in *The Star of the East* 7, no. 1 (March 1985): 8–15.

20. See Gregorios, *Love's Freedom*, 25; and idem, "Poverty of Philosophy and Philosophy of Poverty. The Task of Indian Philosophy Today," presidential address at Madurai Kamaraj University, 27–29 December 1990.

21. Baba Virsa Singh, "In memory of Father Gregorios," *News from Gobind Sadan*, February 1997.

22. Paulos Mar Gregorios, "May the Light Dawn," address delivered at Global Celebration of The Centenary Year of the Chicago Parliament of World Religions, *Khera* 13, no. 2 (July–December 1993); 126–31.

23. Paulos Mar Gregorios, "Education for a New Civilisation in the New Millennium," *Global Learning* 1, no.1 (January-March 1996): 15–19.

24. Gregorios, *Love's Freedom*, 196f.

Chapter 8: The Pioneering Ministry of Stanley J. Samartha

1. Stanley J. Samartha, *Between Two Cultures: Ecumenical Ministry in a Pluralistic World* (Geneva: WCC Publications, 1996), 105–106.

2. Ibid., 132.

3. Ibid.

4. Stanley J. Samartha, *The Hindu View of History: Classical and Modern* (Bangalore: CISRS, 1959).

5. Stanley J. Samartha, *The Hindu Response to the Unbound Christ* (Madras: CLS, 1974).

6. Stanley J. Samartha, *Courage for Dialogue: Ecumenical Issues in Interfaith Relationships* (Geneva: WCC Publications, 1981).

7. S. J. Samartha, "Religious Pluralism and the Quest for Human Community," in J. Robert Nelson, ed., *No Man Is Alien: Essays on the Unity of Mankind* (Leiden: E. J. Brill, 1971), 129.

8. These points are taken from what I had written for the issue of *Current Dialogue* 38 (2001): http:/www.wcc-coe.org/wcc/interreligious/cd38-03.html. A useful summary of Samartha's understanding of the purpose of dialogue is seen in his "The Progress and Promise of Interfaith Dialogue," *Journal of Ecumenical Studies* 9, no. 3 (1972).

9. S. J. Samartha, "Dialogue as a Continuing Christian Concern," in John Hick and Brian Hebblothwaite, eds., *Christianity and Other Religions* (London: Collins, 1979), 164ff.

10. Introductory article in S. J. Samartha, ed., *Towards World Community: The Colombo Papers* (Geneva: WCC Publications, 1975).

11. S. J. Samartha, "More Than an Encounter of Commitments," in *Living Faiths and the Ecumenical Movement* (Geneva: WCC Publications, 1971), 103f.

12. See S. J. Samartha, "Guidelines on Dialogue," *Ecumenical Review* 31, no. 2 (April 1979): 155–62.

13. Ibid.

14. Samartha has himself made a detailed study of some aspects of Hinduism in order to enter into deeper dialogue with Hindus for mutual enrichment. See, for example, "The Significance of the Historical in Contemporary Hinduism," *Indian Journal of Theology* 16, nos. 1 & 2 (January–June 1967): 463-74.

15. Cf. S. J. Samartha, "Ecumenical Issues in Community Relations," lecture delivered at the Centre for Indian and Inter-Religious Studies, Rome, 1978, p. 7.

16. S. J. Samartha, "Can Mount Sinai and River Ganga Meet?," *Tantur Year Book*, 1975–76, 117ff.

17. Samartha demonstrates this in his volume, *The Hindu Response to the Unbound Christ.*

18. S. J. Samartha, "Introduction," in *Dialogue between Men of Living Faiths*, Ajaltoun volume (Geneva: WCC Publications, 1971), 9.

19. S. J. Samartha, *One Christ—Many Religions* (Maryknoll, NY: Orbis, 1991), 10.

20. Eeuwout Klootwijk, *Commitment and Openness: The Interreligious Dialogue and Theology of Religions in the Work of Stanley J. Samartha* (Zoetermeer, The Netherlands: Uitgeverij Boekencentrum, 1992), 157.

21. Ibid., 156–57.

22. Samartha, *One Christ—Many Religions*, 227.

23. In Dow Kirkpatrick, ed., *The Holy Spirit* (Nashville: Tidings, 1974).

24. Samartha, *One Christ—Many Religions*, 110–24.

25. S. J. Samartha, "Partners in Community: Some Reflections on Hindu-Christian Relations Today," *Occasional Bulletin of Missionary Research* 4, no. 2 (April 1980): 80.

26. S. J. Samartha, "The Quest for Salvation and the Dialogue between Religions," *International Review of Mission* (October 1968): 429.

27. Samartha, *No Man Is Alien*, 143.

28. Samartha, "The Quest for Salvation," 432.

Chapter 9: "Only Christ and No Formulation of Christ Can Determine the Frontier"

1. This phrase in the title of this chapter comes from J. R. Chandran, "Christianity and World Religions: The Ecumenical Discussion," *The Indian Journal of Theology* 30, nos. 3–4 (July–December 1981): 186–203, here on 202.

2. This section is a slightly modified version from my contribution "Chandran, Joshua Russell," in Roger E. Hedlund, et al., eds., *The Oxford Encyclopaedia of South Asian Christianity*, vol. 1 (New Delhi: Oxford University Press, 2012), 199–201.

3. See, among other writings, the essays collected in Samuel Amirtham, ed., *A Vision for Man: Essays on Faith, Theology and Society in Honour of Joshua Russell Chandran* (Madras: The Christian Literature Society, 1978); in this a select bibliography of his writings are listed: E. Adiappa, "Writings of Russell Chandran—A Select Bibliography," 19–25. See also Franklyn J. Balasundaram, "India: Joshua Russell Chandran," in *EATWOT in Asia: Towards a Relevant Theology* (Bangalore: Asian Trading Corporation, 1993), 171–87; and L.

E. Sahanam, "'Did You Preach Jesus Christ?': The Christological Focus in the Writings of Joshua Russell Chandran," *Bangalore Theological Forum* 32, no. 2 (December 2000): 27–59.

4. J. R. Chandran, "The Principal's Letter to the Old Students," *The Magazine of the United Theological College, Bangalore* 23 (June 1957): 3.

5. J. R. Chandran, "Mission in Today's Pluralistic Context," *National Council of Churches Review* 114, no. 5 (May–June 1994): 347–61, here on 359–60.

6. J. R. Chandran, "Directions of Christian Theology in India," in Gnana Robinson, ed., *For The Sake of the Gospel: Essays in Honour of Samuel Amirtham* (Madurai: T.T.S. Publications, 1980), 16–28, here on 28.

7. For a summary and analysis of this work, see M. M. Thomas, *The Acknowledged Christ of the Indian Renaissance*, 2d ed. (Madras: CLS, 1976), 131–40.

8. J. R. Chandran, "A Christian Approach to Other Religions," *Bangalore Theological Forum* 7, no. 2 (July–December 1975): 1–20, here on 20.

9. Chandran, "Mission in Today's Pluralistic Context," 358.

10. In Chandran, "A Christian Approach to Other Religions," 13. Chandran's approach echoes the more elaborately worked-out theological position of his contemporary, colleague, and fellow traveller in the ecumenical journey, Stanley J. Samartha, in influential works like *One Christ—Many Religions: Toward a Revised Christology* (Maryknoll, NY: Orbis, 1991).

11. J. Russell Chandran, "Widening Frontiers of Christian Theology—Indian Context," in V. Devasahayam, ed., *Dalits and Women: Quest for Humanity*, The Gurukul Summer Institute 1992 (Madras: Gurukul, 1992), 19.

12. J. R. Chandran, "Christ—the Light of the World," *The Magazine of the United Theological College, Bangalore* 20 (May 1954): 22.

13. J. R. Chandran, "The Christian Style of Living," in David Lyon and Albert Manuel, eds., *Renewal for Mission* (Madras: CLS, 1967), 86–97, here on 96.

14. Part of Chandran's inaugural address as the 1964–65 Henry W. Luce Visiting Professor of World Christianity at Union Theological Seminary in New York, titled "The Theological Task of the Church in India," *Union Seminary Quarterly Review* 20, no. 3 (March 1965): 247–59, here on 259.

15. In J. R. Chandran, "Concern for Man in the Ecumenical Renewal," *Religion and Society* 15, no. 1 (March 1968): 32–38, here on 38.

16. In J. R. Chandran, "Theologizing in the Context of the Marginalized and Oppressed," in *Bangalore Theological Forum* 24, nos. 3–4 (September–December 1992): 3–15, here on 14.

17. See V. V. Thomas, *Conciliar Ecumenism: The Beginning of the Former CSI-CNI-MTC Joint Council* (Bangalore: BTESSC/SATHRI, 2008).

18. J. R. Chandran, "Introduction," in *The C.S.I.–Lutheran Theological Conversations, 1948–1959: Agreed Statements* (Madras: The Christian Literature Society, 1960), 8.

19. In Chandran, "A Christian Approach to Other Religions," 14.

20. In J. R. Chandran, "From an Institution-Based Mission to a People-Based Mission," *National Council of Churches Review* 111, no. 5 (May 1991): 1020–31, here on 1031.

21. In J. R. Chandran, "Principal's Letter to the Alumni," *College Magazine, 1982–83,* 49 (Bangalore: Union Theological College), 7.

22. George A. Lindbeck, *The Nature of Doctrine* (Philadelphia: Westminster, 1984), 134.

23. J. R. Chandran, "Baptism—A Scandal or a Challenge?," *Religion and Society* 19, no. 1 (March 1972) [Issue on "Conversion and Baptism in the Cultural Context of India"]: 51–58, here on 58. For further exploration of this theme, see J. Jayakiran Sebastian, "Baptism and the Unity of the Church in India Today," in Michael Root and Risto Saarinen, eds., *Baptism and the Unity of the Church* (Grand Rapids: Eerdmans/Geneva: WCC Publications, 1998), 196–207.

24. In Chandran, "Principal's Letter to the Alumni," 8–9.

25. In J. R. Chandran, "Congregation Is the Church," *National Council of Churches Review* 112, no. 3 (March 1992): 166–75, here on 171.

26. In R. S. Sugirtharajah, *Postcolonial Criticism and Biblical Interpretation* (New York: Oxford University Press, 2002), 168–69.

27. Preached at the "College Inauguration Service, 1954," in *The Magazine of the United Theological College, Bangalore* 21 (April 1955): 13–15.

28. For the body of this essay, I have drawn and expanded upon my article, J. Jayakiran Sebastian, "Only Christ and No Formulation of Christ Can Determine the Frontier—Chandran's Challenges to Christian Mission," *National Council of Churches Review* 122, no. 5 (June 2002): 493–500.

Chapter 10: Poulose Mar Poulose: An Activist of Alternative Ecumenism

1. V. R. Krishna Iyer, "Bridging the sacred and the secular," book review of Paulose Mar Paulose, *Encounter in Humanization: Insights for Christian-Marxist Dialogue and Cooperation*, in *The Hindu*, 27 November 2001, http://www.hindu.com/thehindu/br/2001/11/27/stories/2001112700100400.htm.

2. While the spellings "Poulose" and "Paulose" have both been used for this church leader, this article uses the spelling, "Poulose" because this is the spelling he used. However, titles of the books and articles referred in this article appear as they were published.

3. See M. M. Thomas, *Response to Tyranny* (Tiruvalla: CSS, 2000).

4. Paulose Mar Paulose, *Spirituality for Struggle* (Tiruvalla: CSS, 1999), 11.

5. Barbara Rossing, "Models of *Koinonia* in the New Testament and Early Church," in Heinrich Holze, ed., *The Church in Communion: Lutheran Contributions to Ecclesiology* (Geneva: Lutheran World Federation, 1997), 78.

6. Barbara Rossing, "(Re)claiming *Oikoumene*," in Shelly Mathews, et al., eds., *Walk in the Ways of Wisdom: Essays in Honor of Elizabeth Schussler Fiorenza* (Philadelphia: Trinity Press International, 2003), 74–87.

7. Harold C. Fey, *A History of the Ecumenical Movement,* volume 2: 1948-1968 (Geneva: World Council of Churches, 1970), 406.

8. Chris Tremewan, *Teatime at the Revolution* (Hong Kong: WSCF Asia Pacific, 1983).

9. Ibid., 12.

10. Ibid., 36.

11. Chris Tremewen, *Out of Control: The Official Report of the Asia Youth Assembly* (Hong Kong: CCA Youth/WSCF Asia Pacific, 1985).

12. Poulose Mar Paulose, "Be a Dissenting Minority," in ibid., viii.

13. Christine Ledger, "Bishop Poulose Mar Paulose: Bishop, Activist, Brother, and Friend," *Praxis*, no. 2 (April–June, 1998): 25.

14. Ibid., 26.

15. Poulouse Mar Poulouse, "SCM Special Lectures," http://www.ibiblio.org/ahkitj/wscfap/arms1974/Leadership%20Formation%20program/HRD/1985%20may-jun/special.htm.

16. Ibid.

17. Ibid.

18. M. M. Thomas, *Ideological Quest within Christian Commitment* (Madras: CLS/Bangalore: CISRS, 1983), 29, 30.

19. Ledger, "Bishop Poulose Mar Poulose."

20. Mar Poulouse, "SCM Special Lectures."

21. Ibid.

22. Paulouse Mar Paulouse, "Movement Report/Message," *Praxis,* nos. 3–4, 1987, 3–4.

23. Paulouse Mar Paulouse, "Workshop Group Report: People's Movement," *Praxis,* nos. 1–2 (1987), http://www.ibiblio.org/ahkitj/wscfap/arms1974/PRAXIS/1987/1987 Q1n2/a.htm.

24. Paulose Mar Paulose, "Development, Special Responsibility, and Christian Values," http://www.ibiblio.org/ahkitj/wscfap/arms1974/Book%20 Series/Ferment&Protest/development.htm.

Chapter 11: Ninan Koshy: An Ecumenical Voice in the World of Nations

1. "The Role of the World Council of Churches in International Affairs," in *The Churches in International Affairs: CCIA Reports from 1983–1986* (Geneva: WCC Publications, 1987), 11–16. See Ninan Koshy, *Churches in the World of Nations: International Politics and the Mission and Ministry of the Church* (Geneva: WCC Publications, 1994), for a detailed spelling-out of what is said more briefly in the document.

2. For a succinct appraisal of the various models that figure in ecumenical social thought, see Ans van de Bent, *Commitment to God's World: A Concise Critical Survey of Ecumenical Social Thought* (Geneva: WCC Publications, 1995).

3. "Statement on Peace and Justice," in David Gill, ed., *Gathered for Life: Official Report of VI Assembly of World Council of Churches, Vancouver, Canada, 24 July–10 August, 1983* (Geneva: WCC Publications, 1983), 131–38, paragraphs 1, 8, 9.

4. Ibid., 255.

5. "Role of WCC in International Affairs," 14.

6. CWME, *Your Kingdom Come: Report on the World Conference on Mission and Evangelism, Melbourne*, Australia, 12-25, May 1980 (Geneva: WCC, 1980); see pp. 179-92.

7. Richard Dowden, "Mrs Thatcher and Africa," *African Arguments,* http://africanarguments.org/2013/04/08/mrs-thatcher-and-africa-by-richard-dowden/. After interviewing contemporaries of Mrs Thatcher, Dowden says that her ambivalent response to the ANC was not based so much on "a crime against humanity as a sin against economic liberalism."

8. See "Address by President Nelson Mandela to the WCC," *Together on the Way*, accessed at wcc-coe.org/wcc/assembly/or-mand.html.

9. Paul Abrecht and Ninan Koshy, eds., *Before It's Too Late: The Challenge of Nuclear Disarmament* (Geneva: WCC Publications, 1983).

10. "Statement on Peace and Justice," paragraphs 20 (d), 25, 13.

11. Koshy, *Churches in the World of Nations*, 1.

12. For this history, see John Briggs et al, eds., *A History of the Ecumenical Movement*, vol: 3: 1968-2000 (Geneva: WCC, 2004), 515-19.

13. See *Central Committee of the World Council of Churches: Minutes of the Fortieth Meeting*, Moscow, USSR, 16-27 July 1989 (Geneva: WCC, 1989), 102-109.

14. Koshy, *Churches in the World of Nations*, 96–103. See also ch. 6: "Ecumenical Diplomacy," 58–78.

15. Ninan Koshy, *The War on Terror: Reordering the World* (Hong Kong: Daga, 2002/Delhi: Leftword, 2003).

16. Ninan Koshy, *A History of the Ecumenical Movement in Asia*, vol. 1 (Hong Kong: WSCF/YMCA/CCA, 2004); and idem, ed., *A History of the Ecumenical Movement in Asia*, vol. 2 (Hong Kong: WSCF/YMCA/CCA, 2004).

17. Donald Shriver, review of Koshy, *War on Terror*, in *Quest: An Interdisciplinary Journal for Asian Christian Scholars* 2, no. 1 (June 2003): 68–73.

18. Ninan's response prompted me to bring out the theology implicit in his book. See D. Preman Niles, "The War on Terror: An Asian Theological Response," *Quest* 3, no. 2 (November 2004): 83–100.